The

Blood Twins

Adelaide Newton

For the Bath Spa Creating Writing class of
2010 - 2013.

Other books by Adelaide Newton

Otaku Trash

Chapter 1

Shots

I can still remember the day Pa died.

Megan an' me'd bin asleep at home. We knew Pa were goin' on 'nother robbery that night but not where. I don't know what time I woke to the sound of crashin' downstairs. Then sumone were shoutin', "Cole! Megan!"

Megan were up an' outta bed while I were still frozen from the fear. Hearin' her holler, "Pa? Pa!" downstairs were enough to snap me outta maself.

I found 'em in the kitchen. Pa were on the floor, his back 'gainst the table, Megan sittin' beside him, an' Dean standin' in the doorway. There were blood everywhere – the floor, the table, on Pa's face, an' on Dean's an' Megan's hands. Pa's shirt an' pants were soaked with it. He were so pale he shined in the candlelight, 'though he were still breathin' despite the blood. While Megan clutched Pa's hand, I sank down on his other side. Ma whole body were like dried grass – brittle an' on the verge of crumblin'.

Everythin' that happened next were like a dream – Pa grippin' our hands an' forcin' a painful smile, Megan demandin' to be told who'd shot him, Dean tellin' her to hush, Pa tellin' Megan not to be angry an' Dean followin' Megan as she went outside.

Pa were talkin' to me, but the words swam by me like fish 'til he grabbed both ma hands inna last show of strength an' said, "Cole, toughen up. Take care of your sis."

An' then his hands went slack in mine, leavin' a trail of blood down ma arm. I screamed Megan's name, but it were too late. Pa were gone. Ma vision blurred with tears.

At the sight of Pa's slumped body, Megan's face crumpled. She looked like she were gonna cry, but she caught herself. Like she always did.

Dean put a hand on ma shoulder.

"Come away now, Cole," he said. Ma legs were numb an' ma knees ached, an' light were streamin' in through the windows.

The three of us laid Pa on the kitchen table. There were bullet holes in his back – two of 'em, one jest below his shoulder blade on the right, an' the other on his left through his ribs.

"Dean," Megan said, her voice low an' dangerous, "tell me. Who did this?"

"Mr Benjamin Scarborough," Dean said. "Your pa broke into his house tonight. Mr Scarborough shot him as he ran. Your pa woke me up fer help."

"He'll die fer this," Megan swore. "I'll never be at peace 'til Benjamin Scarborough lies unner the dust."

"Now, Megan," Dean said, "let's not turn sour. It were hardly Scarborough's fault. He were only protectin' his property an' Miss Cassidy."

Ma stomach lurched at the thought that Pa mighta caused Cassidy harm, an' now that Cassidy might see Pa as sumone bad.

"I don't care," Megan hissed. "He'll pay. They *all* will."

We wanted to bury Pa in the churchyard next to Ma, but the Reverend said we couldn't. By then the whole town knew how Pa'd died, an' the Reverend said Pa's death warn't suitable fer a Christian place of rest. Megan went to hit him, but I pulled her away in time.

We buried Pa in his favourite spot – unner a tree that had the prettiest white blossom in the spring. Pa loved to sit 'neath it an' watch the petals spin away on the wind. The tree were a good ride outta town, but Dean let us borrow his cart to carry Pa's body.

We made a sorry congregation – Megan, Dean, Mary an' me – stood 'round the open grave Dean an' I'd dug. We said our goodbyes an' covered Pa in the red earth.

Megan an' me were sixteen years old.

"It ain't fair," Megan said that night. "Why couldn't Pa be buried next to Ma?"

"You heard the Reverend," I said.

"Pa died tryin' to feed us, Cole. His family. If Gawd refuses to let a man like Pa into his Heaven, then no one oughta be allowed in."

An' fer one of the few times in ma life, I agreed with Megan completely.

When Megan disappears I always know where to find her: The Sleepin' Raccoon. Megan's favourite saloon in the territory, 'cause apparently the whisky there's the finest an' the strongest. I believe her. I've dragged her unconscious body from jest 'bout every saloon in Arizona Territory.

I stop outside The Sleepin' Raccoon's swing doors. The shouts from a table of cowboys – their hair freshly cut an' their beards freshly trimmed, likely restin' after months on the road – are loud enough to drown out the janglin' of the saloon's piano. I can smell their hair oil from the door. All eyes are focused on ma sis an' her drinkin' opponent.

There's folk stompin' an' beatin' their fists an' glasses on the table tops. One key change away from a gunshot.

Saloons make me jumpy. When the feelin's as tense as this you can guarantee the night's gonna end inna fight. I hate goin' in saloons even when they're quiet. Everyone watches you enter, their eyes drillin' into the back of your skull. Megan's always cool in those situations. I stay 'hind her, keepin' ma eyes down an' ma hands clenched at ma sides, 'case I look at sumone the wrong way. But now I've no one to hide 'hind.

I peer over the top of the swing door. Megan's sittin' at a small table, littered with drinkin' glasses. Opposite her's a young fella with short blonde curly hair, wearin' a blue checked shirt. They're both holdin' a shot glass, but Megan's hand's steadier. His is limp an' he's leanin' sideways in his chair, with his other arm danglin' over the ground.

Megan raises her drink to her lips, smiles, tips it back an' swallows. She slams the empty shot glass down on the table. The crowd roars an' men swarm 'round her opponent, pushin' him with their elbows, encouragin' him. The blonde fella raises his glass to his lips, but he's finished. He's pale, his eyes are glassy an' his posture slumped.

The shot glass hits the floor 'fore he does.

The crowd boos as Megan punches the air.

"Thank you, ladies an' gentlemen!" she crows. "Now, pay up!"

Coins an' banknotes're thrown at ma sis, showerin' down on the table an' floor 'round her. Sum men rush 'round the blonde fella an' prop him 'gainst the wall. They slap his face, but git little response.

I rest ma hands on the swing doors, ready to push 'em open, but I stop as fear freezes ma limbs. I don't wanna go inside. It's loud, an' there're too many folks in there with guns. I wanna go home—

Cole, toughen up.

"Coward," I hiss 'tween ma teeth an' then slip into the saloon. I kneel an' help Megan gather the coins.

"Cole!" Megan grins at me. "I gave that jackass a right poundin'. Thought he could out drink me. *Me!*"

I nod an' glance 'round the room. No one seems to've heard her outburst.

"Asshole said he'd drink me unner the table. Well, I sure put him in his place." She punches ma shoulder, makin' me stagger. "Oh, Cole! Ain't you proud of your sis?"

The bartender approaches us. He points to the pile of shot glasses on the table.

"I ain't lettin' you git away without payin' this time, Hayes." It's unfortunate that Joe ain't on duty tonight. He always puts Megan's expenses on her tab. A tab which must now be worth a president's ransom.

Megan points at me. "Ma brother'll pay up. I need to use the can."

I settle ma sis's large bill fer that night. Thankfully the amount Megan's won from bettin' covers it, with a little left over. Megan returns, staggerin' from side to side, wipin' her hands on her pants.

"Woulda made a horse proud," she says.

"Let's go," I say an' head towards the door, but sumone steps in front of us. It's one of the men who'd bin sittin' 'hind Megan's opponent. From the way his chest's puffed out, this ain't gonna be a friendly conversation. I shrink 'hind Megan.

"That money ain't yours," he says, twistin' his mouth like he's holdin' a cigar in there. "Give it back."

"It's ma money," Megan says, tippin' up her chin. "I won it."

"You cheated."

The pianist stops playin' an' the saloon becomes dead silent.

Megan draws herself up to her full six foot an' looks

the fella in the eye.

"I won that money fair an' square."

The man spits at her feet. "There ain't no way a filly like you could—"

Megan's fist punches his words back down his throat.

The man's head snaps back as he staggers into a table. He flings out an arm tryin' to catch himself but ends up flippin' 'nother. He goes down inna shower of broken glass.

"Say I'm a cheater one more time!" Megan roars, advancin' 'wards the man with her clenched fists at her sides. "I dare you!"

"Megan," I say, "come on. Let's go."

The men who'd bin tendin' to Megan's opponent stand. All their eyes say we ain't leavin' the saloon without a fight.

'Nother man who'd bin standin' at the bar walks 'tween Megan an' the men. He's got black hair, brown skin, is short an' hassa gauze stuck over his right ear unner his miller hat. An' he's wearin' a sheriff star. A new stillness comes over the saloon as everyone's eyes fix on that star.

"That's enough of that now," the sheriff says. "You've had your fun. Let the rest of us finish our night in peace."

At the appearance of the sheriff, I expect the men in the bar to back down. Hell, ma insides are already shrinkin' at the sight of that shinin' star. But quite a few of the eyes in the bar travel from the star up to the sheriff's face. There's a tense few moments where backs straighten, chins tip up an' chests puff out. Sumone's neck clicks. The sheriff remains still, keepin' eye contact with the rest of the bar.

Finally, sumone says, "Yes, Sheriff."

Quickly, all three men leave the saloon. Megan whispers, "Cowards," as they stagger through the swing doors, Megan's opponent's bein' dragged by his friends. Sensin' the diminished tension, the pianist recommences playin' an' folks in the saloon start talkin' again, 'though several pairs of eyes stay on us.

The sheriff an' Megan don't move. Ma palms are sweatin'.

"What happened to Robert?" Megan asks. "Last I heard he were sheriff in this town."

"Robert retired," the sheriff says. His accent ain't the same as ours – he sounds fresh off a train from New York City. He turns a little to the left, favourin' that side to listen. Perhaps he's lost his ear unner that bandage. "As of this week, I'm the new sheriff. Name's Antonio Valdez." He sticks out his hand. "Nice to meet you...?"

"Megan Hayes," Megan says, crossin' her arms. "This is ma brother, Cole."

Sheriff Valdez an' I catch each other's eyes an' exchange nods. Sheriff Valdez drops his hand.

"So, what made you choose a backwater town like Helena?" Megan asks.

"Opportunity, and a certain mission to bring those two to justice." The sheriff nods at the wall – or rather at the poster stuck to it.

WANTED
THE BLOOD TWINS
DEAD OR ALIVE
$2,000 cash reward

There're sketches of two people on it, but their faces're covered from their eyes downwards with cloth.

The sweatin's now startin' unner ma armpits. I keep ma expression calm, but inside I'm panickin' like a man caught with his head inna noose.

Does he know?

"The Blood Twins?" Megan laughs. "Those assholes're impossible to catch."

"No one's impossible to catch," the sheriff says.

"They're just more difficult."

"Heard they've stolen more 'n ten thousand dollars," Megan continues, with a dangerous boastful tone in her voice, "an' killed more people 'n the cholera."

The sheriff laughs – a quiet, low chuckle. "I believe the first part but not the second. Although they are an evil pair."

"An' no one ain't gotta clue who they are."

"I wouldn't have a job if they did."

"We should be goin' now," I say. I nod at ma sis. "Need to git sumbody home."

"Right. Let me know if you hear anything about the Blood Twins."

"Course we will!" Megan says.

We leave the saloon togither. Our horses're tied up out front, but I'll be damned 'fore lettin' ma sis ride in her state, so I lead the horses by the reins while we walk down the town's main street. I light a lamp so we've got sum light to see by. 'Round us the crickets're chirpin', hidden in the bushes. The air's still warm, but with the sun gone it's no longer swelterin'.

I'm calmer now we're outside, surrounded by the darkness an' the familiar rhythm of the horse's hooves. Rosie an' Hattie are sisters, an' they're the most reliable an' calm horses I've met. Rosie's coat's dark sorrel, like a newly opened chestnut. Hattie's a lighter dun colour. Megan's dark mare an' ma light steed. I love bein' 'round 'em; their smell, the warmth of their skin an' the way their hair quivers when bothered by a fly. Their graceful natures can't be matched by 'nother animal.

"What a jackass," Megan says. She trips an' falls flat on her face. "Damn!" I move to help her, but she pushes me away. "I'm *fine*! Gawddamn ground jumped up at me!"

Megan picks herself up an' we continue walkin'. I glance at her – road dust's in her hair an' she's a specklin' of blood on her cheek, where the stones've bitten her skin.

"Do you think he's gonna be trouble?" I ask.

"Naaahh." Megan leans 'gainst Rosie, usin' her to stop herself from fallin' again. "He seems like a pushover."

"But he said it were his mission to catch the Blood Twins. Robert only—"

"Cole!" Megan snaps. "Quit worryin'."

I shrink 'gainst Hattie's side, ma heart hammerin'.

"Hayes?"

We freeze. Sumone's on horseback on the road ahead of us. They're holdin' a lantern danglin' on the end of a stick in their hand, which casts their face in shadow.

"Who the hell are you?" Megan says, staggerin' a few paces ferward.

I smiled. "It's Dean."

"Sure as hell it is." Dean's horse moves ferward, close enough fer us to see his tanned weathered face an' the tuffs of grey hair unner his hat. Dean swings himself down. He takes one look at Megan an' sighs. "Bin in The Sleepin' Racoon again, Megan?"

Megan grins at him. "Sure as the sun do rise every day."

Even though Dean turns his eyes on me I refuse to meet his gaze. He's tryin' to tell me I need to stop Megan from doin' this to herself, but he knows as well as I do how you can never stop Megan when she wants to do summit.

"Where you bin?" I ask, desperate to change the subject.

"Next town over," Dean says. "Mary wanted summit from the drug store there. You need any help gittin' her home?"

Megan's head's now lollin' to one side as she leans on Rosie. She says summit, but this time her words're so slurred I can barely unnerstand 'em. Then she doubles over an' hurls on the ground 'round Rosie's hooves. I thank Gawd Rosie's such a calm mare.

"Yes, please," I say.

Fer a man in his sixties, Dean's still strong enough to lift Megan up into the saddle. He rides his horse with Megan slumped upright in front of him. I ride Hattie with Rosie tied 'hind me.

Megan an' me own a house on the edge of Helena, our hometown. The town's in Arizona Territory, on the south-west side near the Gila River an' California. The people here know us. The house's old an' always needin' repairs no matter how much time I spend fixin' it up. It ain't the sorta house you expect two bandits who've stolen ten thousand dollars to live in, an' that's 'cause we ain't stolen anythin' close to that amount. That were all newspaper talk. Anythin' that we do steal goes 'wards feedin' an' clothin' us, or gits drunk or gambled away by Megan.

The house is two storeys, with a kitchen, a parlour an' two bedrooms upstairs, with an outhouse at the back. It's gotta front an' back porch, an' stairs that creak like they're 'bout to collapse. There's a small paddock fer the horses an' a patch of ground where Pa once tried to grow vegetables.

The house'd belonged to our Pa an' Ma when they'd first got married. We'd bin born there. Both Ma an' Pa'd died there.

We git Megan cleaned up an' into bed.

Back outside Dean says, "Mary were sayin' today how much she misses you. Said to ask you to dinner the next time I saw you."

Warmth spreads through me at the thought of one of Mary's home cooked meals. "We'd love to drop by sumtime."

The lines 'round Dean's eyes crease as he smiles. "I'll tell Mary that." He swings himself back onto his horse. "Look after your sis, Cole. It looks like she could do with sum guidance. Gawd bless the two of you."

That night I pray to Gawd. I ask fer His blessin' an' am

met with the same stony silence as always. I long ago accepted that Gawd doesn't give His blessin' to people like ma sis an' I.

Not after all the folks we've killed.

Chapter 2

Deserving

The first thing Antonio felt when he woke up was his belt digging into his hip.

He groaned and rolled over onto his back, but his boot spurs caught in the bedsheets. Hadn't he even taken off his boots? With another groan, Antonio sat up and found he had managed to get one off before he passed out. He kicked off the remaining boot.

He had only drunk one bourbon, and yet his head was pounding. What time did he go to bed last night? Antonio wasn't sure, but he had a feeling he'd only managed a few hours' sleep.

Antonio pushed himself off his bed and over to the washbasin. He washed his face. Some water soaked through the gauze over his right ear. Antonio ripped the thing off and gave the ear beneath it a good scrub.

Towel still in hand, he turned his eyes back to the

Arizona Territory map stuck to his wall. Pins marked all the places the Blood Twins had committed a robbery. Newspaper articles reporting their activities surrounded the map. Last night had been a waste of time. He hoped someone there would have something for him to go on – just a hint as to who the Blood Twins might be or where they might strike next. But apart from the drunken comments from that young woman – Megan Hayes – no one even mentioned the Blood Twins. The people Antonio talked to about them shrugged and just said they hoped the outlaws didn't come to Helena. Antonio spent the rest of the night poring over his map, wondering if he was missing something. Until he collapsed into bed and fell asleep.

Antonio pressed his face into the towel.

It was just day seven. Robert and all the other sheriffs in the area hadn't caught the Blood Twins in the two years they'd been active. He shouldn't expect himself to do something in a few days that they were unable to do in a few years.

Except those men's jobs hadn't been riding on their success.

Antonio had to capture the Blood Twins – to thank Mr Scarborough for giving him this opportunity, to prove to everyone that he was worthy of the star pinned to his jacket and to put those murdering church-burning bastards behind bars.

Antonio clutched the cross around his neck and looked at one of the newspaper clippings pinned to his map. The one titled: BANDITS BURN DOWN CHURCH WITH CONGREGATION INSIDE.

The church was a Protestant one, but even as a Catholic Antonio felt a wave of horror re-reading the title. There was a special circle in hell for those who attacked a place of worship.

"Breakfast," Antonio told himself. "Breakfast first, and then we'll worry later."

The sheriff's office below Antonio's room had a small kitchen out the back where Antonio fried his bacon and eggs. He ate outside, watching the sky turn from a blaze of yellow, red, orange, purple and pink to a bright blue, and thought about the dozens of other desert sunsets he had watched while eating breakfast. Someplace that wasn't too far away that smelt of chipotle, stewed eggs, rice porridge, tomatoes and avocados, and soft bao. A place where the air was always filled with a mixture of chattering Cantonese and Spanish, laughter, music and the screams of playing children.

Antonio slammed his empty plate down on the decking. The memories retreated into the back of his mind. It was easier to get rid of them now – the first few days in Helena had been an assault of the sounds, tastes and sights of his family home. They had flocked to him like a murder of crows. Now they were easier to deal with. Leaving New York, he'd told himself he was never going back home. That he couldn't go back there.

Not after what he'd done.

Antonio washed the dishes and wrote his report on the amount of taxes he had collected the previous day. Being sheriff was a lot more money collecting and picking up trash than Antonio expected it to be.

Wanting some air, Antonio reached for his hat, but as he did the door opened and his deputy stepped inside.

"Mornin', Sheriff," the deputy said, throwing himself into the spare chair. Jason was a pale-skinned man with sandy hair. He always wore a neckerchief – today's was dark blue – and he was consistently late to arrive at the office and early to leave. As Jason had served the previous sheriff, Antonio hoped he would leave so Antonio could make his own appointment. But Jason seemed determined to stick around.

"Morning, Jason," Antonio replied.

"Heard you were at the Racoon last night," Jason said, kicking his heels up onto the desk. The smile on his face made Antonio bristle. "You, er, hear anythin' 'bout those Blood Twins?"

"No. Nothing."

"Ah. Well." Jason reached into his pocket and pulled out his cigar case. "Ain't that a shame? You hear anythin' from that Mr Scarborough yet? Didn't you say he were meant to be comin' back to town?"

"Nothing yet. Mr Scarborough is a very busy man. He'll contact me when he's ready."

There was a hiss as Jason struck a match. "Ah. Well, ain't that a shame. I guess he's got more important things to do in the big city, like appointin' folk to jobs who don't deserve 'em."

Smoke billowed out of Jason's mouth. Antonio kept his face neutral despite the stink and the insult. Jason had made it quite clear since day one that he thought Antonio should not be wearing the sheriff's star, because he was an out-of-towner who had been appointed by an out-of-towner. Not voted in like sheriffs usually were. Turns out Mr Scarborough had enough influence in Helena to appoint whoever he wanted as sheriff, something Antonio now understood had pissed off a lot of people in Helena. Antonio also had a suspicion that Jason had been in the running to be elected the next sheriff and didn't like that Antonio was Mexican. He'd made a few too many jokes about strange smells in the office and loud comments about how immigrants are out to steal American jobs. After a week it still grated even though Antonio did his best to ignore it. He thought it would be best to not bring up the fact that his family had likely been in this part of the country longer than Jason's.

Jason sucked on his cigar, making the tip glow. "But then I guess if you're one of the richest mine-owners in Arizona – hell, one of the richest in America – you can do whatever the hell you want."

"Must be nice," Antonio said.

Jason laughed. "Yeah, I bet it is."

"I was about to head out," Antonio said. "I'll be back in an hour or so. While you're in the office, sort the—"

"Did you fergit, Sheriff?" Antonio blinked. "Me an' the boys are takin' you to Los Angeles today fer your welcomin' party."

"But that's not until this afternoon."

"Ah, Sheriff, you gotta git started early, otherwise it's only half a night!" Jason pushed himself out of the chair. "But if you don't wanna go, then I can tell the boys you've got more important things to do."

Antonio did. He was Helena's sheriff and he didn't trust Jason or his men one bit. This night out was likely going to be an opportunity for them to dispose of him – either by threat or by slitting his throat – but Antonio didn't dare say no out of fear of making their relationship worse. Keep your enemies closer and all that.

"Well," Antonio said putting on his hat, "sounds like we'd better head to the train station."

With a big grin on his face, Jason slapped Antonio on the shoulder. "That we do. Come on, Sheriff, we'll meet the boys there. We're gonna show you a night out that you'll never fergit." Jason released a lungful of smoke in front of Antonio's face and breezed out the door. Antonio held his breath and wafted the smoke away with his hat.

Chapter 3

The Blood Twins

The newspapers called us the Blood Twins 'cause we kill people. The name's fittin' fer 'nother reason 'cause Megan an' me were born in blood. Our ma died givin' birth to us.

I wish I could say I ain't never killed a human being. But I can't. I've killed three. They threatened ma sis's life.

The first man I killed I almost didn't pull the trigger.

But Megan were shoutin' at me, hollerin' fer help, an' I heard Pa's voice in ma head again: *Cole, toughen up.*

An' I pulled the trigger.

Ma bullet took the man through the neck. He drowned in his own blood.

I saw his face everwhere I went fer a week after. I still catch him out the corner of ma eye sumtimes. But I killed again. An' again to save her. An' I'll keep doin' it to keep her safe.

That's how much I love her.

I find Megan lyin' outside next to the horse trough.

She's conscious, starin' up at the sky. Her eyes're so blue they look like they're mirrorin' the heavens. Megan's hair, face an' shoulders're soakin' wet. She must've dunked her head in the water to relieve herself of the headache.

Megan's the exact same shape Pa were; big shouldered, tall an' muscular. She's got dark ginger hair, white skin that's strewn with freckles an' catches easy in the sun.

Accordin' to Pa, I take after Ma. I've her willowy body, long fingers an' sandy hair. Ma skin's tanned from always bein' outdoors an' I've a small smatterin' of freckles along ma arms. Where I takes after Ma in appearance, Pa told us Megan takes after her in personality. Megan's how I imagine Ma'd bin – a free spirit, who could shoot an' drink jest as good as any man.

"I feel like crap," she mutters.

"I ain't surprised," I say, crouchin' beside her. "Can you sit up?"

"Yeah, but I know ma head'll crack like an egg if I does."

"How much do you remember?" I ask.

Megan groans an' clamps a hand to her forehead. "I remember meetin' that new sheriff in the bar, leavin' the Raccoon, walkin' home an'... didn't we meet sumone on the way?"

"Dean," I say, feelin' relieved. If Megan remembers that much, she ain't too bad. There're sum mornin's she remembers nuthin' 'bout the previous night.

"Dean! Yeah." Megan tips her head back an' squints at the sun. "What day is it?"

I think fer a few moments. Keepin' track of the days has never bin one of ma specialities.

"June twenty, I think."

Megan sits bolt upright. "Damn!" She jumps up an' sprints into the house, stumblin' on the threshold, fergittin' her hangover all a sudden. I follow.

I find her rifflin' through Pa's trunk in her room. She's pullin' out our guns.

"What's wrong?" I ask.

"It's today, jackass! The express car!"

Damn. I'd clean fergot. This mornin', I'd bin thinkin' 'bout Cassidy Scarborough – 'bout the time she an' I found an injured cactus wren. I remembered the way she'd cupped the creature in her hands, an' told me kind words when I cried over how much pain the bird musta bin in. The wren died, an' after we buried it, she held ma hand an' cried with me. She didn't tell me boys shouldn't cry – not like Megan woulda done. I'd thought 'bout what she must look like now – tall but a little shorter 'n me, with long-lashed green eyes, hair the colour of fall leaves, perhaps tied inna knot at the back of her head. Ma heart aches to see her again, 'though I know I'll likely never.

"Cole, git the horses ready! We hafta leave fer Barren Post now."

I rush outside. Hattie an' Rosie're munchin' on their hay. Ideally I'd brush an' groom 'em 'fore we started ridin', but Megan's inna rush to git away. I clean their hooves quick. Megan cares nuthin' fer Rosie. It's up to me to look after both horses. Megan doesn't even know how to saddle 'em.

Megan screams fer me to come git ready. I tie the horses by their trough an' go to do ma sis's biddin'.

We always rob masked. That's how we keep our identities separate. There's Megan an' Cole Hayes, two orphans, livin' in their family's house on the edge of Helena. They're pitied by the town 'cause of what happened to their Pa.

Then there's the Blood Twins – two ruthless bandits who rob stagecoaches, carriages an' houses. They've bin terrorisin' Arizona Territory fer two years. They're rumoured to've once bin strung up, cut down an' pronounced dead, only to come alive again. They've stolen more money 'n President Harrison owns, an' they've murdered so many people their clothes're dyed red by their victims' blood. I can tell you, since me an' Megan're the Blood Twins, that none of those rumours're true. We've near bin caught more times 'n I can count, but we've never bin hung. The money we've stolen don't come close to what the president has. An' when we'd bought our clothes they were already red – Megan says our clothes oughta fit the name we've bin given.

Our masks're simple triangles of black cloth that cover our faces from the nose down. Mine's the mask our pa'd worn on his last robbery. Megan refuses to touch it. She hates it an' is disgusted I wear it, but it's one of the few things we have of his.

We pack our red clothes an' masks in saddlebags but put on our guns. I strap mine to ma waist: a Colt Navy. It hugs the outside of ma left leg. The right holster's empty. I lost that one robbin' a stagecoach a few months back. When I killed ma third man. I'm glad that gun's gone. It means I'm carryin' one less murder weapon.

Megan's two guns Smithy an' Florence've killed more 'n three men. She loves her guns like I love Hattie an' Rosie. You can imagine her anger when I lost ma right gun.

"It serves you right fer bein' so careless," were all she said. There'd bin no thanks fer savin' her life. I ain't bought maself a new right gun.

We mount our horses. Hattie seems more nervous 'n usual. I soothe her. Megan tsks as I do so, but I ain't gonna risk gittin' bucked off, an' I hate seein' Hattie in distress. It's in her eyes. Summit's troublin' her. I stroke her nose 'til she calms.

"Are you ready yet?"

"Sure." I put ma left leg in the stirrup an' swing ma

right leg over. Ma saddle's soft an' well moulded from years ridin'. I take the reins in ma right hand an' rest ma other on the horn of ma saddle.

"Let's go!" Megan spurs Rosie into action an' they set off at a canter. Why does she do that? She knows how bad it is fer horses not to take it slow first. There's bin plenty of times we've hadda spur the horses into a canter runnin' away, but there ain't a rush now. Megan's so darn impatient.

I urge Hattie on with a gentle nudge of ma foot. I walk her fer a minute, then urge her into a trot. I take ma time. I don't want her to pull a muscle. Then we're gallopin' full out, flyin' through the desert, kickin' up dust. Megan an' Rosie're ahead. They're quite far, but I urge Hattie on an' we soon catch up. The wind's whippin' ma face, takin' the edge off the day's fierce heat. I smile an' whoop, fer there's nuthin' I enjoy more in the world 'n this.

Chapter 4

Train Robbin'

We robbed fer the first time when we were fifteen – less 'n three months after our pa'd died.

Megan said we were gonna do it. Said we oughta keep Pa's name alive. Said it were what he'd've wanted.

She did it 'cause she missed him an' she wanted summit to take away the pain. I did it 'cause Pa told me to look after Megan. 'Cause I wanted to toughen up like he told me. 'Cause I didn't wanna be a coward.

But then Megan developed a likin' fer the danger, fer the money an' fer the drink. Megan never knew the sins of drink 'til after the third robbery. It were a small store inna town on the California border, one that sold whisky. We'd taken the money an' one bottle. Megan'd drunk the whole thing at home an' thrown up everywhere. I'd taken a sip an' shoved it away, hatin' the burn. But ma sis bought an' stole more, an' got drunk as much as she could.

Nuthin' I said or did could make her stop.

We ride the horses into Barren Post an' hitch 'em outside a saloon. We tell the barman we'll be gone fer a while an' pay him to make sure the horses git all they need. It breaks ma heart to leave Rosie an' Hattie. They watch us go. Hattie snorts an' tosses her head. Summit's still troublin' her. I don't look at her 'case I run back.

Megan doesn't notice. Her eyes're fixed ahead an' her mouth's movin' ever so slight like she's goin' over the plan again. She's always this focused 'fore a robbery. I look down at ma hands. They're tremblin'.

First, we need sumwhere to change. Inside the saloon we find an empty room. We change an' git outta there in two minutes. As well as wearin' red shirts an' pants, Megan's got her hair tied back an' shoved unner her hat. With her wide face an' heavy jaw this makes her look more like a boy 'n a girl. The first reported sights of the Blood Twins described 'em as two men, an' afterwards we didn't see any point in correctin' 'em. It were 'nother layer of protection 'tween keepin' Cole an' Megan Hayes separate from those bandits.

We sneak 'round the backstreets of the town, duckin' 'hind houses an' avoidin' everyone we see. If sumone sees the Blood Twins wanderin' 'round the town, the sheriff'll be on our heads 'fore we can catch the train.

The station ain't too far away, but it takes a painful amount of time to git there. We hide 'round the back an' keep an eye on the rails. Megan's breathin' deep, steady breaths. Her fingers stroke her gun holster, tracin' the stamped leather. I pray she ain't gonna fire 'em today.

The train enters the station inna cloud of steam. We run, usin' the steam as cover to make it 'round the back of the train. The express car's at the front. We wait 'hind it, outta sight of the passengers leavin' an' boardin'.

I go over the plan again. We git on, go in the express

car, hold up the guard, git him to tell us the safe code, git the money, jump off the train at the next stop an' run back to where we'd left the horses. Easy. We've done this a few times 'fore. It's risky – sumtimes there're two guards, once there'd bin three. It'd bin hard keepin' all of 'em in check, 'specially when Megan'd had all her attention on the safe – but the pay fer a train robbery's good. Real good. So good we won't hafta rob fer a long time.

We don't jump aboard 'til the train starts to move, pullin' ourselves up 'hind the express car. We wait fer the train to gain enough speed – when there's no hope of anyone comin' to stop us – an' make ready to enter the express car.

Megan grips her guns. I git out ma Colt Navy. I hate the feelin' of it in ma hand – it's like I'm holdin' a lit stick of dynamite.

Megan nods at the door.

"On three," she whispers. "One..." I grip the door handle. "Two..." I take a deep breath. "Three!"

I push the handle down an' kick the door open. Megan strides into the carriage, guns held up front.

"Hold 'em high!" she shouts.

We expect to see one guard, perhaps two, sittin' inside the express car. Sumtimes we find 'em dozin'. Sumtimes we find 'em readin', or playin' cards. But this time, we find 'em talkin' to Sheriff Valdez an' three other men. All seven of us stare in confusion at each other fer a few seconds.

Sheriff Valdez makes a grab fer his holsters.

"Drop your guns!" he hollers.

Megan fires five bullets. One of 'em hits the back wall an' the others bury 'emselves into four of the men. They go down screamin'. Two on two. It's even now.

I scramble 'hind a crate as bullets fly. Megan's done the same on the other side of the carriage. She's breathin' hard, her back 'gainst the crate, her guns crossed over her chest.

We're trapped.

I flick the hammer down on ma Colt. I don't wanna shoot 'em, but if it comes to a choice 'tween their lives an' mine an' ma sis's, I know whose I'll choose.

Chapter 5

Hostage

Our pa were killed robbin' Mr Scarborough's house. He'd bin escapin' on horseback an' Mr Scarborough shot him twice with his rifle.

Mr Benjamin Scarborough'd bin Pa's employer not two years 'fore when Pa'd worked in his silver mines. Then Mr Scarborough accused Pa of stealin' from him. 'Course Pa were innocent, but he were fired anyway, sent to jail fer a coupla years, an' when he got out he hadda turn to robbin' to feed us, 'cause no one would hire a thief. Pa told everyone he hadda job outta town to cover his tracks. He didn't git one 'cause he were afraid to leave us alone. Even though he did in the end.

Ma sis hated the Scarboroughs – hated 'em fer what they'd done to Pa. She wanted nuthin' more 'n to put a bullet 'tween Mr Scarborough's eyes. She's bin plottin' his death fer years, but with the Scarboroughs in New York she couldn't git at him.

I didn't hate Mr Scarborough. He'd bin protectin' his home an' his family, jest as our pa'd bin protectin' his. But the day Pa'd bin fired were the last day I'd sin Cassidy. We'd bin playmates. We used to run 'round the Scarborough's fields, chasin' birds an' catchin' critters. I missed those days. They were the days when things were simple.

I breathe in an' swing 'round the side of the crate. The carriage is already full of smoke. Blind, I fire all six of ma shots an' pull back. No one screams. Ma aim must've bin off, an' I can't help feelin' relieved. I reload ma gun, droppin' the empty cartridges on the carriage floor. Megan fires 'nother two shots. They're followed by screams an' gasps of pain.

Then I'm no longer in the carriage.

I'm inna wooden church.

Flames're roarin' in ma ears. 'Hind 'em I can hear the screams of the burnin'.

Please. No.

Not now.

Not again.

I can't afford to go back now.

Please.

"Go!" Megan shouts.

Her voice pulls me outta ma head. I emerge in time to catch her backin' out the carriage door. I follow her, still shakin'. The sheriff an' the other five men are lyin' on the floor. Most are still, but the one on the far right's screamin' with a hand on his neck. Blood's pumpin' through it like water from an overflowin' drain. I run after Megan.

We jump the join 'tween the express car an' the next. I try not to look at the blur 'neath me, or on either side. The next carriage's the first passenger one an' it's empty. We pass through to the second.

How the hell we're gonna git outta this mess? What's the sheriff doin' in the express car anyway? Is it jest a coincidence? Or did they know we'd be there?

The second carriage's got two men an' three women in it. Me an' Megan point our guns at 'em. They let us pass. Their eyes burn ma back, an' I hear "the Blood Twins" whispered as we leave.

The third an' fourth carriages're both occupied, but the passengers're smart enough to let us through. I hear our name whispered a few more times as we move through the train. Sumone starts prayin' as soon as we enter their carriage, beggin' Gawd to spare 'em from bein' burnt alive.

In the fifth carriage a man grabs Megan as she passes an' tries to wrestle a gun off her. Megan shoots him through the forehead. A fountain of blood sprays 'cross the carriage windows an' ma face. The man slumps to the floor an' I wipe ma eyes on the back of ma hand.

Sick rises in ma throat. I swallow, feelin' the blood dryin' on ma skin. Ma mask's covered an' every time I breathe in the smell of iron clogs ma throat.

Panic rushes up inside me, clawin' at ma insides as it scrambles fer a way to escape.

It's hard to breathe.

I wanna scream.

I wanna throw up.

I wanna throw maself out the carriage window.

I don't wanna—

Cole, toughen up.

"Brother!" Megan gestures to me. "C'mon!"

I swallow an' step over the man, 'round the chunks of white an' pink. The sounds of screamin' echo in ma ears as I leave the carriage.

No one in the other carriages gives us any trouble.

We reach the last one, which is the first class carriage.

We bundle into it an' Megan bars the door 'hind us.

The carriage's a private one, fully furnished, with blue couches, a small table with two chairs, a blue flowery carpet an' light curtains over the windows. An' sittin' on one of the couches, an open book in her lap, wearin' a dark green dress, is a very beautiful lady. She's no older 'n Megan an' me, an' is starin' at us with wide eyes. She's mostly starin' at ma blood-splattered face.

Megan also sees her. "Hell! Why in Gawd's name can't anythin' go right today? Grab her 'fore she does anythin' stupid."

The woman jumps up an' holds the book like she's gonna swat a fly.

"Don't lay a finger on me!" she hisses. I move 'wards her, but stop. Do I know her? She's really beautiful – breathtakin'ly so. She's got white skin, a heart-shaped face with a prominent jaw an' cheek bones, an' long auburn hair, which is gathered at the back of her head. Her eyes're the same green as her dress.

"Brother!" Megan snaps. "Grab her!"

"Sorry, ma'am." I lunge an' grab the woman's arm that's holdin' the book.

She screams an' drops the tome, but her other hand claws at me. I gasp as her nails rake ma face. They come away bloodied. I try to push her down on the couch. Her fingers hook over the top of ma mask an' pull. The cloth falls away. I freeze. The woman's starin' at me with the same shocked expression I must've on ma face. I don't know what to do. Then Megan sees what's happenin'.

"Jesus!"

I fumble with ma mask, tryin' to git it back on. Ma sis grabs the woman's arms an' pulls 'em 'hind her back. Megan ties her hands there with the curtain cord, an' pushes her back onto the couch. The woman continues to struggle.

Megan slaps her face. Their skin connects with a crack

that makes me an' the woman gasp. Megan points a finger at her.

"Stay there an' keep outta trouble."

"Or what?" the woman spits. Her hair's fallen 'cross her face an' her cheek's turnin' red.

Megan points the barrel of her gun 'tween the woman's eyes. "Or I'll use this."

The woman slouches 'gainst the couch. I turn away from her. She can't be saved, not now she's sin ma face. She hassa die so our identities can remain secret. I know the only reason Megan ain't shot the woman yet is 'cause she hassa use fer her.

"Fer Gawd's sake, brother," Megan says, "wipe that shit off your face."

As I'm usin' a curtain to clean the blood off ma face, the door handle rattles an' there's a thump as sumbody pushes at the door on the other side.

"You in there?" hollers a voice. The sheriff's. "There are ten of us out here and we're all armed. If you come out with your guns at your feet, you won't be harmed. If you resist, we'll be forced to break down the door. You stand no chance."

"We've a hostage!" Megan replies. She's standin' next to the door, one gun out. Her knuckles're white. "If you try to force entry, we'll kill her."

There's silence on the other side of the door.

"Fine! I'll prove we ain't lyin'. Brother, see to her."

The woman glares at me as I approach. I bite ma bottom lip. She wriggles an' strains 'gainst the curtain cord.

"Don't touch me!" she hisses.

I stop. A flash of recognition hits me. Where have I sin her 'fore?

"Brother!" Megan snaps.

I seize the woman's arm. I pinch her, hard, on the forearm. I expect her to cry out, but she jest keeps lookin' at me with those hard green eyes. I keep ma fingers there fer a good minute. Upon removin' 'em a large red mark blooms on her skin.

"Oh fer Gawd's sake!" Megan strides over an' slaps the woman 'round the face. She screams an' cowers 'gainst the couch, sobbin'. The couch's blue material darkens with her fallen tears.

'Nother stab of recognition pierces me, but I swallow an' look out the carriage window 'fore I can break through it. There's a lump in ma throat I can't swallow. I wanna hit summit.

"Were that good enough fer you, Sheriff?" Megan hollers.

"Fine," comes the sheriff's voice.

"Here's the deal," Megan says. "You're gonna cut this carriage loose from the rest of the train. It's gonna stop while the train carries on. Nice 'n simple."

"What about the girl?"

"She's comin' with us."

The woman stares at Megan with wide eyes.

The sheriff asks, "What're you going to do—"

"She ain't your business!" Megan snaps. "Jest know that if you try to come in here now, she's a dead girl. If you cut us, then who knows?" There's 'nother long pause. "Fifty-fifty chance, Sheriff."

"Why don't we trade? Your freedom for the girl?"

Megan snorts. "An' what'd we have to ensure our safety? Nice try, Sheriff, but no thanks."

There's a brief pause. "Fine. We'll cut you loose."

All ma breath comes floodin' out inna whoosh. I glance at Megan. She's leanin' 'gainst the door, exhausted all a sudden. But we ain't outta danger yet.

We wait, an' wait, fer minutes. Then we hear the sound of metal 'gainst metal an' our carriage shifts unner our feet. I pull down the window an' stick ma head out. The train's movin' away from us. Our carriage's slowin' down.

"What now?" I ask.

"We shoot her," Megan says, straightenin' herself.

"Please." The woman's lost all her courage. She's cryin' now – thick streams of tears runnin' down her cheeks. "Don't kill me."

I don't wanna shoot her, but she's sin ma face so she hassa die.

Then the recognition comes back, an' this time I break through it.

I remember sittin' in the desert, lookin' at a girl with two bloody knees. She'd fallen down, but were tryin' not to cry. She'd hidden her face 'hind her long auburn hair, but I saw two tears run down her cheeks. She warn't cryin' 'cause of the pain, but 'cause of what her pa would say when he saw her torn skin.

An' here is that same girl. Now all grown.

The woman I'd bin longin' to see fer the past six years.

Cassidy Scarborough.

Chapter 6

Desert

Cassidy an' me'd once bin best buds an' I thought we'd stay friends ferever. I'd bin blind to our differences.

Cassidy's pa didn't like her wanderin' too far from the house, so we hadda stay on the estate. Cassidy warn't even allowed to go to school. She hadda governess – a nice lady who allowed us to go further away 'n she were meant to. Mr Scarborough didn't know that Cassidy, Megan an' me used to play together, 'cause every time he came home early the governess used to chase Megan an' me away.

Megan an' Cassidy never really got on. Megan wanted to play outdoors all the time, catchin' critters, huntin' fer gold an' playin' cowboys an' Indians. Cassidy were happy to play these games but also wanted to play tea parties, which Megan couldn't stand. I were never any good at playin' tea parties, but I enjoyed the peace an' quiet of 'em. Megan used to stomp off when I agreed to play 'em with Cassidy. I never knew where she went – Megan hated the other girls at school an' the boys always refused to let her join in with their games. They used to invite me to play, but I refused to 'less they included Megan. They refused, even though Megan were better at their kinda games 'n me.

The last day I saw Cassidy were six years ago, on the day our pa were fired by Mr Scarborough an' sent to jail. Dean came to pick us up from the Scarborough estate, summit he'd never done 'fore. He told us to say goodbye to Cassidy an' then we went to his an' Mary's house. When Megan an' me tried to go to Cassidy's house, Dean told us we warn't allowed to go there no more. I cried. Megan warn't fussed.

Then Pa were shot by Mr Scarborough, an' Mr Scarborough took Cassidy to New York. I thought they'd be back soon, that it were only a short visit. But two years'd passed since our Pa's death an' I'd lost all hope of seein' her again.

Megan wastes no time. She presses Florence's barrel 'gainst Cassidy's head. Cassidy shuts her eyes an' starts mutterin' a prayer unner her breath. She's tremblin'. A strand of hair's come outta her bun an' is driftin' 'cross her face.

"No!" I knock the gun from ma sis's hand. It falls to the carriage floor with a loud clatter. Summit pulls in ma chest, the horror of what I've jest done realised. No one touches Smithy an' Florence 'cept Megan. Her blue eyes blaze as she turns her gaze on me.

"Don't shoot her," I say, ma voice shakin'. "Please." 'Hind me I hear Cassidy whimper.

"Why the hell shouldn't I?" Megan says. Her voice's the opposite to mine – cold, low an' controlled. "She saw your face. She hasta die! We're in enough shit already without her gabbin' 'bout what we look like!"

"She didn't see ma face."

Megan's eyes narrow. "What?"

"She didn't see ma face. She couldn't've. Ma mask were off fer jest a second, an' I turned away quick. She don't know who we are. Letta her go."

Megan frowns. "Don't you dare lie to me."

"I swear." I swallow. "On Pa's grave."

Megan straightens her back an' glares' at me with one eye. I wanna cower, but I keep upright. I can't back down or she'll know I'm lyin'.

"We can't let her go," Megan says at last. "It's too risky."

I feel ma heartbeat in ma throat. "Then... let's take her with us."

Megan scoffs. "An' what'll we *do* with Miss Priss?"

"She can look after the house. Do your chores." Megan hates doin' any sorta work that don't involve her shootin' things. This is an offer she'll find hard to refuse.

She don't say anythin' fer a while, then a wide smirk spreads 'cross her face an' her eyes glow like a wolf's. Like she's jest realised summit that pleases her. Ma stomach lurches.

"Fine," she says. "She stays with us."

"What?" Cassidy splutters. "I'm not staying with you! I want to go home!"

"Tough, Miss Priss. Now, let's git goin' 'fore they double back on us."

We walk, not along the train tracks – that'll make us easy to find – but 'cross the desert.

It ain't the hottest I've felt, but it's enough to make me wanna rip ma mask from ma face. The dust swirls 'round ma boots an' soon they're coated. I'm sweatin' in ma heavy clothes, an' a thumpin' headache's started in ma temples. There's sweat runnin' into ma eyes. Ma limbs are heavy. All the energy's run outta me from the train robbery. But even though ma body's heavy with exhaustion, ma mind's whirrin'.

Cassidy's here, walkin' right in fronta me.

I can't believe it.

After six years of wonderin' if I'd ever see her again, she's here.

I wanna holler an' jump fer joy. I wanna wrap ma arm 'round her an' hug her to me, but I can't. 'Cause Megan can't know an' from the hatred in Cassidy's eyes when she looks at me, I don't think she recognises me.

Megan an' Cassidy're ahead of me. Megan's tuggin' Cassidy along by the rope, her hands now tied in front of her. She looks like a cow bein' dragged to market. Cassidy won't shut up. She's complainin' 'bout the heat, the sun, the cryin' birds, the animals – which there ain't none of 'cept the occasional lizard – an' her hurtin' feet. I glance at her shoes. They're the ones with the pointed toes an' the high heels. Not the kinda shoes you wanna be wearin' fer walkin' in the desert.

Cassidy tries to git away a few times, when she thinks Megan's attention's turned away from her. They're feeble attempts – she tries jerkin' backwards to pull the rope from ma sis's hands. But Megan's ready every time an' she pulls back, sendin' Cassidy sprawlin' in the dust. I wanna take Cassidy in ma arms an' carry her, to stop her achin' feet, to dry her face an' calm her fears. But Megan'd never allow me to do that. Cassidy'd never allow me to do that either.

The fourth time Cassidy tries to run snaps Megan's patience. Megan tugs on her rope so hard she pulls Cassidy to the ground, then drags her through the dust. Cassidy screams as ma sis drags her nearer, 'til she's yanked to her feet by her hair. I run towards 'em, ready to innerveen, but Megan gives me a look that tells me to stay back.

"I fuckin' swear," Megan hisses in Cassidy's ear, "if you

don't quit bein' a whiney ungrateful bitch, I'll blow your eyeballs out the back of your head!" Then she throws Cassidy back onto the ground.

Cassidy stares up at Megan with darin' eyes, sayin' nuthin', but she doesn't make 'nother move to escape an' quits her whinin'. She keeps a slow pace, draggin' her feet an' swayin' from side to side like a drunk. She does this fer a while an' I worry she might be sufferin' bad from lack of water, but the other part of me knows she's doin' it to annoy Megan.

We've bin walkin' fer a good hour, an' the sun's near touchin' the horizon. Megan stops an' says, "Gawddammit! We'll be wanderin' 'round here in the dark at the pace we're goin'." She looks at me. "One of us needs to git the horses."

I think quick. If Megan stays here with Cassidy, it's very likely I'll return to jest Megan. "You go. I'll stay here with—" Cassidy's name near slips from ma lips, but thankfully ma throat clogs in the heat. I swallow. "—the hostage."

"Oh, no. I don't trust you. You'll let her go if she so much as bats her eyelashes at you. I'll stay here an' you can go git the horses."

"I can't find the way to town," I lie.

"But it's jest three miles away!"

"I'll git lost."

Megan rolls her eyes. "Fine! I'll git the Gawddamn horses!" She hands me the rope bindin' Cassidy. "An' if I come back to find you've let her escape, Gawd won't stop me from killin' the both of you."

Megan walks briskly off into the dyin' light, leavin' me an' Cassidy alone.

I sit down. Ma feet're two hot coals. The warmth's startin' to lessen with the light, but I'm desperate fer the cooler evenin' air on ma face. I remove ma mask fer a moment an' wipe the sweat away with ma sleeve. There ain't no point in keepin' any pretences 'round Cassidy – she's sin ma face. Cassidy remains standin'. I watch her out the corner of ma eye. She's lookin' at me. I return her gaze an' she turns away quick.

"I'm sorry 'bout ma sis," I say. There's no point pretendin' Megan's ma brother. Cassidy's heard her voice enough to tell she ain't a fellar. "She's a difficult person." Cassidy says nuthin'. She's starin' at the sun, which is slowly disappearin'.

"Why don't you sit yourself down? Your feet must be tired after the walk." Still nuthin'. Near ma hand a lizard scuttles unner a rock. I wish I could do that sumtimes – hide unner a rock to git away from the world.

"It were the only way to save your life," I say, "by sayin' you ain't sin ma face. I didn't want your blood on ma hands."

"I've got enough information for them to do a good drawing of the two of you." Her accent's changed. She speaks like a lady. Her western drawl's gone. "Especially since I know your partner's your sister, not your brother." A long pause follows. "Are you really the Blood Twins?"

I nod.

Cassidy shuts her eyes an' breathes deep. "What are you going to do with me?" she whispers.

"I... I don't know."

There's 'nother pause. While I trace the toe of ma boot in the dust, Cassidy's eyes turn on me. It ain't a hateful kinda look, or a bored expression. She's lookin' at me like I musta bin lookin' at her on the train, when I were tryin' to work out who she were.

Does she recognise me?

I mean, I've grown a lot in six years, but I haven't changed that much. An' how many pairs of brothers an' sisters are there that look like Megan an' me in this part of Arizona? Cassidy spent most days with us when we were kids. Surely she'll know who we are.

I wanna tell her. I want her to know who I am, that I know who she is, but ma throat's sealed togither from thirst. I put ma mask back into place.

"I've sum advice fer you," I say. "Don't tell ma sis who you are."

"Why?" Cassidy frowns. "Do you know who I am?"

"Jest trust me on this. If you wanna live to see your pa again, don't tell ma sis your real name."

To ma surprise, Cassidy kneels in front of me. I lean back, amazed by the greenness of her eyes. There's no green like it in the desert. I can see every freckle 'cross the bridge of her nose.

"Then let me go," she says. "Don't give your sister the chance to kill me." She bites her bottom lip an' ma hands loosen on the rope. I lean ferward. Her voice's low. "You don't have to do everything she says. You're so much better than her and you know it. You know this is wrong." The curtain cord starts to slide outta ma hands. "Wouldn't it be so easy to just..." The rope lurches. Ma senses return an' I grab it. Cassidy tries to pull it from ma hands, but I pull harder. She loses her grip an' falls back in the dust. She screams in frustration an' turns her back on me.

We give up on talkin'. I don't know whatta say. As much as I wanna comfort her, I can't. She won't accept anythin' from me. I watch the sun set an' listen to the sounds of the desert. Crickets're chirrpin' an' there's a wolf howlin' sumwhere.

Then I hear the faint thunder of hooves an' Megan comes into sight ridin' Rosie, with Hattie in tow. Both horses look tired already. I click ma tongue. Will she ever learn?

"Well done, brother," Megan says, as she pulls up beside us. She ain't wearin' her bandit clothes no more, but her mask's on. Megan looks at Cassidy, her eyes alight in the same way as when I knocked the gun from her hand. "You're ridin' with me, Miss Priss."

Cassidy clambers up onto Rosie inna ungraceful way, an' as soon as she's up Megan's canterin' away. I pull maself onto Hattie an' follow 'em at a slow trot.

Chapter 7

Competence

He'd blown it.

The Blood Twins were right there, in the palm of his hand, and he'd let them go.

"Sheriff." Antonio jerked upright and looked at the train conductor and driver. If they were surprised to have found the sheriff sitting on a crate with his head in his hands they didn't show it.

"We've finished our count of the passengers," the conductor said. "One dead, an' one missin'. Otherwise, all unharmed an' accounted fer. 'Though, a lot of 'em are in distress."

"That's to be expected, I guess," Antonio said.

"I've telegrammed the head office," the driver said. "Told 'em 'bout our accident. They'll telegram the other stations to let 'em know we're runnin' late. They've cancelled the next train an' are sendin' sumone to collect the detached carriage, but we need to git goin' again soon. Can't sit here much longer."

"I guess not," Antonio said. "The man who was murdered, I've spoken to his wife. They were travelling back home to El Paso, so could you take the body with you? Perhaps telegram ahead so there'll be a coroner waiting for you to take the body."

"Not a problem, Sheriff." The conductor tipped his hat. "Train robbery's always bad business, but to blow an innocent man's head clean apart, an' to take a poor lady hostage... Well, the devil musta bin possessin' those two fer 'em to do such things. Didja find out who that lady might be?"

"Er, no. No, I'm still looking into it."

"I hope you catch the varmints soon, Sheriff," the driver said.

"Thank you," Antonio said.

The driver and conductor walked away. Antonio ran a hand down his face and sighed. He allowed himself a few more minutes to sit quiet, then forced himself to his feet and walked back to the station.

After the end carriage had been cut, the train continued onto the next station, where Antonio made the driver stop and assess the damage. Two of the three men the Blood Twins had shot in the express car were dead. The express car guard had taken a bullet to the leg. He'd live, but he wouldn't be walking anytime soon. Like Antonio, Jason avoided the spray of bullets.

Instead of checking on the passengers like Antonio had told him to, Jason leant against the side of the train, smoking a cigar.

"Bit of a mess, eh, Sheriff," he said.

"Yes, I guess."

"An' jest after a week on the job. Well, guess this is what happens when you appoint folks to jobs that don't deserve 'em."

Antonio pressed his back teeth together.

"I'm sure Robert wouldn't've made as big a mess as you jest did. Two train guards dead. Three citizens, includin' two of ma best friends, dead, an' the other missin'." Jason took one last pull on his cigar and threw it away. Shaking his head, he said, "Guess that fancy map of yours with all those pins an' readin' all those newspaper articles ain't much use at all."

"We're going to ride back along the railroad," Antonio said, doing his best to keep his voice level, "to find the cut carriage. They might have left the hostage in it."

"If it's all right by you, Sheriff—" Jason pushed his hat down. "—I'm gonna stick 'round here. Wanna see that ma boys git home safe."

It was not alright. Going into a potentially dangerous situation, Antonio needed backup, but it would be callous to tell that to Jason when the bodies of two of his friends lay inside the station. So he nodded and went to find a horse.

The cut carriage was a way back down the railroad. Antonio drew his guns the moment it came into sight. In the vast desert there was nowhere to hide his approach, so he kept his eyes sharp and his guns trained on the carriage. He scanned the windows for any signs of movement.

None came.

Antonio dismounted at the back. He crouched and slowly cracked open the door. He waited, turning his left ear to the carriage interior. Nothing. He pushed the door open further. Still nothing. He stood up and stepped inside.

It was empty.

At least of people. The carriage was still full of boxes and bags, likely belonging to the hostage. Shoving his guns in his belt, Antonio began checking the luggage, hoping to identify the hostage. Then at least he could contact the girl's family.

Then he saw the name stamped on the outside of one of the luggage cases and knew that was not an option.

Tracking the Blood Twins was impossible. Antonio had never been the most competent tracker and it was impossible for him to do so across the desert, where the wind kept shifting the dirt. He gave up quickly and galloped as fast as he could back to Helena.

A telegram waited for him on his desk.

Antonio ignored it until he had washed and hydrated himself. Then he read the name of the sender and the feeling of nausea in his stomach doubled.

It was from Mr Benjamin Scarborough, saying Cassidy had taken the train from New York and was expected to arrive in Helena in the next few days. And that he wanted Antonio to look out for her arrival and ensure she had everything she needed.

The telegram crinkled in Antonio's fist. He pressed his forehead into the table, sucking in deep breaths.

"Shit," he said.

Chapter 8

Fishin'

I realised Megan warn't like other girls when she were eight. By then most girls were wearin' dresses, playin' with dolls an' learnin' to paint, but Megan were still wantin' to kick up dust all day.

If the boys at school'd given her a chance, they woulda liked her more 'n me. She were always up fer a dare, never baulked at throwin' stones to knock off a gent's hat an' were never called a yellow belly. I've bin called coward in every way you can be.

Pa said that Megan'd settle down in her own time, but 'cause he never tried to change her I'm sure he didn't want her to stop bein' like Ma.

We'd go out togither a great deal, the three of us. We'd go huntin' fer cottontail, quail an' other small critters fer eatin' an' sellin'. In the fall we'd hunt turkey, but ma preferred thing to do were fishin'. I still hated seein' a fish gasp fer breath as we hauled it onto land, but it were less chillin' 'n hearin' the cries of a shot animal. I hadda look away an' put ma hands over ma ears each time Megan or Pa slit an animal's throat, or smashed a fish over the head.

Pa'd made me promise dozens of times that I wouldn't leave Megan 'til she were settled. It seemed that every time we found a quiet moment togither he hadda remind me of ma promise. I jest nodded each time, unable to imagine ever havin' a life without Pa or ma sis.

The night after the first time Pa made me promise, he went on his first robbery. He came back with enough money to feed us fer a week, an' three bullets in his backside. Megan an' me picked 'em out an' that night we et better 'n we'd done in weeks.

We return to the house after dark. I see to Rosie an' Hattie, while Megan locks Cassidy in the parlour – a room of the house we never use. Cassidy's never bin to our house – her governess never let her go beyond the boundaries of her pa's property, an' since Cassidy's pa didn't even let her outta the house, Cassidy knew not to push her luck an' go further – so I don't worry 'bout her recognisin' the place an' therefore us. I stable the horses an' wash the blood from ma face.

"Run into town an' buy a bolt fer the door," Megan says. "An' sum wood fer boardin' up the windows if we don't got any."

I don't like the idea of leavin' Megan an' Cassidy on their own, but I've already played that card once today an' I can't play it again. So I change ma clothes as fast as I can an' run into town to the store. I git there jest as Mr Bergman's closin' up. He takes one look at ma panicked red face an' turns back the key. Thankfully, he's got sum locks an' bolts in stock. I tell him to keep the change an' sprint back to the house, half expectin' to find Cassidy dead when I git back. But she's still in the parlour, sittin' in one of the chairs opposite Megan, who's got Smithy an' Florence pointed at her. They're starin' daggers at each other.

"Fix the bolt to the door, brother," Megan says, not takin' her eyes off Cassidy, "an' then board up the windows on the outside."

I work fast by lantern light to cover the windows with the wood I were plannin' to use to fix the fence, an' then secure the bolt to the outside of the parlour door. Megan keeps her guns trained on Cassidy as she backs out the room. Then she slams the door shut an' pushes the bolt 'cross with more force 'n necessary.

"That'll do fer now," she says, takin' off her mask. "Go fix us sum supper."

I find sum bread in the cupboard that's only a few days old an' a can of beans. As I'm pullin' the usual two plates from the cupboard, ma fingers brush the third in the pile, an' I think 'bout Cassidy locked in the parlour. Megan won't like me takin' Cassidy food, but the thought of Cassidy locked in the dark, alone an' hungry makes ma stomach cramp. So I make up a small plate fer her, hide it an' call Megan in fer supper. The beans'll be cold by the time I take 'em to Cassidy, but it's better 'n nuthin'.

"I still can't unnerstand," Megan says, chewin' her bread, "how the sheriff knew we were gonna be there."

"Perhaps he didn't," I suggest. "Perhaps it were jest a coincidence."

"Hmm. Seems unlikely."

"But they seemed jest as surprised to see us as we did 'em," I point out, rememberin' the look on the sheriff's face when we burst through the express car door.

"Hmm," Megan says again, but says nuthin' else 'bout it. From her expression, I can tell she's thinkin' things over. To me, the whole thing seems like a coincidence. No one apart from us knew we were plannin' to rob the express car. 'Less the sheriff guessed we were gonna be there? Perhaps he's one of those clever folks who can always think several steps ahead of everyone else. If so, things fer the Blood Twins're 'bout to git a lot harder.

I wait fer Megan to go to bed an' take Cassidy her meal. I crack open the door, slide the plate 'round the side an' shut it again.

"It's dark." Her voice comes from the other side of the door. "Could I have a candle and some matches? And... and a chamber pot?"

Ma face flushes red, but I manage to keep ma voice level as I say, "Sure." I bring all those things to her, includin' a blanket, an' deliver the candle to her already lit. I hear Cassidy cross the room an' pick everythin' up, but she says nuthin' else to me. I lean ma forehead 'gainst the parlour door, wishin' more 'n anythin' else that things could be different.

I manage to stay awake long enough to ask Gawd fer fergiveness fer all the sins we committed that day. Ma words even sound hollow to me.

It feels like as soon as I fall asleep I wake to light streamin' through ma bedroom window. Fer a coupla minutes, I lie in bed enjoyin' the warmth of the early mornin' sun on ma face an' the sounds of the wakin' world outside, then I remember everythin' that happened yesterday. I groan an' roll outta bed.

I traipse down the stairs an' outside, stretchin' ma achin' limbs. I wash the last of yesterday's blood outta ma hair. I don't have time to wash ma mask, which I hafta put on 'fore goin' to see Cassidy. It crunches in ma hand an' it smells like iron. I'd rather have her see ma face 'n wear it, but I put it in ma pocket anyway.

The chamber pot an' candle stick've bin moved, but the plate of food is untouched. Cassidy's pushed the two armchairs togither an' is lyin' in 'em like a bed. Her hands're still bound an' she's facin' the wall. I can't tell if she's asleep. I watch her fer any signs to tell me one way or the other, but as I watch I become hypnotised by the steady rhythm of her breathin'. The rise an' fall of her body's like the gentle blowin' of summer grass.

"Are you going to have your way with me?" I blink. Cassidy's still got her back to me, but the voice's hers. It's quiet an' shakes a little. Her back an' shoulders that were relaxed a moment ago're now tense.

"No," I say. "Why'd I do that?"

"That's what men do, isn't it? When they have power over a woman. Anyway." She rolls over, fixin' me with those green eyes. "I thought you were a Blood Twin. Isn't that the sort of thing you do?"

I swallow an' look at the floor.

"We ain't 'bout that at all," I croak, but a little voice in ma head says: *You're only one step away, though.*

All a sudden ma head's filled with the screams, the heat, the crackle of the flames...

Cassidy's voice cuts through it, pushin' the memory back into the dark corners of ma mind. "I can't believe that. Not after what I've heard."

"Folk talk. Rumours spread. Things git outta control."

"You're not wearing your mask."

"Ain't no point."

"I thought I hadn't seen your face."

"We both know you did."

"Does this mean I can never go home? Will I be here forever?"

I shake ma head. "You'll be here 'til we think you can be trusted not to gab," I lie, though I hope Megan'll come 'round to this way of thinkin'.

"Your sister will never trust me."

We stay in silence fer a long time. I stare at ma feet, an' out the corner of ma eye I catch Cassidy lookin' at the animal carvin's on the shelves. They were Pa's. Megan put 'em in here after he died, 'cause they're too painful fer her to look at. Pa taught me to carve an' I've done a few of ma own, but they're not as good as his.

There's a sudden bang from upstairs, which makes both me an' Cassidy jump. Megan musta fallen outta bed – she tosses an' turns so much durin' the night she often falls out. Even in Pa an' Ma's double bed she still can't keep herself in one place. I look back at Cassidy, an' find her starin' at me. I pull ma mask outta ma pocket an' over ma face. I don't want Megan catchin' me without it on 'round Cassidy.

"Your face looks familiar," she says. "And I swear I've heard your sister's voice before. Who are you?"

I shift from one foot to the other. Tellin' Cassidy who we were'd be a relief. She might even remember me. Heck, she might even care, but tellin' her would put our lives in more danger.

"How much do you value your freedom?" I ask.

"My life is worthless without my freedom."

Cassidy's words take me by surprise. She's certainly not the girl I'd known six years ago. She's a real grown-up, sayin' grown-up things. Even though she's a captive in this room, she's still sumhow able to maintain the air of a lady. It makes me feel... small an' worthless.

"If I tell you our names, you'll never be free. It'd be one ounce of information too many."

Cassidy flops back down onto her makeshift bed. "Then perhaps I don't want to know."

The silence returns.

"I'll empty your chamber pot," I say at last, "an' bring you sum breakfast later. Do you wanna wash?"

Cassidy says nuthin'.

I do as I said I would, also cleanin' her untouched dinner plate. Her candle's nearly burnt out, so I bring her 'nother, as well as a basin of water an' a towel.

"Knock when you're done," I say, an' bolt the door 'hind me.

Megan doesn't come downstairs 'til late into the mornin'.

"Mornin'," she yawns.

"Mornin'," I say.

"Is she still there?" Megan asks, pointin' at the parlour door. I nod. Megan sighs. "I'd rather hoped it'd all bin a bad dream. Guess not. Make a pot of coffee, wouldja? An' what's fer breakfast?"

"We're outta food," I say. "I need to run to the store." Ma stomach grumbles, an' with it comes an idea. "Wanna go fishin'?"

Megan glances at the parlour door.

"I don't know, Cole. I don't know if we should leave her..." Then ma sis's stomach grumbles so loud that I hear it.

"She'll be fine in there," I say. "She can't escape."

Megan chews her lip fer a minute more. "Fine," she says.

"I found out her name," I say. "It's May."

"Don't matter what it is," Megan says. "She's Miss Priss."

We grab our fishin' rods an' hats an' set out. The river's only a short walk from Helena, so we let the horses rest. We rode 'em hard yesterday.

Megan an' me walk outta the town, headin' south.

"There's summit familiar 'bout that girl," Megan says. "I can't think what it is. I tried talkin' to her, but she kept her stubborn mouth shut."

I kick a stone. It tumbles over an' over in the dust an' hits a cactus.

"She's pretty," Megan says.

"Yeah, she is." I glance sideways. Megan's lookin' down at her large calloused hands. She's got thick hard fingers – jest like the rest of her body. "You're pretty too, sis."

Megan gives me a hard stare. "Shut your mouth."

We soon reach the canyon. Pa'd showed us the way to git to the river. There's a section of the canyon wall that's worn into a series of natural shelves. You hafta lower yourself backwards over the edge of the cliff, find the ledge below you, an' then do the same thing goin' all the way down. Ma heart's in ma mouth all the way down, but it's the only way down to the water, 'less we travel miles to 'nother section of the river.

By the time I reach the canyon floor I'm sweatin' an' shakin'. Megan's no better, though she tries to hide it.

It's worth it. The river runs slow through the canyon, the waters shinin' an' sparklin' in the sun. I rush to it an' stand in the shallows, the water splashin' over ma boots an' up ma pants. I scoop sum water onto ma face.

"Gawd's sake, Cole. You didn't take off your boots!"

I grin at Megan, an' she grins back. No longer the Blood Twins. Jest Megan an' Cole Hayes, fer an afternoon at least.

We sit on the riverbank an' cast our lines. 'Cause the river's runnin' slow we don't hafta worry 'bout recastin' 'em. I watch ma cork float bobbin' on top of the water an' listen to the hush of the river. Downstream two men're standin' in the shallows, pants rolled up to their knees, backs bent, their attention focused on the pans in their hands.

"It's too far down river fer gold," Megan comments. "They ain't gonna find anythin'."

"Remember when Pa took us prospectin'?"

Megan snorts. "We didn't find anythin' 'cept sum rocks, but then everybody'd be rich if they found summit every time they went prospectin'."

"You tried to catch a fish with your hands, but you fell on your face."

Megan snorts. "Broke ma nose. Took ferever to heal, but I also remember you thought it'd be funny to try it too."

"I never thought a fish tail slap'd hurt so much."

Megan laughs. It's good to hear her laugh.

We return to our own thoughts.

"You think Pa'd be proud of us?"

I watch ma float bobbin' up an' down, wonderin' what Pa'd think if he saw us now. "I guess he would," I say, 'though I ain't sure."

"I miss him."

"So do I."

"I wish he warn't dead. I wish he'd stayed with us." I hear the crack in her throat. I've never sin Megan cry, not even when Pa'd died, but I check fer tears anyway. There's none, an' when Megan next speaks her voice's cold. "But he did an' I'm gonna make Benjamin Scarborough pay fer what he's done."

We could stop now, move away, to a city where no one knows us. We'd jest be Cole an' Megan Hayes. But Megan'll never rest 'til Benjamin Scarborough's dead. An' she'll want me to feel the same. Anyway, I can't leave her. She's family. We were born togither. We oughta stay togither.

Chapter 9

Reunion

Antonio searched every hideout. He'd had the locations of potential places stuck to his map for some time – abandoned houses, caves, ghost towns and disused mines – but wanted to wait until he had a good band to back him up before he checked them out. But with the Blood Twins holding Cassidy hostage Antonio couldn't waste time.

He didn't know when that good band might come along. Jason was still off sick, grieving for his friends, although Antonio had seen him staggering a few times out of The Sleeping Racoon, singing and laughing. Antonio hoped he'd stay away. When there was a job to do, if he did it himself Antonio knew it would get done, which was not a guarantee when he delegated to Jason.

But Antonio needn't have worried about that good band because after two days of searching he discovered all the potential hideouts were empty. Antonio's frustration grew with each one he crossed off his map.

Finding the final one empty left him with a sick heavy feeling in his stomach.

Once again, he was at a dead end.

Antonio rode back into Helena, caked in dust and sweat, parched and in a foul temper. Soon he would have to answer the telegram from Mr Scarborough. He didn't know what he was going to say. Should he lie and say Cassidy was here safe and well? Or that she hadn't arrived but he had no idea where she was? Should he tell the truth? The thought of writing any of the three options made Antonio's stomach churn.

What had Cassidy been doing on the train past Helena anyway? If she was meant to be travelling to Helena, she would have alighted at Barren Post. Was there something else going on that Antonio wasn't aware of? Or was it all just a cruel twist of fate?

Riding into town, Antonio pushed his foul temper down and smiled and tipped his hat at passers-by. Two returned his greeting. Everyone else ignored him or looked away as soon as Antonio met their eyes. Antonio gritted his back teeth and rode on.

As dusty and thirsty as Antonio was, he needed food supplies. He stopped his horse outside the general store and heard voices arguing inside. Through the window, Antonio could see the storekeeper, Mr Bergman, and a customer shouting at each other over the counter, both of them red-faced. Antonio sighed, took off his hat and walked inside, ensuring he put his feet down hard enough that they heard his spurs click.

"What's going on here, gentlemen?"

At first Mr Bergman's face relaxed, but his facial muscles tensed at the sight of Antonio standing in the door to his store. His eyes flicked from the star on Antonio's chest, up to his face and back to the star. Antonio tensed, but he forced his expression to remain neutral, waiting for

Mr Bergman to make the first move.

The confusion passed, but Mr Bergman didn't meet Antonio's eyes. "This gentleman is wrongly accusin' me of short changin' him," he said.

"T-this, this thief," the hat-wearing man blustered, pointing his finger at the storekeeper, "has cheated me outta a nickel."

"Sir," Mr Bergman sighed, "you gave me two dollars an' fifty cents fer items that cost two dollars an' twenty-three cents. Therefore, I gave you back twenty-seven cents change."

"You did not. I gave you two dollars fifty-five. Therefore, you shoulda given me thirty-two in change."

"Sir, you did not. You gave me two dollars fifty."

"You lyin' cheatin' th—"

"Gentlemen," Antonio said loudly, "let's talk this through like civilised human beings, shall we?"

They checked over Mr Bergman's books and compared them to the amount in the change box. It turned out the customer hadn't been cheated out of any money. Upon realising his mistake, the customer offered no apology – just stormed out of the store with a red face and his supplies crushed under his arms.

"Thank you, Sheriff," Mr Bergman said. "I'd love it if he stayed away fer a while, but the problem with bein' the only store in town is that they always come back."

Antonio bought his supplies and left the store. Outside, he took a moment to bask in the sense of a job well done and then headed back to the office, carrying his supplies and leading his horse by the reins.

A movement caught Antonio's eye down the end of an alley. A figure stood in the gap between the store and the building next door. They leaned to the side, like a puppet with one of its strings cut. Antonio waited for the figure to say something or to walk on, but they continued to stand there. Antonio dropped the reins to reach for his gun.

"Are you all right?" he asked.

"Antonio?" The voice that came out of the figure was raspy, as dry as the desert sand. Then they crumpled to the ground.

Antonio dropped his supplies and rushed over. He knelt down and pulled the person's head into his lap. Their hat rolled across the ground. A pale, sweat-drenched face stared up at Antonio. A familiar face that Antonio hadn't seen in a decade.

"Hu?" he asked.

"Hey, Tonio." The edges of Hu's mouth began to lift into a smile, but then he gasped and gritted his teeth. His dry lips cracked from the effort, splotching his mouth with blood. Antonio moved Hu's hand from his side and found a ragged wound underneath that had soaked his shirt and pants with blood.

"What in the blazes happened?" Antonio asked in Cantonese. "And what are you doing here? How did you even know I was here?"

"The newspapers," Hu rasped. "They... reported Helena... had a new sheriff... called... Antonio Valdez." He tried to laugh, but it turned into a dry cough. Antonio held him as still as he could until he finished. "We couldn't believe it."

Antonio swallowed the thickness in his throat as he imagined who "we" was. His mother. All the aunties, uncles and cousins he had left behind that day. Alejandro.

Juanita.

Dozens more questions crowded to the front of his mind, demanding to be asked, but the sight of Hu's blood on his hand brought him back to reality.

"You need to get to a doctor," Antonio said. "We'll have plenty of time to catch up later."

Antonio moved to pick Hu up, but the youth clasped his arm.

"Listen, Tonio," Hu said. "The fort's been taken over.

This... gang stormed it yesterday. They... killed dozens of us – Auntie Emilia, Uncle Wan, Uncle Javier, Xiu and... Little Lan. Tried to kill me—" he let out a strangled laugh "—but I got away... Had to get away... Had to... warn you so you could... help them."

"We need to get you to a doctor," Antonio said. The repeated words came out automatically, because his brain couldn't process what Hu had said. That his family were in danger.

That some of them were dead.

Hu's eyes fluttered and Antonio felt his grip on his arm grow weak.

"Don't fret about... that. Just... glad... I got to... warn you."

His eyes shut and his hand fell from Antonio's arm. Hu's body grew very heavy in his arms.

Antonio wasn't sure how long he sat there with Hu's body weighing down on him, turning his legs numb – he just concentrated on taking the next breath.

At last he picked up Hu's body in his arms, carried him to his horse and then to Dr Fallon's.

The doctor confirmed Hu's death, citing infection from the bullet wound in Hu's gut and blood loss as the cause.

Antonio left Hu's body at the doctor's and went to the undertakers to order a coffin, then to the Reverend to secure a plot of land in the churchyard and book a date for the funeral. He slipped the Reverend some extra dollars to ensure he would look the other way to the fact he would be burying a non-Christian on Christian burial ground. Antonio had read about the Rock Springs and Hells Canyon massacres. The Chinese Exclusion Act had given people an excuse to act cruelly towards their fellow countrymen, and Antonio wasn't sure what the Reverend's response would be to Hu. In the end, the Reverend didn't blink. Just took the money and started preparing for the funeral.

Antonio knew Hu would have preferred to be buried at

the family fortress, in the plot of land out the back where they'd buried Hu's grandparents, but there was no way Antonio could go back. He wanted to ensure his family member was laid to rest somewhere safe and given a proper headstone.

It was only once Antonio got back to the office that he remembered he had left his purchases from the store dropped on the ground somewhere. The thought of going back outside sent a wave of exhaustion through Antonio's body.

Then it hit him.

Hu was dead.

Members of his family were dead.

The remaining members of his family were in danger.

And Antonio was the only person who knew they were.

His knees collapsed and he slumped against the wall. Tears bubbled up behind his eyes.

What was he meant to do?

He had to find Cassidy.

He had to track down the Blood Twins.

He had his job as sheriff of Helena.

He had to feed himself, wash himself and sleep.

And now he had to rescue his family.

But he couldn't go back there.

He just couldn't.

Not just because it would mean facing what he had done, but also because he was afraid that his family might not want him back. Even if he rescued them from this gang.

The world was dark outside by the time Antonio hauled himself to his feet. He dragged himself upstairs to his room. He took one look at the map on the wall, then kicked off his shoes, stripped off his clothes and crawled into bed.

Chapter 10

Dinner

Dean an' Pa met when Pa were sixteen an' Dean were thirty-one. They met while workin' fer Mr Scarborough in one of his silver mines. Pa'd jest started work there as a miner, an' Dean'd worked fer Mr Scarborough since the end of the war, guardin' his mines 'gainst robbers an' raiders.

Dean'd fought in the war. He'd joined the Confederates at the age of twenty-four. He'd bin at Gettysburg unner Lee's command, an'd bin one of the few lucky ones to walk away. Pa'd bin alive durin' the war, but he'd bin too young to fight. The fightin' didn't make it far enough west fer Pa to've sin any of it, but Dean'd enough stories fer the both of 'em.

They'd got to talkin' 'tween work hours, an' then down at The Sleepin' Racoon. They became fast friends, an' when Pa married Ma, Dean handed over the rings, an' Pa handed over the rings at Dean's weddin' to Mary.

Dean'd bin at Pa's funeral. He an' Mary'd taken us in when Pa'd gone to jail.

I didn't mind when Dean an' Mary took us in. At first Megan hated 'em an' she let 'em know it. 'Fore Pa went to jail, Megan'd loved spendin' time with Dean, but'd always bin wary 'round Mary. Megan an' me didn't know how mothers worked, an' Mary so wanted a little girl to dote on. But there warn't no way Megan were gonna fill that role despite all Mary did to make Megan into the little girl she'd always wanted. She bought Megan dolls, tried to git her to help with the cookin' or with the sewin'. She didn't know Megan at all.

I ended up helpin' Mary 'round the house while Megan stayed in her room all day an' when she were older snuck out at night to gamble at The Sleepin' Raccoon.

Neither me or Megan knew how to act 'round Mary. Pa'd taken us huntin', fishin' an' ridin'. He'd bin messy an' fun. Mary were kind but tidy. She'd buy the meat from the store an' always do the dishes 'fore goin' to bed. She'd tuck me in at night an' wake me in the mornin' by openin' the curtains, an' sayin', "Rise an' shine!" Pa'd let us sleep in as long as we wanted.

One day Dean said he were gonna go huntin', an' asked if we wanted to come. Mary laughed an' said Megan wouldn't wanna go. But Megan jumped at the chance.

Dean took Megan huntin' twice a week fer the time we stayed with 'em. Megan stopped playin' dumb an' started talkin', an' her nightly visits to The Sleepin' Raccoon grew fewer. But they didn't stop.

Megan falls asleep quickly. She's leanin' 'gainst a rock, her hat over her face an' her rod fergotten in her hands. I keep ma eyes on ma bobbin' float, watchin' fer the tell-tale signs of a nibble. A bite doesn't come fer a long time, not 'til the sun's startin' to sizzle ma brain like a steak over a fire. I drift ofta sleep.

Ma line snaps an' ma rod jerks ferward. I wake up in time to pull it up. The fish ain't that big, but it takes a few minutes to land. It's a Gila trout – a small brown fish with a yellow belly an' black spots.

The sight of it gaspin' an' flappin' makes ma stomach churn, but the thought of endin' its life makes ma skin prickle with cold. I reach to throw the fish back into the river—

Cole, toughen up.

Ma hands still as I remember 'nother time me an' Megan went fishin', back when Pa were still alive. Megan landed the first Gila trout. I were laughin' an' celebratin' along with her an' Pa, an' then Megan struck it over the head with the handle of her knife. I howled an' cried an' clung to Pa, afraid.

"You're such a coward," Megan spat at me.

Pa laid one of his big hands on ma head inna gesture that were meant to be comfortin', but when I looked up I saw the disappointment in his eyes.

The memory of that moment makes me reach fer ma knife.

I whack the fish quick over the head with the handle.

I don't waste any time boastin' to Megan 'bout ma catch, but spear 'nother insect on ma hook an' recast ma line.

'Nother long time comes an' goes then a second trout takes the bait, but it gits away. I curse ma bad luck as I rebait.

While waitin' I think 'bout the problem I've bin ignorin' since the train robbery. What am I gonna do 'bout Cassidy? I can't tell Megan who she is. Megan'll either shoot her or will ransom her back to her pa an' then shoot her in front of 'em. Megan wants Mr Scarborough to pay fer our Pa's death an' that means either he, or sumone dear to him, hassa die. Cassidy's his only child. The dearest thing he possesses. No, Megan can't find out who Cassidy is. I'll hafta make sure she doesn't.

I think of Cassidy, alone in the house. She's bin left on her own all day, shut inna room with nuthin' to do 'cept stare at the walls, after bein' kidnapped by two notorious criminals. She must be so scared.

Gawd. What've I done? Wouldn't it've bin easier to shoot Cassidy rather 'n put her in danger from Megan's vengeful wrath? But I'll never allow Cassidy to die while I'm alive. I love her, as sure as the sun do rise every mornin'. She'll never love me back, but I wish I could jest tell her ma name. Maybe then at least she wouldn't hate me anymore.

The third fish doesn't git away, 'though he's a long time comin'. It's 'nother Gila trout, a little smaller 'n the first, but nuthin' to be sniffed at. Two hours later I've got six trout on the ground next to me, an' Megan's still sleepin'. Her float hasn't moved inna long time, which means a fish most likely snatched her insect long ago. I'm desperate to git outta the sun. I reach to give Megan a shake, but ma eyes fall on the pile of fish. An' grin as an idea comes into ma head.

I pick up the largest trout I've landed an' I creep up to ma sis.

Clutchin' the head, I draw ma arm back an' slap the tail 'cross her face. It makes a lovely crackin' sound.

I'm already laughin' as Megan jerks awake, like sumone's pushed her from 'hind.

"You shoulda sin your face," I wheeze, bent double. "It were—"

I stop, 'cause Megan's shoved Smithy an' Florence in ma face. Megan's breathin' heavy. Her arms're steady, but her eyes're bleary with sleep. The laughter dies in ma throat.

"Sis," I says nice an' calm, starin' cross-eyed at the barrels, "it's me, Cole. Put the guns down." There's confusion in her eyes as she looks at me. The muscles on her fingers bulge as they squeeze the handles. Ma chest's tight. Ma heart's hammerin' in ma ears.

Then Megan lowers her guns.

"Idiot!" she shouts. She sticks her guns back in their holsters an' stands up. Her face's red from sunburn where her hat ain't shaded her. "I coulda shot you!"

"But you didn't," I say, shakin'. "So it's fine."

"It's not fine, Cole!" Megan spots ma pile of trout. "Good, you've caught summit. Let's go." She leaves her rod an' storms back to the canyon wall. Ma whole body's shakin' an' I'm cold. I pick up our rods an' the fish an' follow ma sis home.

Megan don't say a word on the walk back. She won't look at me. I wanna say summit, to tell her it's fine, that I shouldn't've surprised her like that, but I'm jest makin' excuses. I've never bin afraid of her like that 'fore. I've never bin on that side of Megan's guns. I unnerstand now how her victims feel – how *our* victims feel.

Dean's waitin' fer us on the front porch, a tin on his knees which I guess is full of Mary's sugar cookies. He waves his hat as we approach, smilin' like the sun. I can't force one back. I rub ma sweatin' palms on ma pants. How long's Dean bin here? Has he noticed the boarded up parlour window an' looked inside? Or has Cassidy heard him outside an' shouted fer help? I risk a glance at Megan. Her face is stony.

"There you are! I were 'bout to head home." Dean stands, leavin' the tin on the deck. If he an' Cassidy've spoken, he ain't showin' it. "I thought you might be havin' an afternoon nap inside, but I see you've bin fishin'."

"Yeah, Cole did a good job." Heat flushes ma cheeks, though I shouldn't be surprised. Megan only ever compliments me in front of other folk.

"I came to bring you sum cookies," Dean says, handin'

the tin to Megan. "Mary insisted, an' she also told me to invite you to dinner tonight. An' by invite I mean demand that you come."

I glance at the boarded up parlour window. We can't really leave Cassidy alone fer much longer. I should turn down Dean's invite.

"We'd be mighty glad to come," Megan says.

Dean smiles. "I'll run home an' tell Mary. You come 'round when you're ready." Dean tips his hat an' strides home, whistlin' a cheery tune.

"Do you think he suspects summit?" I ask.

"No," Megan says. "I don't think he does, but go check on Miss Priss jest to be sure."

"What should I do with the trout?"

"It's still hours 'til supper," Megan says. "Cook those fish while they're still fresh."

"Should we really be leavin' May alone tonight as well?" I ask. "Won't she git lonely?"

"Fer Gawd's sake, Cole. Stop fussin'. She's a hostage, not a guest."

She's also a human bein', but I remember Megan's guns pointin' at ma face an' I keep quiet.

Dean an' Mary's house is on the edge of the east side of town. It's much better lookin' 'n ours. Mary's very proud of her home. Everythin's jest so. There ain't a frayed rug in sight, they've got couches with fabric on 'em, the curtains're clean an' there ain't a speck of dust to be sin.

Dinner's jugged hare. Neither Megan or me're good cooks – Pa'd often said how good a cook Ma'd bin, but she hadn't taught him, so he didn't teach us. The jugged hare tastes like summit from a dream. I can't remember the last time I tasted summit so good. At the same time I can't help but think 'bout Cassidy locked in the dark with only a candle fer company. She must be so hungry...

"It's lovely seein' the two of you again," Mary says.

"It's bin too long since our last meal togither."

"Far too long," Dean says, reachin' fer the pot. "I thought after I retired I'd have all the time in the world fer socialisin', but the days run by faster 'n they ever did 'fore."

"Guests first!" Mary says, slappin' Dean's hand. Dean scowls at her but offers the pot to me an' Megan.

"Wouldja like sum more?" he asks.

"I'm full, thanks," I say, but Megan has her third helpin'.

"So," Mary says, fillin' the silence that settles over the table, "what've you bin up to lately? Cole, didja git anywhere with John Sanders?"

"Er," I say, "no. No, I didn't."

"It's a cryin' shame," Mary says. "You're so good with horses. He's a fool fer not takin' you on to help on his ranch. I'll tell him that maself!"

"No," I protest. "It's all right. It were ma decision. I realised that Hattie an' Rosie were enough work fer me. I ain't fussed 'bout workin' onna ranch no more."

Ma face glows hot with the lie, but Mary doesn't notice. "Ah, well, if it's your decision, then I guess that's fine. But it's a cryin' shame, Cole. It were always your dream to work onna horse ranch, an' you'd be perfect fer the work."

I jest nod an' keep ma eyes on ma empty plate, tryin' not to cry.

"An' what 'bout you, Megan?" Mary asks. A smile spreads 'cross her face. "Has any young man caught your eye yet?"

"No," Megan says through a mouthful of food. "Neither will he."

"Megan," Mary says, disapprovin' enterin' her voice, "you can't waste away your life. Or your brother's, fer that matter."

"What's Cole gotta do with it?" Megan snaps. Dean an'

I exchange looks. We know this argument. We've sin it play out dozens of times 'fore.

"He can't very well move on with his own life while he has his unmarried sis livin' unner his roof."

"*Our* roof," Megan hisses. "An' I ain't got any intention of gittin' married. Pa said I didn't hafta git married if I didn't wanna."

"Your pa woulda wanted you to be happy."

"An' marriage is gonna make me happy?"

"A woman ain't complete 'til she hassa home an' a husband to care fer."

Megan's chair topples over as she stands up. Her face's red an' I swear her hair's doubled in size. But even though she towers over Mary, Mary seems the same size as Megan as she returns her stare.

"Cole," Dean stands up, his chair legs scrapin' 'gainst the wooden floor, "come keep me company outside while I have a smoke."

"Yeah," I say, an' follow Dean outside as fast as I can.

Even though Dean closes the back door 'hind him, we still hear Megan an' Mary shoutin' at each other inside. The fight will only end once Megan reminds Mary that she ain't her ma, an' then Mary'll burst into tears, an' the two of 'em'll sit in separate parts of the house to cool down.

Dean an' I sit on the back porch, lookin' up at the starry sky.

"How're you really, Cole?" Dean asks, strikin' a match. "You can tell me now your sis ain't here."

I force a smile. "I'm fine. Really, Dean. Never better."

Dean holds the lit match up to his cigarette, an' then shakes it out. "Looks like you caught a good haul on your fishin' trip."

"Yeah. Went to the Gila River. We saw sum folks prospectin' while we was there."

A plume of smoke curls 'round from Dean's lips as he laughs. "They won't find gold that far down river."

"That's what Megan said."

"You shoulda joined 'em," Dean says. "Prospectin's in your blood. You mighta found summit."

"I doubt it," I say. Pa'd told us 'bout his pa – 'bout how he'd come over from England fer the California gold rush in '49. Pa didn't remember his pa 'cause he'd died when Pa were only a baby, murdered by sumone in the minin' camps. Cassidy's grandpa an' pa'd also come over from England durin' the gold rush. Her grandpa'd died soon after they arrived in America, but Mr Scarborough'd struck lucky an' bin one of the few to make his fortune. I'd always wondered if ma grandpa an' Mr Scarborough'd met each other durin' that time, but thought it unlikely since there were thousands of folks lookin' fer gold back then.

But Dean's family's bin in America fer centuries. His grandpa's family were pilgrims, then his grandpa became one of the mountain men, trappin' beavers fer their fur. 'Cause Pa didn't have many family stories – apart from the knowledge his pa were a gold prospector – Megan an' me'd grown up on stories from Dean's family. Dean'd never met his grandpa, but his ma'd told him plenty of stories of his adventures in the mountains.

In return, Dean's always askin' us 'bout our family's time in California. He'd obviously done the same to Pa, 'cause Pa'd always joke, "Guess what Dean wanted to talk 'bout while fishin' today?" In the end, though, we don't have much to tell him. Pa's ma'd not bin well enough to keep any of the stories – we jest know where our grandpa'd come from, an' that he'd died in the prospectors' camps. Dean's got sum sorta gold prospectin' obsession. When he retired, I expected him to run fer the hills with a pan an' shovel.

"I bet you wish you coulda bin old enough in those days to try your luck," I say with a smile.

Dean laughs. "I wouldn't've minded makin' a lifetime's amount of money in one lucky strike." A small puff of dust rises up 'round Dean's foot as he grinds his finished cigarette unner his boot heel.

"I wonder how different ma life woulda bin if ma grandpa'd made his fortune like Mr Scarborough'd done," I muse, restin' ma hand in ma chin.

"How indeed," Dean says.

"But," I says, still starin' out at the desert, "I'm glad that he didn't. If he had, Pa might've never met Ma, an' Megan an' me might've never bin born. An' I'd never've met you an' Mary. I'd rather have you all 'n a pile of gold."

Dean sighs, an' smacks the back of ma head with his hat.

"You're too damn pure, Cole," Dean says. "Jest like your pa."

There's a pause where we both admire the stars.

"You know," Dean says, "your pa were worried 'bout you."

I know.

I know Pa were worried 'bout me. I'd heard him talkin' to Dean once, right here on this porch. We'd come over fer dinner. Mary were entertainin' Megan an' me while Pa an' Dean smoked out the back. I slipped away to see 'em an' heard 'em talkin' 'bout me. Heard Pa tellin' Dean how worried he were 'cause I were soft. 'Cause I cried at the sight of dead animals. 'Cause I preferred playin' tea parties with Cassidy, an' spendin' time with horses 'n playin' with the boys at school. He told Dean how he were worried I warn't gonna survive in this world 'less I toughened up. I heard Mary say summit similar to Dean when we were livin' with 'em while Pa were in jail – heard her say that she were worried I warn't like other boys, an' Megan warn't like other girls.

"But I'm glad to see that you're copin' all right in the world." Dean shoots me a smile. "You've done him proud, Cole."

Chapter 11

Trust

I take Cassidy food an' water every day, empty her chamber pot, ensure she has fresh candles, an' try to talk to her, but she always turns her back to me. I don't wear ma mask 'round her when it's jest the two of us, even though Megan'll shoot me if she finds out I ain't. I tell her I've told Megan her name's May, an' she's only to go by that name now, but that gits no response.

Cassidy doesn't eat fer three days, then her hunger must take over 'cause I find her plate on the fourth day licked clean.

"She can't do no harm," I say to Megan. "Anyway, I thought you wanted her to do your chores. She can't do that if she's stuck inside the parlour."

Megan stays silent as she cleans her pistols. "Fine," she says at last, "but if she escapes..." Megan draws a finger 'cross her throat.

I keep a rope tied 'round Cassidy's waist an' take her onna tour of our pitiful home. It's nuthin' compared to the size of the Scarborough estate. I show her the small stable an' paddock where Hattie an' Rosie live, where she needs to go to git water an' the outhouse. I'm embarrassed to show her this last part, rememberin' the indoor plumbin' at the Scarborough estate.

Cassidy keeps lookin' at her feet, which she scuffs in the dirt. Her hair's knotted, her clothes still dusty from the walk 'cross the desert an' her eyes're red an' blotchy, like she's bin cryin' a lot. I wanna draw her a hot bath an' give her clean clothes, but Megan watches us from her perch on the porch fence, cleanin' her pistols. So I set Cassidy to work washin' our clothes.

I tie the other end of her rope to the fence. As I'm walkin' back to the house, I hear three thunks an' then a loud crack. By the time I turn 'round, Cassidy's leggin' it, the rope trailin' from her hands, the broken fence post splintered on the ground where she kicked it 'til it shattered.

From the back porch Megan fires twice. Cassidy sprawls in the dust with a cry. Breathin' hard she raises a hand to her cheek. A thick trickle of blood runs through her fingers.

"You're a fuckin' idiot," Megan shouts at me. "What in Gawd's name made you think she'd stay where you left her?" She storms over to Cassidy, pistols raised. Cassidy scrambles to her feet.

"No!" I scream.

One shot bites the dust next to Cassidy's leg, the other whizzes over her head. Cassidy cries out an' falls back down. I reach her 'fore Megan does. I'm mighty glad our house's so far away from the others in Helena, an' that our neighbours're used to Megan's shootin' practice.

"What is it with you an' this girl?" Megan asks. "What good is she? Let's shoot her an' have done with it."

I help Cassidy stand. She tries to push me away, mouthin' summit no lady of her class oughta, but I grab hold of her wrist, not wantin' to risk her escape again. Megan's eyes fix on ma hand an' her eyes light up. She laughs a dangerous low chuckle.

"I see now, brother," she says. "I see now why you wanna keep this girl alive."

Cassidy looks as horrified as I feel.

"No!" I protest, the heat rushin' up ma neck.

"I'm not judgin' you, but if your piece of fun escapes again—" Megan stares at Cassidy over the top of her mask "—I'll put a bullet in her back. An' this is ma last warnin'."

From then on either me or Megan keep an eye on Cassidy when she's outside. I make Cassidy a pair of wooden shackles that keep her feet locked togither so she can't run. An' she wants to. She's always watchin' when I put 'em on in the mornin' an' when I take 'em off at night, lookin' fer a moment to break free. It scares me that after Megan's sworn to kill her the next time she tries to escape, Cassidy's still tryin' to find a way. Don't she care 'bout her life? Don't she unnerstand Megan ain't jokin'?

But she unnerstands. She knows all too well what she's riskin'. She doesn't wanna stay with us, she wants her home an' her family. She wants her freedom. An' I wanna give it to her. But I can't, not without riskin' losin' everythin'.

One afternoon, I lock Cassidy in the parlour an' go into town to replace the wood that we used to board up the window so I can repair the fence. Apart from goin' to dinner with Dean an' Mary the other night, an' ma hurried rush to buy a lock fer the parlour door, this is the first time I've bin anywhere public since the train robbery. The moment the busy main street of Helena comes into sight, it's like sumone's pressed a gun barrel 'gainst the back of ma head. I check to be sure there ain't sumone there, but it's only ma mind playin' tricks on me.

Walkin' along the main street, I could swear all eyes're on me. Ma arms itch an' ma head pounds as I make ma way to the store. Can everyone tell? Can everyone see the guilt written all over ma face? I'm sure they can. Like they're all talkin' 'bout me an' Megan – whisperin' 'bout how we're keepin' poor Cassidy in shackles an' workin' her like a slave.

I can't look Mr Bergman in the eye as I buy an' pay fer the planks of wood. I keep ma head down as I walk home. Ma breathin' quickens as I pass the sheriff's office, an' the board of wanted posters.

The sight makes me slow.

'Cause on the same board are also missin' posters. How long is it gonna be 'fore sumone reports Cassidy missin'? I don't know why she were on that train when she's meant to be in New York, but there's no way her pa doesn't know she were headin' back to Helena.

An' when he reports her missin', sumone's gonna work out that the train Cassidy were on were the train the Blood Twins tried to rob. Then it's only gonna be a matter of time 'fore there's a massive man hunt in the area tryin' to track her down.

Five more days pass without Cassidy an' Megan breakin' the peace. Cassidy still won't talk to me, let alone look at me. I've got her onna routine, givin' her breakfast 'fore work, then lunch, then a sleep when the sun's too strong to be outside, then a few more hours of work 'fore dinner. It hurts that she don't talk to me. I've tried to clean the cut an' burn on her face from Megan's bullet, but Cassidy hit me away.

On the eighth day Cassidy finally speaks to me.

I'm cleanin' out the stable. The smell of hot hay's in the air an' I've stray strands in ma hair, down ma back an' stuck to the front of ma shirt. Cassidy's standin' a few feet away, 'hind the paddock fence. She's finally given up wearin' her jacket, but she's still got her sleeves rolled down an' her shirt collar buttoned up to her throat. I don't unnerstand how she can work in those clothes an' not faint from the heat.

Cassidy's s'posed to be cleanin' the house, but she's watchin' me, an empty bucket danglin' in her hands. I smile at her. She doesn't smile back. She doesn't notice me. She's starin' at Hattie an' Rosie 'hind me. Ma cheeks flush an' I look down at the rest of the hay I need to shovel.

"What are their names?" she asks.

I'm so shocked I almost drop the shovel.

"Hattie an' Rosie," I reply, grippin' the handle tight to ensure I don't lose ma hold again. "They're sisters."

"I wouldn't have guessed. Their colouring is so different."

"Well, not all siblings are born in the same colours."

Cassidy holds out a hand an' starts clickin' her tongue. Hattie an' Rosie look up from their food. They see Cassidy's got nuthin' to offer 'em an' return to their eatin'. I lean ma pitch fork 'gainst the stable wall an' pull two apples from ma pockets. I hold 'em out to Cassidy.

"Here, they'll be more interested if you give 'em these." Cassidy snatches the apples from ma hands, like I'm gonna bite her.

I return to ma shovellin' but watch out the corner of ma eye as Cassidy feeds Hattie an' Rosie the apples. I remember she used to own a pony – a sweet little thing with a white an' brown coat. It'd bin useless fer ridin', but she rode it anyway with me leadin' her 'round the estate. Perhaps this were the opportunity I'd bin waitin' fer to git Cassidy to finally talk to me.

"They're mighty fine horses," I say. "Hattie's ma horse, an' Rosie's Meg— Ma sis's." I bite ma tongue, angry at maself fer almost sayin' Megan's name.

"I don't see your sister helping you muck them out," Cassidy says, strokin' Hattie's nose.

"She's busy doin' other things."

A shot sounds from the front of the house. Cassidy starts, but the horses don't even snort. I hear a clink of a tin can fallin' off a fence.

"What in God's name was that?" Cassidy exclaims, lookin' 'round, doubtless fer Megan advancin' with drawn pistols.

"Shootin' practice."

"And that's more important than looking after her horse?"

I shrug. "Sumone's gotta be a good shot 'tween the two of us."

Cassidy strokes Rosie's nose. "The horses didn't spook at all."

"They're very good-natured. Calm as two deaf cats."

"I used to own a horse," Cassidy says. "It were only a small thing, and I could never go too far on it. But..." She sighs an' runs a hand along Hattie's neck. "I used to enjoy the little riding I was allowed to do. In New York I couldn't ride at all. I miss it."

"We oughta go ridin' togither sumtime." I regret the words as soon as they're outta ma mouth. We can't go ridin' togither, you coot. I can't risk Cassidy runnin' off on one of the horses. But the look on Cassidy's face at the suggestion melts ma heart.

"I'd love to!" she cries. "But wouldn't your sister mind me using her horse?" 'Nother two shots sound from the front of the house. I raise an eyebrow. Cassidy smiles. "I guess not."

I pick up ma pitch fork. Cassidy says, "What your sister said about... about your intentions for me... Are they true?"

"No!" I protest. "No. 'Course they ain't. I'd never harm you."

"But you'll keep me here against my will? Keep me shackled and working with no way out?"

The accusation in her tone makes ma insides shrink. I try to meet her gaze, but her hands are on her hips an' I can't bring maself to meet her eyes.

"It's not like I wanna," I say, "but mine an' ma sis's identities are a secret. We can't let you go with you knowin' what we look like."

"What if I promised not to tell?"

"We can't take your word fer it."

"You can't, or your sister can't?"

"Ma sis," I mutter.

"Then why should I take your word that you will not hurt me?"

"You'll jest hafta trust me."

Cassidy's silent fer a long time. "Then you can at least have the decency to do the same thing for me," she says.

She leaves me feelin' two inches tall.

Chapter 12

True Colours

Eight days.

Cassidy had been missing for eight days.

Mr Scarborough's telegram had sat buried on Antonio's desk unanswered for eight days.

And Antonio was no closer to solving either problem.

Several times Antonio picked up a pen to reply to Mr Scarborough's message, but each time he put it down, went upstairs and stared at his map, trying to find new possible hideouts. He'd found and checked a few, but they were all empty.

At each new failure the sense of panic doubled in his chest, pulling it tighter and tighter.

Sleeping, never Antonio's strongest pursuit, had become almost impossible. His mind would not stop whirring. The map on his wall was so imprinted in his mind he still pored over it in his dreams.

It wouldn't be long before Mr Scarborough wrote to him again, demanding to know where Cassidy was. And at that point, Antonio would either have to reply, or Mr Scarborough would come to Helena early and see what a mess Antonio had made of everything. Either way, Antonio wasn't sure how he was going to escape being fired or sent to jail.

Unless he could find Cassidy before either of those eventualities happened.

But as much as he wanted to spend all his time searching for Cassidy, he still had his responsibilities as Helena's sheriff to fulfil. The Blood Twins were not the only outlaws in this part of Arizona – just the most infamous. There were cattle rustlers to catch, highway men to apprehend and the regular bar brawl at The Sleeping Racoon to break up. And with Jason still absent from work, he had no one to watch his back or protect his right side. Not that he would ever trust Jason to protect him. Juanita always had, though...

Antonio didn't allow himself to think about Juanita.

Whenever he did, tears were never far behind.

Jason finally returned to work. Antonio came in from a patrol to find Jason sitting in Antonio's chair behind his desk, reading the telegram from Mr Scarborough.

"This the prospector that gave you the job?" Jason asked, waving the telegram.

"Put that back where you found it," Antonio said.

"Has his daughter turned up?" Jason asked.

Antonio snatched the telegram from Jason's hand and the sound of ripping paper tore the air. For a second, Jason's face fell with shock. The sight sent a pleasing ripple of goosebumps across Antonio's skin. That was until Jason's mouth curved back up into a sneer.

"Well, well, well," Jason said. "Showin' our true colours now, are we? You Mexicans are always—"

"Get out of my chair!" Antonio snapped.

"All right, all right, Sheriff. You're the boss." Jason swung his feet down from Antonio's desk. Antonio's body stayed tense until Jason was on the other side of the small room.

"So," Jason said, leaning against the windowsill, "what'd I miss? Sorry you hadda go eight days without ma help."

All the tension drained out of Antonio's body. He sighed and ran a hand over his face.

"Err," he said, struggling to get his thoughts into order, "nothing much."

"Ah. Well. Nice to know that you warn't strugglin' without me. Nuthin' turned up 'bout that hostage that were taken on the train?"

"No. Nothing. I er... I've searched the surrounding area for any potential hideouts. But nothing."

"Ah. Well. She's likely dead now."

Antonio swallowed the wave of nausea that rolled up from his stomach.

He hadn't considered the possibility that Cassidy might be dead.

There was a knock at the door.

"Come in," Antonio said.

Donal from the telegram station opened the door.

"Urgent message for you, Sheriff," he said and handed Antonio a piece of paper.

"Thank you."

A quick scan of the message was enough to make Antonio's heart sink.

"Bad news, Sheriff?" Jason asked.

"It's from Sheriff Conner in Little Point. They were attacked by a gang of outlaws. Saloon burnt down. Folks gunned down in the street."

"Geez. How awful," Jason said, not sounding horrified in the least.

But Antonio was harbouring enough horror for the

both of them.

It was them.

Antonio knew it was them. The gang who had taken over his home.

He pushed the swelling tide of panic down and stood up. "I'm going to Little Point. Sounds like they need some help."

"Want me to come, Sheriff?" Jason asked. He was leaning back against the window, his thumbs hooked into his belt.

Antonio's hand rested on his hat while he considered what would do the most damage: Leaving Jason here to snoop through his things? Or leaving Helena without any law enforcement?

"Best you stay here to look after the town," Antonio said. "In case there's any trouble."

"You got it, boss."

Antonio left him with his feet up on his desk, smoking a cigar.

Little Point was a small settlement a few miles west on the other side of the Gila River. On his approach, Antonio saw the smoking ruin of the saloon. There was little left of it. Just some blackened timbers reaching up like grave markers. Ash covered the ground like snow on the streets of New York in winter while embers floated on the wind. It was a miracle none of the other surrounding buildings had caught fire. Torn sacks, scattered grain, dented cans and smashed produce from the general store littered the main street.

Sheriff Neil Conner was a small white man with a style of beard that Antonio had seen a lot of in New York, with long sideburns and a shaved chin. He also had the same guarded look in his eyes that a lot of well-to-do New York men got when they first saw Antonio. Antonio drew himself up to his full height as he walked towards the other sheriff. He didn't offer his hand, knowing he wouldn't be offered one back.

"Sheriff Conner," Antonio said. "My name is Antonio Valdez. I'm the sheriff over in Helena. I got your message and thought I should come over to see if you needed any help."

"Ah, Sheriff Valdez. So good of you to come, but as you can see we've dealt with most of the trouble."

Antonio had a feeling Sheriff Conner wanted him gone as soon as possible, but he didn't want to leave until he was certain this gang was the same one that had taken over his family home. "What happened?"

"A band of outlaws ran through our town. Didn't give us a warning. Strode into the saloon and then set fire to the place. They gutted the general store and stole the silverware from the church." Sheriff Conner spat on the ground. His face flushed red. "Vermin."

"How many were there?"

"Around twenty. Perhaps. There was so much chaos it was hard to tell."

"Anything distinctive about them?"

"They were a mixed bunch. White and coloured folk. Men and women." The sheriff met Antonio's eye. "Had some Mexicans in there too."

Antonio's throat felt very thick. "And what direction did they ride off in?"

"West. Towards California. I've got an acquaintance in San Diego. Got a telegram from him the other day warning me about a gang of outlaws who'd been causing trouble in California. The call themselves The Reckoners. Led by a man called Clint. Ex-sheriff, although the bastard still has the gall to wear his star. He stoked up some trouble with his posse in his old town. Started taking the law into their own hands, now the whole gang's got a hefty bounty on their heads. They match the description of the ones that attacked us today."

"And you would like help tracking them down?"

"No, not so much. I doubt they'll be back to Little Point, but I wanted to give you a fair warning of what might be coming. It'll only be a matter of time before they cross the river. With mines closing, more towns are being abandoned, and rats always run to where they can find food. Unless you know something about this particular band of outlaws?"

Antonio felt the other sheriff's gaze on him, but he didn't meet it. "They're not one I've heard of before. I've got my eye on the Blood Twins."

"Of course you do, and I've heard your efforts to capture them are going very well."

The sly tone in Neil's voice sent a kick through Antonio's stomach.

"As well as any sheriff's efforts before mine." Antonio pushed his hat down. "Thank you for the warning, Sheriff. I'll make sure Helena is prepared for an attack. Did you manage to kill any of these gang members?"

"Think we got one of the vermin. There was a shootout at the church. If we got any of them, their body will be there. We're still cleaning up so haven't had a chance to look."

"I'd like to take a look, if that's all right by you, Sheriff Conner?"

"Be my guest." Sheriff Conner called over a ruddy-faced man from the group combing through the saloon rubble. "Vincent, show Sheriff Valdez the way, will you?"

Vincent nodded.

The church was a simple rectangular wooden building with a porch but no steeple. The remains of the intricate pattern carved into the door showed around the bullet holes that now riddled its surface.

Vincent stayed on his horse. Antonio kissed the crucifix around his neck, crossed himself and went inside.

The church interior looked more like a saloon after a

brawl than a place of worship. Pieces of splintered pew scattered the aisle. The altar was on its side, the surface peppered with bullets where it had been used as a barrier.

Special level of hell, Antonio thought as he looked around at the destruction.

Then he heard someone cough.

Antonio dropped behind one of the pews. He waited, twisting to catch any other sounds of movement. For a long time – long enough that Antonio wondered if he had imagined the cough – he heard nothing, and then he heard another one. And then a groan.

He wished Juanita was here. She'd be able to tell him exactly where the noise was coming from. But with his limited hearing, Antonio guessed it was coming from behind the upturned altar.

Whoever was there, it didn't sound like they had much of a fighting spirit. Although it could be a trap...

Antonio looked up at the eastern window, crossed himself while gripping his crucifix, drew his gun and crept towards the next pew. He made his way through the church, using the disarrayed pews to keep himself out of sight of the altar, freezing every time the wooden floor squeaked beneath his feet.

He reached the altar and paused with his back against its side. His heart was beating so quickly in his chest he felt sick.

He counted down from three and swung himself around the side.

And almost dropped his gun.

"Silvana," he whispered and sunk to his knees beside her.

For a moment, Silvana's eyes remained glazed with confusion then, slowly, the fog lifted. She coughed.

"Toni?" He nodded. The edges of her mouth quipped up into a smile. "Ha. I almost didn't recognise you. You're all grown up."

"So are you," he replied to her in Spanish. "Where are you hurt?"

Silvana tried to laugh but it turned into a hacking cough that left her lips flecked with blood. "Everywhere."

"Let me see?" She nodded and Antonio unbuttoned the front of her blood-soaked shirt. There were three bullet holes in her chest and one in her shoulder. It was a miracle she was still alive. And only a miracle could save her.

His thought must have shown on his face, because Silvana said, "That bad?"

"Nothing a bao from Auntie Ju couldn't cure." That made Silvana's smile stretch a little wider. "What are you doing here?" he asked. "I thought the gang that had taken over the fortress had done this."

"How do you know about that?"

"Hu." Silvana's eyes widened. "He found me in Helena. Told me what had happened."

"So he escaped." Silvana slid further down the altar. "Thank God. We all thought he'd died in the desert."

"Why are you here, Silvana?"

"Hostages." A chill ran through Antonio. "To make the others left at the fortress behave. If someone causes trouble on one side, they'll shoot the others."

A deep hacking cough took over Silvana's body. She bent double, sounding like she was going to cough up her lungs. Blood dribbled from her mouth. Antonio gritted his teeth while he rubbed her back.

"You're not just hostages," Antonio said. "Not if you were caught in the crossfire."

"They're making us join in," Silvana rasped. "Said we got to... earn our... keep. Apart from Ale..."

"What do you mean? What about Alejandro?"

Silvana swayed. Antonio caught her and held her against him. Her breathing slowed and even though her eyes were open, Antonio knew she couldn't see him anymore. Couldn't see anything anymore.

"Glad you're here, Toni," she said. "I didn't... want to... die... alone."

Her chest stopped moving and her eyes turned glassy. He prayed – prayed for God to welcome Silvana into His Heaven. And prayed for the strength for what he knew he needed to do, but was too afraid to do.

Then he carried her body out of the church, back to Helena, to lay her to rest beside Hu.

Chapter 13

Anniversary

I wake to the usual mornin' sounds of the desert – there's a pair of coyote fightin' sumwhere, an' not too far away a cactus wren's singin'. I lay in bed thinkin' what needs to be done that day. It ain't 'til I open ma door an' find Megan's bedroom door ajar, that I remember what day it is.

Usually I don't pay attention to the days, but there're two dates I make sure I know're comin': April 17, Megan an' mine's birthday, an' today. July 1. The day Pa died.

If today's gonna be anythin' like last year, then it ain't gonna be easy.

Sure as sure can be, I find Megan sittin' on the back porch in Ma's rockin' chair, a bottle of whisky in her hand.

"Good mornin', sis," I say. But Megan ignores me. She keeps starin' at the flat Arizona desert that stretches beyond our back porch.

"Have you eaten?" I ask, tryin' to git her to notice me.

"Wouldja like sum? I could git May to make you an omelette. Her cookin' gittin' better. She don't git any egg shell in her food no more. Or I could ask her to make flapjacks. Your favourite, flapjacks."

Megan takes a deep swig of whisky.

I go an' git Cassidy up.

'Round midday Megan disappears, leavin' 'hind a half-empty bottle of whisky. She doesn't take Rosie with her, fer which I'm grateful. I know where she's goin', an' I ain't lookin' ferward to collectin' her from The Sleepin' Raccoon this evenin'. In the meantime, I've ma own place to be.

"You wanna go fer a ride this afternoon?" I ask Cassidy.

Cassidy's eyes shine almost as bright as the sun, an' she smiles at me inna way I've only sin her do in ma dreams. "Of course!"

I saddle Hattie an' begin to saddle Rosie, but notice Cassidy' watchin' me. I know that look. It's the same one I wear when watchin' sumone do summit I wanna do. So I call her over an' show her what to do. She does a quick job an' is kind to Hattie, talkin' to her an' respondin' to her inna way I've never sin Megan do. Cassidy's a natural born horsewoman.

I've thought 'bout the next bit fer a long time – how to git Cassidy on her own horse without riskin' her escape. Even though she ain't tried anythin' fer a while, she's still waitin' fer a chance to run. So, I tie Hattie an' Rosie togither with a short length of rope, which means I can keep an eye on what Cassidy's doin'. Cassidy pulls herself into the saddle. I tie her hands togither an' her feet togither unner the horse.

"Don't you have a side saddle?" Cassidy asks. She's squirmin' in her seat. She's probably never ridden with her legs either side of a horse. Megan refuses to ride side saddle. I don't blame her. It looks real uncomfortable.

"No, we don't." I smile to say sorry, but Cassidy ain't lookin'.

"I forgot your sister rides like a man."

I pull maself into Hattie's saddle. It's bin a while since I've ridden a long distance – not since the failed train robbery – so I'm lookin' ferward to this as much as Cassidy.

"Don't you mind?" Cassidy asks.

"Mind what?"

"That your sister rides like a man. She dresses like one too."

"I don't have a say in what ma sis wears an' does."

"Don't you find it embarrassing?"

"Why would I?" Why's Cassidy askin' all these questions?

"Aren't men supposed to be in charge of their wives and sisters?"

"I ain't married, an' ma sis's a free woman. I can't tell her what to do."

I nudge Hattie's side with ma foot, an' she begins to walk. There's a short tug on the rope then Rosie follows her sis.

"I saw her drinking this morning," Cassidy says.

"So?"

"Don't you mind?"

"Sure I do—"

"Then why don't you stop her?"

"Why don't you?"

Cassidy purses her lips an' lifts her chin. "I don't want a bullet in my back," she mutters.

"Neither do I."

"She'd do that to her own brother?"

"She'd do it to anyone who got in her way."

"Why do you stay with her, then?"

"I made a promise once," I explain, "to sumone very special. An' that promise means more 'n anythin' else in the world."

"Anything?"

Cassidy's lookin' at me, with one of her eyebrows raised. I'd fergotten she could do that. Ma heart stumbles over itself inna missed beat.

Well, perhaps not anythin' in the world.

We ride side by side. Cassidy's suddenly as talkative as a jay bird. Is she startin' to like me? I doubt it. She's probably lonely. It's nice to hear her talk again, like when we was children. We'd talk 'bout the future, what we wanted to be, what we wanted to happen. Back then I never woulda guessed this were how we'd end up.

"Where are we going?" Cassidy asks an hour into the journey.

"To see sumone."

"Who?"

"Sumone special."

Pa's gravestone's jest a wooden cross. We didn't have enough money to afford a proper engravin'. It's summit I'd sworn I'd do if I ever had the money. The tree's finished flowerin' fer the year, but there're new red flowers growin' on the grave, which annoys me. There'd bin enough red in Pa's life.

I jump down from Hattie an' tie her to the tree. I untie Cassidy's feet an' offer her ma hand to take, but she refuses it. Then she realises how different it is gittin' down from a horse when you ain't ridin' side saddle. She ends up sittin' facin' out, ready to slide down Rosie's side.

"That's not the way you're s'posed to git off a horse," I say.

"I know it isn't," Cassidy snaps, "but this saddle is stupid and I can't get down with my hands tied. Help me."

I place ma hands on her waist an' lower her gently to the floor. I'm ashamed to say I don't take ma hands away as quick as I shoulda done. When I do a new rush of heat comes to ma cheeks that's nuthin' to do with the hot sun.

I take hold of the rope that's attached to Cassidy's tied hands an' walk to Pa's grave.

I nod at the cross. "Do you mind if I have a moment alone?"

Cassidy swallows an' nods. She's very sombre all a sudden. "Of course not."

I talk to Pa, tellin' him how much I miss him – how much we miss him. I point out Cassidy to him, tellin' him how beautiful she is now, how scared I am Megan'll find out who she is an' what she'll do when she does. I tell him 'bout the new sheriff, an' how I'm worried he'll be trouble. I empty every last thought in ma head to him. But he don't say nuthin' back. He can't, yet I wish so hard that he could.

I wanna be held. I want sumone to wrap their arms 'round me an' hug me.

I think of Cassidy standin' 'hind me an' wish more 'n ever that we hadn't lost what we'd had as children. If only I hadn't bin born who I was. If I were sum rich landowner's son, sumone respectable, then we could be togither. But no, I'm jest a bandit's son. Despite what I'd said to Dean, perhaps I do sorta wish that ma grandpa'd struck it lucky in California.

Tears prick ma eyes. I wanna let 'em fall, but I push 'em back. "Men don't cry," Megan'd told me whenever she caught me weepin'. So I wipe ma nose an' eyes on ma sleeve, take a deep breath an' turn 'round.

An' find Cassidy's no longer there.

She's gone.

As has Rosie.

In the close distance is a shrinkin' cloud of dust.

I throw maself at Hattie an' take after Cassidy.

Chapter 14

Escape

I expect Cassidy to head to the sheriff's office. That's where I woulda gone if I'd bin kidnapped. Ma palms sweat as I think 'bout her staggerin' in there, sobbin' with relief, an' then the sheriff callin' up his men to storm our house.

But ma panic calms when I notice Rosie's hoofprints ain't headin' 'wards town, but to an old house on the edge of it.

The Scarborough estate.

The house's stood empty fer six years, but Mr Scarborough musta bin payin' sumone to maintain it while he's away. The windows're clean, the wood freshly painted, the yard neatly maintained. It's like steppin' back in time. I half expect the front door to open an' fer a young Cassidy an' her governess to step outta it.

But instead I find Cassidy slumped on the front porch, her back 'gainst one of the columns. She ain't bothered to tie Rosie up, but the mare's munchin' on sum of the scrubby grass in the front yard. I hitch Hattie up, secure Rosie, an' slowly approach Cassidy.

"Go away," Cassidy says. "I've escaped. You can't touch me now."

"Sorry," I say, "but this don't count as escapin'."

Cassidy looks up at the big empty house, with its round tower, triangular rooves an' white balconies.

"No," she says, "I don't suppose it does." A tear tracks down her face. "I have nowhere else to go. But now I'm here..." Her lower lip trembles an' she digs her nails into the sleeve of her dress. "I've realised there's nowhere else I'd like to be less."

I look away while she composes herself.

"Why didja come back here?" I ask once her breathin's calmed. "Why not go to the sheriff's office? Tell 'em everythin'? Turn us in."

"Because if I do," Cassidy says, "they'll send me back to New York. Back to my father. And I can't go back to him, not now that I've finally gotten away. I thought I'd come back here for a while, gather myself before finding a way to Los Angeles, start a new life there, but now that I'm here..." She laughs. "I've realised there's no hope for me. Even if I go to Los Angeles, I know nothing of the world. I wouldn't even know where to begin setting up a new life. Father would only find me and lock me inside again.

"You know—" she traces the join between the wooden planks with her finger "—the day I left New York was the first day I'd been anywhere on my own. The first time I'd been allowed to leave the house without my father attached to my arm. I'd dreamed of coming back to Helena for so long, and when I was finally allowed to get on that train I saw my chance to escape."

"Then why didn't you git off at Barren Post?" I ask. But then it hits me. "You were runnin' away," I say, 'fore Cassidy can reply. "You shoulda got off the train when we got on it, but you stayed 'cause you were headin' to Los Angeles."

"Yes." Cassidy lets out a small laugh. "I stayed when I should have gotten off, and because I stayed I got captured by the two of you. And now Father hasn't heard from me in over a week, there's no way he'll allow me out of sight again."

"I can't let you go," I say. "If I come home without you, ma sis'll hunt you down."

"Yes," Cassidy says, "I can imagine Megan doing that."

The world stills. I don't breathe. I don't hear anythin' 'cept Cassidy's last words rotatin' 'round an' 'round ma head.

Then the wind whips 'round us an' everythin' comes back into motion. Ma stomach clenches.

"How long have you known?" I croak.

"I had my suspicions the moment we arrived in Helena. There are hardly many brothers and sisters in this town that match yours and Megan's descriptions. But I didn't want to believe that it was you because—"

Cassidy's lips make a thin line. I study the carvin' on the white wooden columns as I wait fer her to reply, even though I already know what she's gonna say.

"Because you'd... changed too much," Cassidy says at last.

I nod, holdin' back tears.

"When I was in New York," she says, "I dreamed of you coming to rescue me. My knight in shining armour sweeping me off my feet and stealing me out my bedroom window to freedom." She laughs again. "And then my knight in shining armour kidnaps me off the train and holds me hostage. Turns out it was nothing more than a girlish fantasy cooked up from reading too many books and spending too much time alone." Fresh tears track down her face. She continues laughin' as she wipes 'em away, but the laugh's too high an' strained. Ma fingers dig into ma leg an' ma jaw clenches.

"I'm sorry that I've changed," I say. "That I've become a monster."

"Not a complete monster," Cassidy says. Her gaze meets mine an' the sight of those dark green eyes makes ma pulse quicken. "At first I was afraid that I might have lost you completely, but there's some of the old Cole still in you."

She's wrong, but hearin' her say that makes me happy. There's none of the Cole left in me that Cassidy were friends with as a child. He died two years ago the moment he took his first life.

"When you first took me hostage," Cassidy says, "you told me not to let Megan know who I am. Why?"

I toe the gap 'tween the porch boards. She deserves to know the truth. She deserves to know that the woman she's livin' with hassa vendetta 'gainst her pa - even if Cassidy don't hold him very high in her favour. But how can I tell her that? How can I scare her even more?

"Is it to do with my father?" Cassidy asks.

I suck inna breath.

"Yes," I say.

"Is it to do with the fact my father killed yours?"

"Yes."

"Right." Fer a while, Cassidy stays sittin' on her front porch, lookin' out into the desert. Ma stomach squirms while I wait fer her reply. In the end, she stands an' says, "Shall we head back?"

I blink. "You're comin' back to the house?"

"Well, there's no point in me sticking around here, and there's nowhere else for me to go. But—" she faces me with her hands on her hips "—if I do come back, things are going to change. I will not be wearing these anymore—" she holds up her bound hands "—and I will have your full trust to do what I want and go where I want. I will not leave the grounds without you, but I will not be locked in that dingy parlour at night any longer. I will have full run of the house. And I expect to be paid, because this is only a temporary arrangement until I can leave for Los Angeles, which I will do whenever I want. Not when it is appropriate for you and Megan."

"All right," I say, 'though I ain't sure if I can accommodate all, or any, of Cassidy's requests. But I will do ma best.

Cassidy holds out her hands, an' I remove the rope.

"Let's go," I say. Cassidy gits back onto Rosie without ma help an' we're soon walkin' back towards Helena.

"What day of the week is it today?" Cassidy asks.

"Err, Monday, I think."

"You didn't go to church yesterday." Ma skin prickles as Cassidy gives me a look out the corner of her eye. "You used to love going, and I hear you praying before bed some nights." Ma cheeks grow hot. "Why don't you go anymore?"

"Megan don't believe no more," I say. "Not since Pa died an' the Reverend refused to bury him in the churchyard."

"I didn't ask about Megan. I asked why *you* don't go anymore."

Ma stomach grows cold. I rub Hattie's neck. Her warmth an' the feelin' of her pulse 'neath ma fingers soothes me a little.

Does Cassidy know? Why else would she be askin' these kinds of questions 'less she knew...

"It don't worry me not goin'," I say. "I can do ma prayin' at home."

Hattie snorts. Even she can tell I'm talkin' horseshit.

"The grave we visited," Cassidy says, "was that your father's?"

"Yes," I say. Ma throat cracks.

There's a long pause. Is Cassidy as aware of the house 'hind us – the place where Pa were shot – as I am?

"You picked a nice spot, Cole," she says at last.

On the way back home, we pass a stall sellin' lemonade. Cassidy's eyes light up at the sight. We've drunk most of the water in our canteens an' I'm thirsty as well. Sugary sour lemonade's always the most refreshin' thing to drink durin' the summer.

"Want one?" I ask, pointin' at the stall.

"Yes, please," Cassidy says. I start to git down from ma saddle. "Can I buy it?" Cassidy blurts out.

I'm so taken aback that I only stare at her fer a few seconds, watchin' her face turn redder 'n redder. Finally I snap maself back an' say, "Sure."

I give Cassidy sum money. She stares at it.

"What do all these coins mean?" she whispers.

I tell her. Cassidy repeats what each one is an' then dismounts.

As she walks 'wards the stall, a panicky thought enters ma head. What if the stall owner recognises her? What if he runs to the sheriff an' tells him he's sin Cassidy Scarborough in the company of Coles Hayes?

But then I remind maself that it's bin six years since Cassidy were last in Helena, an' when she were here she never left the Scarborough estate. There's little chance anyone in town'll recognise her.

A memory of Cassidy watchin' me an' Megan walk away from the estate comes to ma mind, her eyes sad an' her mouth downturned. I asked Pa once why Cassidy warn't allowed to leave the house – why she warn't allow to go to school like the other kids. He said her pa were scared of what might happen if she did, which I thought were strange since Megan an' me left the house all the time, an' Cassidy always looked like she wanted to leave. Ma heart gives a pang as I watch Cassidy come back from the stall, carryin' two cups of lemonade. She's beamin'.

"I've never bought anything before," she says, handin'

me a cup.

"Never?" I ask, confused.

"No," Cassidy says, sippin' her lemonade.

Is that what Cassidy's life'd bin like in New York too? Had she bin confined to her pa's house?

We drink the rest of our lemonade in silence. Cassidy's the first to drain her cup.

"Are you finished?" she asks.

I look down at ma half-finished cup, an' then drain it in one gulp. Ma face puckers from the sourness. I hand the cup down to Cassidy who returns 'em to the stall. The vendor tips his hat at us as Cassidy pulls herself back into the saddle.

"If you wanna," I say, "I could try an' take you out with me when I go places." Cassidy's eyes grow wide. "It won't be anywhere very excitin'. But on days like today when Megan ain't 'round, it would mean you git away from the house."

"I'd like that," Cassidy says. "I'd like that very much."

Chapter 15

Drinking Buddy

Nine days.

And Antonio was no closer to finding Cassidy.

He'd finally relented and composed a telegram back to Mr Scarborough, saying he would keep an eye out for Cassidy's arrival. It wasn't the truth. Or a lie. Although by the time Mr Scarborough got it he would no doubt figure that if Cassidy was taking this long to get to Helena, something had gone wrong. Hopefully in that time Antonio would find her. At least Antonio knew Cassidy wouldn't tell her father what had really happened. If she did, her father would take her straight back to New York, or send her somewhere far away.

Antonio sent the telegram and returned to the map on his wall, desperately searching for something he might have missed. But soon his eyes started gliding over the lines and words. Antonio rubbed them, sighed and sat down on his bed. He was so tired he felt on the verge of collapsing into a pile of broken bones. But if he tried to sleep, he would end up staring at the ceiling, his mind whirring but empty.

A change of scene. That's what he needed.

So he grabbed his hat and walked down to The Sleeping Racoon.

A couple of customers turned as he entered. A few tensed at the sight of the sheriff's star, thinking that he was here to hurry them home. But when Antonio leaned on the bar and ordered a drink, all the shoulders in the saloon fell. Not for the first time, Antonio appreciated how lucky he was that Helena's saloon was owned by a man who didn't take against people because of the colour of their skin. Plenty of places in New York had barred him from entering.

The Racoon was busy. Tables were full of men and women playing poker and faro, drinking, laughing and shouting. Women with painted lips and rosy cheeks flirted with the men, pushing their hips against theirs in hope of securing a patron for the night. The saloon's madam entertained a wealthy looking gentleman at a private table. The pianist was really going for it in the corner, accompanying a woman singing an upbeat song, which had a few of the saloon's customers tapping their feet.

While Antonio nursed his drink, he swept the room, picking out people he knew and trying to remember the names of everyone else. In the corner, he saw a familiar head of ginger curls. Hayes, was it? Megan Hayes. Had a brother called Cole. The brother was nowhere to be seen, but the sister looked like she was ready to keel over. Her table was scattered with empty bottles and glasses. She held a half full glass but was just staring with a half blank, half murderous expression at a spot on the floor.

"Got anyone joinin' you?" An older man stood beside Antonio. He nodded at Megan. "I've come to keep an eye on her, but it looks to me like you could use sum company."

"No. Please." Antonio gestured to the bar on his left side. No one stood on his right, but Antonio hoped the man would take the hint. It would be hard enough to hear with all the background noise without him standing on Antonio's right. The man leaned beside Antonio on his left and spat out his chewing tobacco into the spittoon. The older man dried his face on one of the towels hanging on the bar and held out his hand to Antonio.

"Dean Carson," the older man said. Antonio shook the proffered hand.

"Antonio Valdez."

"Want another?" Dean nodded at Antonio's glass, which Antonio found was empty. When had that happened? So he nodded and Dean ordered two whiskies from the barman, Joe.

"Miss Hayes looks like she's struggling through something," Antonio commented.

"It's the two-year anniversary of her pa's death," Dean said. "She's doin' better 'n last year. She'd already torn up half the saloon by this time."

"I'm sorry to hear that," Antonio said, although made a note to keep an eye on the young woman in the corner for the rest of the night. It sounded as though this wasn't going to be the quiet drinking session Antonio wanted it to be.

"It were a sad occasion," Dean said, as Joe slid their whiskies down the bar to them. Dean caught them and placed one in front of Antonio. Antonio raised his glass to Dean in thanks and took a sip. "He was shot by your employer."

Antonio's eyebrows shot up. "Mr Scarborough?"

"Yeah. Megan an' Cole's pa'd fallen on hard times. Took to robbin' houses. Chose Mr Scarborough's on the wrong night an' got two bullets in the back fer it."

"Oh," Antonio said. He felt less sorry for the Hayes siblings now.

Dean asked Antonio something, but one of the tables close by broke into raucous laughter, drowning out his words.

"Sorry," Antonio said, pointing to his covered right ear. "Can you repeat that?"

A familiar stab of fear pierced Antonio's stomach as he waited for Dean to roll his eyes, or sigh, like so many people did when Antonio asked them to repeat themselves.

But Dean just said, "How you findin' Helena?" and showed no signs of annoyance. Antonio paused, thinking about his reply. Dean started laughing. "Like that, huh?"

"It's not—"

Dean waved his hand. "Don't worry, Sheriff. You don't need to protest. I know how people in this town react to strangers. They haven't changed in twenty-five years. They've got that small town mentality – if you ain't an original settler, they'll take years to accept you. That's even when the town's only bin here fer fifty years."

Or when your skin's a tone too dark, Antonio thought. Or your first language isn't English. But instead of speaking he took a drink.

"As sumone who's bin a stranger maself," Dean said, "if you ever wanna talk, I'm here to listen. 'Though, I unnerstand there are things that a sheriff can't tell normal folk like maself."

"Where are you from?" Antonio asked. "You talk like a southerner."

Dean laughed and scratched his face. "Only 'cause I wanted to do all I could to fit in. I was born in what is now Montana but ran away to New York when I was still a kid."

Antonio smiled as he sloshed the amber liquid around the inside of his glass. His face was very warm. "I also ran away to New York."

"Really? Ain't that a coincidence. Why'd you leave home?"

"I come from a big family – well, two families that make up one big family, I guess. Something happened and I had to leave."

Dean raised his eyebrows. "Summit?"

"Yes." Antonio took another sip of his drink. "What about you? What made you leave home?"

A look passed over Dean's face that was so dark it made the hairs on the back of Antonio's neck stand on end. "Ma pa warn't the kindest of men. I got fed up of his beatin's, an' Ma an' me didn't see eye to eye either. Thought the east would've summit better to offer folks like me who never felt like they fitted in anywhere."

"Did it?"

"Did it fer you?"

They exchanged an understanding look, then knocked their glasses together and drained them. Antonio thought about his own father, who had also not been the kindest of men. After draining his glass, he felt a bond connecting the two of them, the kind that was forged between people who had lived through similar experiences.

"What did you do after you got to New York?" Antonio asked.

"Did sum work here an' there," Dean said. "Then did what everyone else ma age were doin'."

"What's that?"

"Joined the army."

"Union?"

"No."

The silence that stretched between them only lasted for a few moments, but to Antonio it was so heavy it compressed his chest. Antonio had met plenty of ex-Confederates, and he always got the same sense of bitterness from them when the war was mentioned, like they couldn't let it go.

"Ah, well." Dean took a long drink, and just like that the tense atmosphere disappeared.

Cole Hayes had come to pick up his sister. He was crouched by her side in the corner, trying to get Megan to talk to him, but she was still staring at the same spot on the floor, the now empty glass clutched in her hand.

"Gotta see plenty of the east durin' those four years 'fore I came out this way," Dean said.

"I bet," Antonio said.

"You done much travellin'?"

"Only to New York, but my family's in California."

"Ah, California. Came over fer the gold rush, by any chance?"

"A tale as old as time," Antonio said.

"Any luck?"

"Would I be sitting here if they had?"

Dean laughed, which made Antonio laugh. As the sound died on his lips, he stared at the rows of bottles behind the bar. His attention moved to the back of his mind, where it found a memory of a tale told in another room full of bottles.

"My family has a story," Antonio said, "about something that happened to them during the gold rush."

"Yeah?" Dean asked.

"Yeah..." Antonio furrowed his brow, trying to remember the story his parents had told him time and time again. "Apparently, one of my great-uncles found a treasure of lost Spanish gold in the California mountains along with a couple of others – but they were all murdered by one of the men who found it with them." Antonio swirled the dregs of his drink in his glass. "Ridiculous, isn't it?"

Looking over at Dean, Antonio expected to find the older man raising his eyebrows in disbelief, but instead Dean's face was grave.

"The man who murdered your uncle, what was his name?"

"I..." Antonio blinked. He was sure he had been told

the name, but it had been so long since he had heard the story he couldn't remember. "I don't know. Why?"

"No reason," Dean said, although Antonio got the sense that there was a very big reason behind his question. Perhaps another drink might get him to spill it.

As Antonio raised his hand to flag down Joe, he heard shouting. Megan was on her feet, yelling and throwing insults at the people sitting closest to her. Her brother tugged on her arm, but Megan pushed him away.

"Excuse me," Dean said and moved away from the bar.

Antonio listened to the commotion while staring at his empty glass. But soon he noticed the rest of the saloon had fallen silent. The hairs on Antonio's neck stood on end.

He swivelled around to face the room. Everyone stared at the saloon doors.

Where stood a group of men and women. Antonio knew some of their faces – or could see in them the shadows of their childhood selves that he had grown up knowing. Ai. Xin. Lorenzo. Fang. Rou. Tu. Fen. The majority of the group Antonio had never seen before, but he knew they were the gang that had taken over his family home. Who had been responsible for the deaths of Hu and Silvana.

The Reckoners.

Chapter 16

Intruders

I stand in front of the saloon swing doors, fightin' down the panic of steppin' through 'em again. After last year, I'd delayed comin' here as long as possible.

I don't wanna see Megan in that state again.

The fear I feel each time I put a gun in ma hand's nuthin' compared to the fear I felt last year findin' Megan after a day of drinkin'. Ma ribs still hurt from where she broke 'em punchin' me. At least this year Dean's keepin' an eye on her.

I take 'nother coupla deep breaths, an' then push ma way into the saloon 'fore Pa's voice hassa chance to enter ma head. The eyes of a coupla folk turn ma way as I walk inside, but I keep ma head down an' move fer the table in the darkest corner where Megan'll be.

"Megan," I say, crouchin' beside her, "it's time to go home."

But Megan don't move. Jest keeps starin' at a spot on the floor an' clutchin' her empty whisky glass. Her knuckles shine white 'gainst the glass. I swallow.

"Sis," I say, "shall we go home?"

"Don't wanna," Megan says, so low an' quiet I almost miss it.

"All right. All right," I say. What can I do to git Megan to leave without settin' her off? I glance 'round the room. Dean standin' at the bar. I'm 'bout to call out to him an' then I see who he's talkin' to. I shrink back 'gainst the wall, not wantin' to catch the sheriff's attention.

"Assholes," Megan mutters. "They're all assholes. Every last one of 'em."

"Megan." Ma voice trembles outta fear fer what's comin'.

"ALL OF YOU!" she bellows, standin' with such force several bottles roll off the table an' smash on the floor. "You're all assholes! None of you care. NONE OF YOU!"

Springin' to ma feet, I grab her arm, tryin' to git her to sit down, to calm her down 'fore the sheriff hassa reason to arrest her, but she pushes me away, yellin' at me to let go.

"Megan!" I hiss. "The sheriff's here. We can't—"

"Fuck off, Cole!" The next shove's a hard one. Ma arm rips away from hers. Next thing I'm lyin' on the floor, covered in spilt drinks an' ma back smartin' from collidin' with a table edge. Through ma daze I hear Megan shout, "You're the fuckin' worse of all 'em, Cole!"

"That's enough, Megan." Dean's hand grips her upper arm. Megan tries to hit him, but Dean's grip's stronger 'n mine. I stand, sticky from the alcohol, ma face burnin' from Megan's words an' from the looks I'm sure everyone in the saloon's givin' us.

But when I look 'round, everyone's starin' at the saloon doors, where stands a group. They're a collection of folk from all walks of life, an' all of 'em with guns on their hips. One tall Chinese man's gotta bow an' arrow slung across his back.

A heavy feelin' drops into ma stomach as the air begins to crackle with tension.

I glance 'wards the sheriff, expectin' him to be alert, but he's jest starin' at the new arrivals, his face ashen. Looks like we ain't gonna git much help from him.

"May we help you?" Joe asks, leanin' on the bar, his palms flat on the counter.

"That depends on what you hafta offer," says the white man at the front. He's got a salt an' pepper beard, an' he's wearin' a sheriff star on his jacket, 'though he an' those 'hind him don't look like law keepin' folk. I've heard stories 'bout sheriffs an' their posses gone bad.

"Whisky. Rum. Beer. Gin. Bourbon."

A Black woman with white hair an' crow's feet laughs. "We ain't talkin' 'bout alcohol," she says. "We're talkin' 'bout materials. Money, mostly. But we'll take anythin' that's of value."

"If you've gotta bank, we're happy to clear it out fer you," one of 'em says, which makes a couple in the group laugh.

"We don't tolerate outlaws in this town," sumone in the saloon spits.

"Outlaws?" the white man says. "Don't think of us as outlaws. What we're here to propose is more of a relationship. You give us what we want an' we leave you all in one piece."

The woman lets out a laugh that booms 'round the saloon, but it ain't enough to cover up Megan's words.

"Don't you know this here is Blood Twins' territory?"

A new stillness sweeps over the bar. Megan's glarin' at the group of newcomers. The drunkenness seems to've retreated. She's holdin' herself up straight, her eyes gleamin', clear an' full of fire. Ma stomach rolls. I dig ma fingernails into the sides of ma pants as ma hands shake.

"They ain't gonna be happy with you bargin' in on their turf," Megan continues.

"The Blood Twins?" The white man scratches his cheek. "Never heard of 'em. Ever heard of the Blood Twins, Annie?"

"Nope," the Black woman says. "Oh, wait. Aren't they those two cowards who refuse to show their faces?"

"Oh, yeah." The white man laughs. "Those two. Why would we worry 'bout 'em?" He meets Megan's eye. "We're not afraid of cowards."

Megan smiles an' ma stomach drops outta fear she'll start runnin' her mouth off. But instead she does summit worse.

She pulls out Florence an' Smithy.

Or she tries to, but Dean grabs her arms.

The gang reacts, pullin' all their weapons free. I find maself facin' into a dozen gun barrels, as well as a notched arrow.

Joe says, "It's a policy in ma bar that weapons are kept in their holsters."

"You didn't tell her that when she drew her weapon," Annie says. "One rule fer us an' one rule fer everyone else."

"As far as I can see, Megan's guns are still in their holsters."

"Ladies an' gentlemen," Dean says, his hands still on Megan's arms, "let's not git carried away. I'm sure we can talk this through like civilised folk." Dean looks at the sheriff. He wants back up, but the sheriff doesn't meet his eyes. He looks dazed, like he's bin hypnotised. What's up with him? Dean must see the same thing I do, 'cause he frowns an' turns back to the gang. "What do you say to a drink?"

"We don't serve their kind in here," sumone in the saloon says. Their comment causes a ripple of agreement. A few more hands move 'wards their holsters. I take a small step 'wards Megan, ready to jump in front of her if necessary. Things're 'bout to git ugly.

But the change in atmosphere snaps the sheriff outta his daze 'cause he takes a step ferward, his expression focused. He opens his mouth to stay summit, but 'fore he can git it out Megan pulls her guns free an' fires into the fray.

Folks scream an' dive unner tables as Megan's bullets fly. I throw maself onto the floor, arms over ma head. Dean hollers Megan's name an' then the bullets stop flyin'. The moment Megan stops, the other side fires back at us, but it's fer only a few moments. From unner ma arms, I hear a chorus of shouts an' the sound of fists hittin' bodies. I glance up an' find the customers in the saloon settin' upon the gang.

"Cole!" Dean's gesturin' at me from 'hind the bar. I scramble 'cross the floor through the melee of screamin', shoutin' an' explodin' guns. 'Hind the wooden counter, I find Megan slumped 'gainst the side, a rag doll once again, Joe loadin' a shotgun, Dean with his revolver out an' the sheriff breathin' deep.

Smoke fills the saloon along with the sulphuric smell of gunpowder.

I cower unner the counter, ma hands over ma ears.

I tell maself to breathe.

If I breathe, I'll stay in the moment.

If I breathe, I won't go back there.

But as the gunshots echo in ma ears, ma heartbeat pounds faster an' faster, an' flames rise outta the ground. The saloon walls narrow an' stretch.

The screamin' starts, an' Jesus stares down at me from his cross on the wall.

I press the heels of ma hands into ma eyes an' wait fer it to pass.

Chapter 17

Bar Fight

A bullet whizzed over the bar, hitting a bottle on the shelves. Antonio covered his head. Glass rained down around him, mixing the smell of sweet rum with the stink of gunpowder. Antonio watched the glass bounce off the toes of his boots, but his mind was across the room where his family fought for their lives with the gang who were holding them hostage.

Antonio needed to protect his town. But he needed to protect his family. Did The Reckoners know his connection to his family? Is that why they had come to Helena? If he started picking off the gang members, would they harm his family because of him?

On the other side of the bar there was a cry of pain and a high-pitched scream. Antonio's gun handles dug into his hands as he gripped them tighter.

What could he do? What was he meant to do?

Pulled by the sense that someone was looking at him, Antonio turned his head towards the others crouched behind the bar. Dean's mouth opened and closed, saying something to him, but the words were lost to Antonio among the rest of the noise.

"What?" Antonio asked, cupping a hand around his left ear.

"You all right there, Sheriff?" Dean repeated.

Antonio looked at Dean – at Joe crouched beside him with his shotgun in his hands, Megan slumped against the back of the bar and Cole with his hands over his eyes.

Antonio gritted his teeth and turned himself around.

"Never better," he said and clicked back the hammers on his revolvers.

Slowly, he raised himself up and peered over the top of the bar. The room was emptier than he expected – it looked like a lot of the saloon customers had managed to get out. There were two small forts made of overturned tables and chairs on opposite sides of the bar. The one closest to the bar sheltered the remaining saloon customers, who used the gaps in the fort to shoot at the other fort near the door. Behind that one, he could just about make out the figures of the gang. On the floor between the two forts lay three bodies. One of them he recognised as the man from the general store – the one who had been convinced the storekeeper had cheated him out of a nickel. There was a bullet hole through his neck.

Joe jumped up beside Antonio and rested his gun on the top of the bar. His shot ripped through the gang's fort, splintering wood. Someone screamed. Ai. Antonio would know her scream anywhere. She always used to scream from the top of the fort roof, frightening the adults half to death every time she did. She went without dinner each time she did it, but she kept doing it because she got such a kick out of making them panic.

But the scream she let out was unlike anything he'd

heard before.

God, he didn't want anyone else to die. Please. Don't let anyone else die.

The gang must have turned all their guns their way, because Ai's scream was followed by a wave of bullets against the counter. Joe dived behind the bar, covering his head as glass bottles exploded on the shelf above them.

"Ceasefire!" Antonio screamed. "Ceasefire and let's talk!"

Slowly, the bullets stopped.

With Antonio's heart slamming against the inside of his chest, he shouted, "This is the sheriff of Helena speaking. If you lay down your guns now, I will ensure your safety as I take you into custody. If you continue to shoot, then I cannot guarantee that you will leave this building alive."

"What makes you so sure you're gonna leave this buildin' alive?" someone shouted. The woman named Annie, Antonio guessed.

Antonio heard someone hush her, and then a man shouted, "We're not backin' down, Sheriff. We don't give ourselves up to anyone who wears a shiny star." Antonio guessed that was Clint, the sheriff turned outlaw.

"Sheriff!" Dean's warning shout made Antonio look in his direction. He knew his mistake when he saw Dean's eyes looking behind him. He turned his head. A tall young man crouched on the top of the bar, sighting Antonio down his pistol barrel. The look in his eyes chilled Antonio to his core.

"For my brother," he snarled.

Alejandro.

Antonio's body froze as the shock of recognition seized his limbs. Even as he stared into the black circle of Alejandro's pistol muzzle, he still couldn't move to defend himself.

A shot rang out across the saloon. The bullet ripped

through Alejandro's right hand, spraying blood. Screaming, Alejandro dropped his gun and clutched his bleeding hand to his chest.

Antonio fired a warning shot over Alejandro's shoulder. Alejandro fled back to the fort.

As Antonio turned his head to see where his saving shot had come from, the saloon back doors burst open and a group of armed men and women rushed inside.

"Thank Gawd," Joe muttered. "Sumone must've gone fer help."

It took another minute of gunfire to drive The Reckoners from the saloon. Antonio was reloading his gun when he heard the bang of the saloon doors and the sound of running feet as the gang made their escape.

"After 'em!" someone shouted, and the customers of The Sleeping Racoon ran out. Joe and Dean followed, Antonio right behind them, but as he was crossing the saloon he felt a pair of eyes on him.

A cloaked and hooded figure stood on the balcony that ran around the side of the saloon's first floor. They held a rifle and the shadow of their face looked down towards Antonio.

"Who—" Antonio began to ask, but then a shot sounded from close outside the saloon doors. By the time Antonio looked back from checking for danger, the hooded figure was gone.

All but one of The Reckoners escaped from the battle outside the saloon. She toppled from her horse with a bullet in her back as the rest of the gang cantered into the night. Several of the townsfolk readied their horses to chase after them, but Antonio stopped them. There had been enough bloodshed for one night and he didn't want a Helena resident to follow The Reckoners all the way back to his family fort.

By the time they'd finished cleaning up the saloon,

they'd uncovered five bodies, three townsfolk, one unknown man who was thought to be a member of The Reckoners and Ai. Wrapped in sheets, the bodies were taken to the undertakers, who Antonio slipped some money to ensure Ai was laid to rest beside Hu and Silvana. Antonio spent the rest of the night speaking to everyone in the saloon to gather as much information as he could about The Reckoners.

It didn't escape him that he had done little during the fight. As sheriff, it was his responsibility to protect Helena in these situations – to organise the townsfolks to drive the invaders out – but all he had done was hide behind the bar and called for a ceasefire. He should have ordered for someone to go for reinforcements. He should have organised the townsfolk in the bar into better offensive positions. He should have made his way across the saloon to try to take out their leader. But he hadn't.

Mr Scarborough had handed him this position on a silver platter and Antonio was proving what he knew all the townsfolk were thinking – that he wasn't worthy of the position.

Being a sheriff was all Antonio had ever wanted – even from when he was a small kid. The desire to see that dream come true had driven him through the dark times in New York, when he was living on the streets, trying to survive. And now that it had come true, Antonio was wasting it.

Early morning light stretched across the desert as Antonio made his way back to the sheriff's office. What had started out as a night off had turned into one of the longest working days of his career.

Antonio closed the door of the sheriff's office behind him. He resisted the urge to slide down the back of it and sleep on the floor. Instead he dragged himself upstairs. As he climbed the stairs, he heard a guitar playing in his room.

Slowing his movements, Antonio drew his gun from its

holster. The door to his room was wide open. A lit gas lamp sat on his bedside table, casting light on the brown-skinned woman sitting on his bed tuning his guitar. She was dressed in loose-fitting pants and a shirt, with a cloak wrapped around her shoulders. The silver pins holding up her long black hair caught in the lamp light, winking like stars. In the corner of his room, Antonio saw a guitar case, a canvas bag and a rifle – the same rifle he had seen on the saloon balcony hours before.

The sight loosened Antonio's grip on his gun, so much so that it began to slide out of his hand. He caught it before it hit the floor. The young woman looked up.

"You bought a new one," she said, tapping his guitar. "Although, you've been neglecting it. It's horribly out of tune."

Antonio returned his gun to its holster. Moving closer to her, Antonio felt a little thrill up his spine as the side of her mouth curved into a smile, in the way it did when she was pleased by something. He was glad that thirteen years later she still had that habit.

"Hello, Juanita," Antonio said in Spanish.

"Hello, Toni," she replied. "Seems like I came home just in time."

She strummed a chord and it was perfectly in tune.

Chapter 18

Dreams

It takes all ma courage to knock on Megan's bedroom door. She's sittin' up in bed, but hassa sheet over her head, blockin' out the hot sun streamin' through the window. The shadows unner her eyes stand out 'gainst her sickly pale skin. I can only imagine how nauseous she must be feelin'.

"You all right, sis?" I ask. All I git in reply is a deathly stare that makes ma bowels clench. "Do you want me to git you anythin'? Water?"

"Who do those Reckoner bastards think they are?" Megan mutters. "Hustlin' in on our turf like that. How dare they. We're gonna hafta teach 'em a lesson, Cole. The Blood Twins can't be sin to be weak, otherwise we'll have every damn gang comin' down on our heads."

I bite ma bottom lip. This were what'd kept me awake all night – the thought of what Megan's reaction were gonna be to this new gang. The Reckoners, as folk'd called 'em last night. I feared she'd go on the war path to wipe 'em all out. How can the two of us take down a whole gang that look to be more skilled an' better equipped?

But once Megan gits an idea into her head, there's no gittin' it out. No matter what I say or do, I ain't gonna be able to persuade her to walk away from the challenge. The whole reason she started the Blood Twins were to keep Pa's memory alive, an' seein' this new gang determined to take over our turf is like seein' sumone pissin' on his grave. To Megan at least it does. As long as Megan's alive, I'll be happy with whatever lot life gives me, but if Megan's determined to take these hustlers out then I'm gonna be there beside her, protectin' her all the way.

"We need to find out where their base is," Megan says. "Take 'em out there rather 'n waitin' fer 'em to come back. We'll ask 'round – sumone's gotta know summit 'bout that gang."

I think 'bout the way the sheriff acted last night. He might know summit, but after what Megan said in front of him I don't want her talkin' to him, so I don't say anythin'.

"I'll take sum of that water," Megan says.

As I'm 'bout to leave, I pause in the door. I ain't sure where the small surge of courage comes from, but I find maself sayin', "You shouldn't talk 'bout the Blood Twins so openly in front of the sheriff. You'll give him ideas."

"Shut up, Cole," Megan snaps, an' jest like that the surge of courage retreats back into its corner. I duck ma head, close Megan's door 'hind me an' go downstairs.

Cassidy's cleanin' out the stove. She rocks back onto her heels as I enter the kitchen. She's got ash smudged 'cross the bridge of her nose. I press ma hands 'gainst the sides of ma pants, surpressin' the urge to wipe it away.

"How's the patient?" Cassidy asks.

"Like a hibernatin' bear that's bin woken too early," I say. Cassidy an' me exchange a knowin' look.

"I need to go sumwhere this afternoon to buy food fer the horses," I say. "Do you wanna come with me?"

"Are you not worried I'll try to escape again?"

I lower ma voice as I say, "You know you're free to go whenever you want."

Cassidy tips her head to one side. "Is that so? Have you told Megan that I have a free pass?" I clear ma throat an' shuffle ma feet. Cassidy sighs. "I thought not. You know, Cole, that free pass is not worth much unless the person with the guns knows about it."

"I'll tell her!" I object. "I will." Cassidy gives me a look that confirms she knows as much as I do I won't be tellin' Megan I've given Cassidy permission to leave whenever she wants. 'Though I didn't lock Cassidy in the parlour last night an' I've found a jar that I can put money aside in to pay Cassidy fer her work. Not that we have any spare money to give her, but I promised her, so I'll make it work.

Cassidy sweeps the last of the soot into the bucket. "Lucky for both of us, then, that I'm not itching to go anywhere yet. But one day I will be taking that train to Los Angeles, so you need to tell her soon that I'm not here for life."

I nod, 'though I've no idea how I'm gonna do that. There's no scene I can imagine Megan lettin' Cassidy go.

"So," I say, "do you wanna come?"

The bucket clangs 'gainst the side of the stove as Cassidy stands up. "Of course I do," she says, an' sweeps outside, leavin' me with ma heart thumpin' so loudly in ma chest I'm surprised it doesn't vibrate the floor 'neath ma feet.

Old Man Coady runs a small horse ranch on the outskirts of town. He lives alone in the large farmhouse. All his children either died in the war or left to start a life elsewhere. Now he runs the place with the help of sum farm hands, 'though he can break a wild horse on his own at the age of eighty.

We approach the farmhouse, walkin' 'tween the paddocks holdin' dozens of horses. Most look to be Cerbat mustangs, like Hattie an' Rosie, but I see a few American Paint Horses an' Appaloosa. Close to the farmhouse a Black man leans on one of the fence posts lookin' out at a paddock of horses. He squints up at us from unner the brim of his hat.

"Cole?" he calls. "Cole Hayes, is that you?"

Swallowin' down the lump in ma throat, I raise a hand an' call back, "Hey, John."

"Well I'll be." John Sanders runs over to us. "How you doin'?"

"Good." Feelin' uncomfortable talkin' to sumone on the ground while I'm so high 'bove 'em, I dismount. Cassidy does the same, if a little awkwardly. "How you doin'?"

"Really good," John says. He jerks his thumb over his shoulder at the ranch house. "I'm here to talk to Old Man Coady. He's thinkin' of sellin' up, an' I'm thinkin' of buyin' him out."

"An' sellin' your ranch?"

"An' keepin' ma ranch! I've got the money to run two. Jest need the extra man power to make it work. I, er, don't suppose you'd think of comin' back to work fer me again?"

John's words make me wanna holler, "Yes!", but I squash the excitement 'fore it can show on ma face. I shake ma head instead.

"Sorry, John," I say. "I can't."

"Ah, well." John gives me a sad smile. "Let me know if you change your mind." Then he notices Cassidy fer the first time. He sweeps off his hat, holds it to his chest an' gives a small bow. "Good afternoon, ma'am. John Sanders at your service."

"A pleasure," Cassidy says.

"This is ma cousin, May. She's from Phoenix," I say, playin' out what Cassidy an' me'd agreed if sumone should ask who she were. She's wearin' one of ma hats that dips down lower 'n it's s'posed to, coverin' much of her face. I'm hopin' it's enough to throw off anyone who might otherwise recognise her.

"Helena must seem mighty small in comparison," John says.

"It's a welcome change," Cassidy says. There's a slight western twang in her words. Summit I haven't heard in her voice since we were children.

"We'd better go see the old man," I say, strokin' Hattie's neck. "Gotta buy sum feed fer these two."

"I won't keep you, then. Cole, don't ferget ma offer."

I jest nod in reply, 'cause of course I ain't gonna fergit his offer. I've regretted turnin' it down since the day I did – the day Pa died an' I knew I hadda give up ma dream to protect Megan.

We walk the horses up to the house, then go in search of a ranch hand to sell us hay. I give Cassidy the money an' let her do all the talkin'. She hands the money over an' is presented with sackful of hay. She turns to me with shinin' eyes.

"I did it," she mouths. I smile at her childlike delight in doin' summit so simple.

We carry the hay back to the horses an' strap 'em on their sides an' back, ensurin' the weight's distributed evenly. John's talkin' to Old Man Coady in the shadow of the house as we leave the ranch. I look away quickly outta fear of ma heart breakin' fer the life I coulda had.

"Why didn't you take his offer?" Cassidy asks. She's lookin' at me with too much knowin' in her eyes, like she's already guessed the answer. So there ain't no point in lyin'. Not that I would lie to her. Not again at least.

"I gotta look after Megan," I say. "I promised Pa I would."

"Surely getting a job would be a better way of looking after your sister, until she gets married."

I snort, then see the affronted look on Cassidy's face. "Sorry," I say, "it's jest that Megan ain't gonna git married. An' what I do now fer her... Well, that's the best thing I can do to ensure she stays safe. More 'n workin' onna ranch at least."

"But you wanted to take John up on his offer, didn't you?"

"I did," I admit. "I... I were meant to go work fer him, but when Pa died I hadda put Megan first. I'd always dreamed of ownin' ma own ranch – thought it'd be fun bein' 'round horses all day, every day. Couldn't think of anythin' I wanted more."

"Do you still think that?"

I sneak a glance at Cassidy out the corner of ma eye. There is one thing I'd like jest as much as ownin' a ranch, but it wouldn't be appropriate fer me to voice it. So I say, "Yeah."

"Then you shouldn't let your sister take that away from you."

"Oh, she's not takin' anythin' away from me. I wanna stay with her. She's... more important to me 'n anythin' else."

"Then you lied."

Ma face falls as I look at Cassidy, who's got that knowin' look on her face.

"When you said you wanted nothing more 'n to own your own ranch. It sounds like you want nothing more 'n to keep Megan safe."

I blink. I guess I ain't thought 'bout it like that, but now that Cassidy said it, it's obvious. Megan's more important to me 'n anythin' else in ma life. Ma own life included.

Then I smile. "'More 'n.' Miss Cassidy Scarborough, you've only bin back in the West fer a few days, an' you're already losin' your New York airs."

This time it's Cassidy who looks taken aback. To ma

surprise, a deep blush spreads 'cross her face. The sight of her bein' embarrassed makes me embarrassed.

"It slipped out," Cassidy mutters.

We both walk with our eyes on the ground fer a while, leadin' the horses, each unable to look at the other. I open ma mouth a few times, tryin' to restart the conversation, but it takes me at least ten attempts to finally say, "What's the thing you want more 'n anythin' else?"

It takes a long while fer Cassidy to reply. Her voice's so muffled I barely hear it.

"I want to go into politics."

I blink. "What, like, bein' the mayor?"

"No, like..." She sighs an' runs her hand along Rosie's neck. "Making decisions about our laws, making new ones that will make things better, and... being trusted by enough people to do that."

"But how can you do that when women can't vote?"

A hard look flashes in Cassidy's eyes.

"Not all women have the vote *yet*," she says. "Neither do all men. But they will. The suffrage movement will see that all women, and men, across the country – no, all over the world – will get the vote. One day, you and Megan can go to the polls together."

"I don't think Megan cares 'bout votin'," I say.

"Well, she should," Cassidy says. "Everyone should care about voting. It's the one chance you get for your voice to be heard."

Bein' too young to vote, I'd never thought 'bout what I'll do when I finally git there. It all seems too far outta reach. Too fanciful fer me to do. What do I hafta do with those educated men sittin' in their offices 'hind those big desks? Folks like me don't matter to folk like 'em. We're told what to do. Ma small life meant nuthin' to 'em.

But summit in Cassidy's voice ignites a feelin' in ma chest that I've never felt. A feelin' that perhaps ma small life's worth summit. An' that ma voice deserves to be heard. 'Cause how could I not be inspired when Cassidy's eyes're shinin' with such clarity as they are now? It's like she's seein' a path straight to the future.

It must be nice to be able to see the path ahead so clearly.

Chapter 19

God's Gift

As ever, Antonio woke first.

Juanita was still fast asleep on her bed roll in the corner of the room. Even though the sun streamed onto her face she slept on. Even when they were children she'd always been able to sleep through anything. Antonio still took care to be quiet as he left the room.

Checking the cupboards, he found only a can of beans and a slice of bread. Enough for him, but not enough for two. So he grabbed his hat and went down to the general store.

By the time Juanita emerged from upstairs, dressed in a shirt and long skirt, Antonio had a hot skillet of sausage, fried eggs and bread, bacon and beans sizzling over the fire.

"No congee?" Juanita asked. "Auntie Zhu would be disappointed."

"It's near impossible to get rice out here," Antonio replied. "And chilies. Here." He handed her his one plate. They sat out the back of the sheriff's office, Juanita eating off the plate and Antonio directly out the skillet.

"So bland," Juanita said.

"You're welcome," Antonio muttered, chewing on his bacon.

"If you're happy to eat food like this, you've been living away from home too long."

Guilt stabbed Antonio's chest. He pushed his beans around his plate. "I guess thirteen years is a long time," he said.

"It is," Juanita said.

They sat in silence, chewing their breakfast. From the way Juanita's chin tilted upwards, Antonio knew it was up to him to break the silence with the right words. Otherwise he would get nothing more out of her.

But as he struggled for words, he found himself captivated by her appearance. Antonio remembered Juanita as he had last seen her – eight years old, stick-thin, a bag of clacking bones in a body always drowned in baggy clothes into which she pulled herself like a tortoise. But now, he saw none of that awkwardness. She lounged on the decking, legs crossed, head thrown back and tilted in a way that made him unable to look away. She was all confidence and grace.

"You look good," he said.

Juanita's mouth curved up into a smile that made heat rush to Antonio's cheeks.

"Thank you," she said. "Although, talking about appearances, what's up with that gauze stuck over your ear? You making a fashion statement?"

"No," Antonio said. "I thought it would help people understand that I can't hear out of that ear." Juanita frowned. Suddenly the idea that Antonio thought was genius felt very stupid. He sighed. "People find it easier to understand something if they can see it. It stops people from acting funny if I ask them to repeat something, or turn my head to the side."

"Does it help?"

"Sometimes. I still get a lot of eye rolls or frowns when I ask people to repeat something. And I've made up some great stories about how I lost it."

Juanita's eyebrows raised. "Give me an example?"

"Got it shot off by a bandit while saving a stage coach that was carrying the president. He then awarded me a Medal of Honour."

"People actually believed that?"

Antonio shrugged. "Yeah. They were pretty drunk at the time, though." He stood up and collected her plate.

"Coffee?"

"If you're offering."

Antonio rushed into the office and grabbed the kettle, coffee and mugs. He glanced at the clock and for once was glad that Jason was never on time for work.

"So," Juanita asked as Antonio's coffee brewed over the fire, "what were half our family doing with a gang of outlaws last night?"

Antonio frowned. "You don't know? Weren't you at the fort when The Reckoners took over?"

"The Reckoners? Who the hell are they?"

"A gang from California."

Juanita shrugged. "Never heard of them. And no. I left the fort right after you did. Haven't been back since." That stab of guilt came back. And this time it was double the strength. There was a long pause.

"So, this gang have taken it over?" Juanita asked.

Antonio nodded. "They're using the fort as a base. They..." He swallowed. "They took it over by force. Some of our family died trying to stop them."

"Toni." Juanita's voice cracked and Antonio could sense her heart breaking with his.

For a long time, they sat in silence watching the kettle over the fire.

"How did you find out if you haven't been back?" she asked.

"Hu. He escaped from the fort the night the gang took over. Came to Helena to warn me. He's buried in the churchyard," he said. "Next to Silvana, who I found in Little Point after the gang raided the town. Ai was killed last night. They're using half the family as hostages to make the others left at the fort behave. That's why The Reckoners were there last night at The Racoon."

Steam billowed from the kettle spout. Antonio removed it from the fire with a hand wrapped in a towel and set it on the ground. While he waited for the water temperature to drop, Juanita crossed herself and whispered a prayer for their dead family members. He wished she had been there when he buried Hu and Silvana.

After counting to thirty, Antonio stirred the coffee grounds into the kettle. He and Juanita sat in silence as they waited for the coffee to brew. After stirring and waiting again, Antonio added a cup of cold water to the kettle to help the granules sink to the bottom, then slowly poured the coffee into two mugs.

"Ale seemed to be enjoying himself," Juanita said, accepting her mug.

"Silvana tried to give me a warning about him," Antonio said. "I don't know what it was, but it seems Ale might be an exception to the rule."

"You think he's in league with the gang?"

Antonio raised his mug to his lips and blanched at the heat. "I don't know, but it might be the case. So," he said, brightening his tone, ready to change the subject, "if you haven't been at the fort for the past thirteen years, where have you been?"

"I went on a bit of a journey. With you gone, there

wasn't a reason for me to stay. And, well, I wanted to meet people like me."

"Did you?"

The grin that split Juanita's face was brighter than the sun. "I went to all over – New Mexico Territory, Oklahoma, Colorado, Montana, South Dakota. Anywhere there were first nation territories." Her expression darkened. "What I saw wasn't pleasant, Toni. The sorrow my people felt at the loss of their land – at the loss of their way of life. It was unlike anything I know I'll see again. It made me feel like such a fraud – walking around in these clothes with a cross around my neck." Her fist gripped a handful of her skirt. "Some of them looked at me with such hatred, thinking I was a puppet of the people who had put them on those reservations – an advert for what a good Indian should look like." Her lips pressed together. "It didn't help that the white people I ran into on the reservations tried to put me on a pedestal in front of the others. I thought about changing my clothes to fit in, wearing the same clothes my ancestors would have worn, but decided I would feel like even more of a fraud."

Antonio didn't know what to say. He couldn't understand what it must have been like for Juanita over these past thirteen years. Growing up surrounded by his biological family, in a body he felt comfortable in, he had always felt at home. He knew it had been different for Juanita, but it hurt to hear that even meeting other Native Americans hadn't been the reaffirming experience he guessed she had wanted.

"Was it not helpful at all?" he asked.

Juanita paused for a long time, thinking. Finally, she said, "A little, yes. I think. Those that were willing to listen to my story were sympathetic and allowed me to stay with them. I learnt a lot about where I might have come from, although I wasn't able to identify my tribe. I hoped someone would recognise me. You know, someone who knew me as the child of their long lost brother, or sister, or something. But no one did. It would have been a nice extra, finding something out about my parents or my family."

Antonio's father had found Juanita in the wreckage of a stage coach. There had been no traces of any other people, just a lot of blood and torn clothes. Whatever had taken her family had left her crying in the upturned carriage. Antonio's father brought her home and the family had raised her with the other children.

The aunties and uncles had argued over what name to give her. In the end she was given one name that meant God's gift in both Spanish and Chinese. Because that's what Antonio's father said she had been – a gift from God. When they were six, Juanita told Antonio she was a girl and told him not to call her that name anymore, but to call her Juanita instead. Antonio had heard Juanita praying every night to God, asking Him to turn her into a girl, so when she told him he hugged her tight because he knew how much courage it had taken her to tell him. From then on, he noticed the pain it caused her when their family called her the wrong name, but by the time he had run away there had been no sign of her telling the rest of the family who she really was.

"Even before you left I was feeling lonely," Juanita admitted. "I loved everyone in the fort like family, and everyone treated me like family, but at the same time being the only Native American in a house where everyone else had someone they looked like..." She sighed. "It could be so exhausting at times. I wanted to meet people like me. I wanted to connect with my heritage. I thought living with the tribes might help me figure myself out..." There was another pause. "So, where have you been this whole time?"

"New York," Antonio said.

"And is that shiny star on your jacket the reason you're back here?" Juanita leant over and flicked the sheriff star. Antonio had to catch himself before he tumbled head over heels, even though there had been very little force in her movement.

"I met a man in New York – a miner from Helena. Saved his life after someone tried to hijack his carriage. He gave me the job."

"Lucky break," Juanita said.

Antonio laughed. "It was until I lost his daughter."

The look Juanita gave him made him laugh harder, but even Antonio heard the hysterical note. He told her everything. Juanita kept silent as he talked, apart from when Antonio name-dropped the Blood Twins for the first time – at which Juanita whispered a curse and reached for the cross at her neck. She knew what they had done at the church. By the end he felt he could finally take a breath that filled every inch of his lungs.

"Ah," Juanita said, "so it hasn't worked out, then."

The stab of guilt was back again with a crippling revenge, and this time Antonio knew he couldn't ignore it, or the heavy weight hanging between him and Juanita that needed to be addressed before it crushed them both. He took a deep breath.

"I'm sorry," he said. "For breaking our promise."

"What promise?" Juanita stared at the bottom of her coffee cup. Even though she was acting aloof, Antonio knew there was no way she would have forgotten the promise they had made.

"The promise that we would see the country together," he said. "I left you behind and fled to save my worthless skin. But after that day—" he ran his fingers through his hair "—I couldn't stay."

"You ran," Juanita muttered, "without a word to anyone. We all thought you'd come back, and when you didn't we thought you'd been kidnapped. But then you still didn't come back... By the time I'd left, most of them had pronounced you dead."

Antonio nodded.

"What happened that day?" Juanita asked. "The day you left? I mean, I've heard versions from people who were there, but I want to hear it from you."

For a while, Antonio stared down into the dregs of his coffee, swirling the grains around the inside of the mug. Then he put the cup down and laced his fingers between his legs.

"Do you remember that day?" he asked.

Juanita nodded. "How could I forget? It was scorching hot and I was ill in bed while the rest of you got to go to the lake."

"I begged Mother to let us go." Antonio's voice cracked. "None of the adults could go with us, but I begged her to let us go to the lake to cool off. In the end she agreed. She put me in charge. Said I was responsible for everyone." He took a deep breath. "So we go to the lake – me, Ale, Hu, Fang, Silvana, Ai, Xin and Elìas. We swim. Mess around. Then come back to shore to dry off... And notice Elìas is missing."

A cold shiver ran through Antonio's body as he remembered that moment. The ripple of horror that had run around the group as they realised, and the sense of mounting panic that had grown in Antonio's chest the longer they called for Elìas without a reply. Ale had been the most frantic. He had called the loudest. Screamed his brother's name until his throat was hoarse. Antonio remembered the tears on his cheeks as he bellowed across the waters.

"Xin found him. Brought him to shore. He was already dead, drowned. We tried to revive him, but nothing we did woke him. Ale turned on me. Screamed at me. Told me it was my fault he was dead cause I had been in charge. Said he was going to kill me."

"So you ran," Juanita said.

"I panicked, because Ale was right. I had been put in charge that day. It was my fault Elìas had drowned. I should have kept a better eye on him. On everyone, but I wanted to have fun. I didn't want to go home – couldn't bear the guilt at what I would find there. The disappointment of my mother, or the blame the rest of the family would put on me. And I was scared of what Ale would do to me."

They sat in silence, listening to the sounds of the town slowly coming to life – the rattle of carts in the street, the opening of window shutters, talking voices and frying breakfasts.

"Ale always had a violent side to him," Juanita said. "But Elìas was always there to reel him in. I only stayed for a few months after you left, but in that time I could see how much worse he was becoming. He'd disappear for days sometimes into the desert and come home covered in blood... No one asked him what he did out there. We didn't want to know."

"He tried to kill me last night," Antonio said. "Your shot stopped him."

"Let's hope I don't have to shoot him again." There was another long heavy pause. "You really hurt me, you know," Juanita whispered. "That day you left without me."

"I know," Antonio said. "And I'm so sorry. I know words don't mean much, but maybe I can make it up to you? If you're planning to stick around, that is."

"Hmm." Juanita tipped her face up to the sky. "I'm not sure. It depends on what's in it for me. I'm a busy person, you know. Got places to go. But—" she tilted her head to the side and met his gaze "—I guess I need to stick around until we've put those Reckoners in the ground."

Yes, Antonio guessed that they should do that. Guessed they needed to rescue their family. To put an end to The Reckoners for the safety of the people of Helena. But the thought of going back to the fortress, back home, sent Antonio down a spiral of dread.

A loud noise from inside the office pulled him out of

himself. Both of them tensed as they turned their attention to the building.

"That must be my deputy," Antonio said, standing. "It's probably best if you stay here."

Juanita raised her eyebrows. "Worried he might judge you for entertaining a lady in the early hours of the morning?"

Antonio's cheeks burned. He cleared his throat. "Of course not."

Trying his best not to run, but moving as fast as he could, Antonio made his way into the office. As he opened the door that separated the office from the small kitchen at the back, he almost ran into Dean, who was stood on the other side with his hand raised and ready to knock.

"Sorry, Sheriff," Dean said. "I couldn't find you in your office, or in your room, so thought you might be back here. I'm... er, not interruptin' anythin', am I?"

He looked past Antonio to Juanita sitting on the decking out the back. She smiled and waved.

"No," Antonio said, too quickly. "Juanita's a family friend. What can I do for you, Dean? Actually, I guess I should thank you for your help last night."

"Think nuthin' of it. Glad to've bin of help. I came here today with a bit of a proposition. After our talk last night, I realised that sum of our goals might be aligned."

"How so?"

Dean smiled. "What if I told you I know the identities of the Blood Twins, an' I am willin' to help you capture 'em in exchange fer sum information?"

For a few seconds, Antonio stood blinking at Dean, speechless from the shock. Once the words had registered with his brain, he almost tripped over his feet in his hurry to stand aside.

"I think you'd better come through," he said.

Chapter 20

Proud

Megan strides outta the house the moment Cassidy an' me git home. 'Though her skin still looks ashen, at least she's outta bed. As soon as I see her, I pull ma mask over ma face, which has a permanent place 'round ma neck these days.

"Brother," she says. "Git inside. Now."

Panickin' that summit urgent's happened, I leave Cassidy to unpack the hay an' tend to the horses, an' follow ma sis inside.

"What's wrong?" I ask in the kitchen. Then Megan turns to me with a smile on her face an' ma stomach sinks.

"I've had an idea," she says. "An idea of how we're gonna git back at those invadin' bastards who *think* they can trample all over our turf."

"Megan—" I begin but stop at the manic gleam in her eyes. You don't bring Megan down when she's in one of these moments. Not 'less you wanna end up bleedin'.

"Ma thinkin'," Megan continues, her words comin' faster an' faster, "is that we need to hit back at 'em. Bump up the Blood Twins' reputation to stop us from gittin' eclipsed by these varmits. Git ourselves on the front pages of the newspapers. Be the talk of the town. An' to do that, we need to do summit big." Her smile widens. "Summit like a bank robbery."

While Megan looks at me, waitin' fer ma reaction, I pray. Beggin' Gawd fer his fergiveness fer Megan's ways, fer ma weakness of not bein' able to stand up to her. Fer all that we've done, an' fer what we're 'bout to do.

"Megan," I say, carefully, "robbin' a bank's... dangerous."

"Yup. That's why it's gonna git us on the front pages of all the papers around. Heck. We might even git on the front pages of the papers in New York." She laughs. "I'd love to see the faces of those bastards when they realise the Blood Twins are the rulers of this turf."

"Also," I say as the sweat beads on ma palms, "I don't think it's a good idea to pick a fight with those people. I doubt we saw 'em all last night. They could've dozens – hundreds of folk. We can't win that battle, Megan. Perhaps it's time we—"

Megan slams her fist down on the table. I look at ma feet.

"We *can*," she hisses. "An' we *will*. They fuckin' started this, an' we're gonna end it. An' when we kick those varmits off our turf with their tails 'tween their legs, Pa's gonna look down on us from Heaven an' be proud. He's gonna be proud of us, Cole, 'cause there ain't no way that if he'd bin alive today he woulda put up with their shit. Remember why we do this – to keep Pa's memory alive. An' how can we keep his memory alive if we can't do our jobs as the Blood Twins?"

Her eyes're on me, burrowin' unner ma skin. I keep

ma gaze on ma shoes, usin' every ounce of strength I have to stop ma body from shakin'.

"Don't you want Pa to be proud of us, Cole?" Megan asks.

An' even though ma mind's clouded with the same confusion it always is when Megan reminds me why we're livin' our lives the way we do, I nod.

"Do you have a bank picked out?" I ask.

Megan's looks at the horizon, her fingers tracin' Florence's handle.

"I know jest the one," she says.

Needin' to clear ma head, I go outside to check if Cassidy needs any help. But she's already put the horses away, filled their troughs, topped up their feed an' put their equipment away.

I find her pumpin' water, a pile of washin' on the ground beside the washboard an' tub.

"Need a hand?" I ask.

"No," Cassidy says through gritted teeth. "I've got this."

I hang 'round, feelin' like I should be of sum use to her, but not knowin' what I can do. Cassidy finishes pumpin' the water an' sits down in the shade to scrub.

"Stop hanging around like a fly," Cassidy says.

Ma cheeks burn. "Sorry," I say. "I'll git outta your way."

"You can't let her boss you around like that," Cassidy says. "We're not children anymore."

"I don't mind," I say. "Really, I don't. Megan don't force me—"

Cassidy's eyes're piercin'. "So did you want to commit all those robberies?"

Ma mouth goes dry. "No!" I say. "No, of course not. But... Megan knows what to do. She knows much better 'n I do how to go 'bout things. She's much cleverer 'n I am."

"That's not true, Cole," Cassidy says. "If you had the

courage to stand up to her, then I think you'd see she's the cause of all your misery."

Cassidy's words let sum uncomfortable thoughts into ma head, so I go back into the house.

Chapter 21

Partnership

They sat in a circle, Antonio and Juanita on the decking, and Dean crouched on the floor next to the fire. While Antonio brewed a second batch of coffee, Dean and Juanita made small talk. Antonio half listened to their conversation, but marvelled as he did so at the confidence in Juanita's voice. Thirteen years ago, if someone she didn't know had asked her a question, she would have mumbled something and rushed away. But now she conversed with Dean like she was talking to an old friend, laughing at his jokes.

Dean took a big gulp of coffee and sighed in satisfaction.

"Wonderful," he said. "Thank you, Sheriff."

"No problem," Antonio said. "Now, if you don't mind me being so forward, I'd like us to discuss your proposition."

"Ah, yes. Well, here are ma terms." Dean looked Antonio dead in the eye. "I will tell you the identities of the two masqueradin' 'emselves as the Blood Twins, in exchange fer sum information on that gold you were talkin' 'bout last night."

For a moment, Antonio's brow furrowed in confusion. Then he remembered. "Oh, the Spanish gold?"

"The very same."

"As I'm the sheriff, you should be telling me the names of the Blood Twins without any information exchange," Antonio said.

"Perhaps," Dean said, "but ma father taught me to give nuthin' away fer free."

It was an odd request, but Antonio didn't mind exchanging information about a family legend for the names of the outlaws. Not if it meant he could rescue Cassidy.

"What sort of information do you want?" he asked.

"Jest fer you to tell me everythin' you can 'bout it." Dean took another long gulp of coffee. "I've an interest in findin' that gold."

Antonio laughed. "It's just a legend. There might not be any gold."

"But there might be," Dean said, and the gleam in his eye made Antonio believe for a moment that perhaps there might be some method to Dean's madness. "Call it a retirement project. What else is a man meant to do with his time at ma age?"

"All right," Antonio said with a shrug. "It's your time you'll be wasting."

"Are we talking about that stupid gold rush story?" Juanita asked. Antonio nodded, and Juanita rolled her eyes. "That whole tale is a load of trash. There's no way it's true."

"Humour me," Dean said. "Start from the beginnin' an' tell me everythin' you know."

"Well," Antonio said, thinking about the best place to start, "my family have always told this story about how my great-uncle and three other men found a pile of lost Spanish gold during the gold rush. One of the men from China, and the other two were from England. They banded together and agreed that if one of them struck lucky they would share the spoils between them.

"Instead of striking gold in the hills, they found the trove of gold, lost from the time of the Spanish conquest of California. They agreed to split the treasure, but one of the English men turned on the others, killed them all and made off with the gold."

"Do you know the names of the two English men?" Dean asked.

Antonio paused. "No, I don't think we do." Antonio looked at Juanita, but she shook her head.

"Any idea what they looked like? Where they came from?"

"No idea what they looked like, but I remember my grandfather joking he had trouble understanding what they were saying. Said their accent was so thick he didn't realise at first they were speaking English."

"North," Juanita said. "I think both of them were from Northern England – at least that's what Antonio's grandfather said they told him."

"Good memory," Antonio said. Juanita raised her eyebrows at him.

"Any idea what happened to the one who made off with all the gold?" Dean asked.

Antonio sighed. "Likely set up a cosy life for himself. My family lost track of him when he fled. They tried to get the widow of the second Englishman to come with them, but... Well, her husband's murder drove her to madness. She disappeared from the camp one night with her young son."

"An' the gold, what were it?"

"Coins, I think, and jewellery."

"Anythin' else you can remember?"

"That's all," Antonio said, and Juanita shook her head.

"All right, then." Dean drained the last of his coffee. "The names of the Blood Twins," he said, setting the mug on the ground, "are Cole an' Megan Hayes."

Antonio sat back, clutching his coffee mug. He thought about the brother and sister in the bar last night, and then the outlaws on the train.

"Are you sure?" he asked.

Dean raised his eyebrows. "Quite sure. They haven't told me they're the Blood Twins, but a great deal of things add up if they are. I've known Cole an' Megan since they were babies. Their pa was an outlaw – started robbin' folks fer money after he were fired from the mines. It would jest be the sorta thing Megan would do."

"Not Cole?"

Dean laughed. "Cole's only doin' it to look after his sis. She's the leader of that pack."

Antonio thought about the comments Megan Hayes had made about the Blood Twins. And the way her eyes flashed when she told The Reckoners they were on Blood Twins territory.

"All right, I think it does make sense," Antonio admitted. "Thank you for the information."

Dean tipped his hat and stood up. "Ma pleasure, an' I'm much obliged fer the story."

"Sorry that it's not anything more substantial." As Dean made his way towards the door, Antonio asked, "Would you mind keeping an eye on Cole and Megan for me? Let me know if it looks like they're planning something."

"Happy to," Dean said. Then with one last tip of his hat he went inside.

Antonio waited until he heard the front door of the office shut.

"I can't believe it," he said.

"That those two are the Blood Twins?" Juanita asked, switching back to Spanish.

"That I might finally have them." Antonio ran a hand down his face. "I've been trying to work out who they are for weeks."

"I know," Juanita said, "I saw the crazy man diagram on your wall."

"That map is a comprehensive tracking system."

"It looked like the inner workings of a mad man to me." Antonio went to correct Juanita again, but found her smiling at him. The sight made the heat rise to his cheeks again, so he looked away.

"Well," Antonio said, running a finger around the inside of his shirt collar, "now we just have to catch them in the act and unmask them."

"Why not just go to their house and arrest them?"

"I want to be sure it's them. I don't want to send innocent people to hang. And there's the matter of Miss Cassidy."

"You're worried about them using her as a hostage?" Juanita asked. Antonio nodded. "If she's still alive."

A sick feeling rolled in Antonio's stomach. "I can't consider another possibility."

"And when you say 'we', do you mean you and your deputy?"

Antonio cleared his throat. "Well, erm, I was wondering, since you're in town, if you would be interested in helping me capture the Blood Twins?" He searched for some flicker of emotion in Juanita's face, but her expression remained passive.

"And what's wrong with your deputy? I assume you also have a band of men you can call on for this sort of thing."

"Well, to be honest, my deputy's not the most reliable."

"Really?"

"He's late, and when he does turn up, he rarely does

any work."

"Is that so?"

"Capturing the Blood Twins is of paramount importance. I would hate for anything to go wrong."

"Hmm..."

"And... and you're worth ten of any hired men... or women. There's no one else I would trust to guard my right side more."

"Any other reason?"

Antonio scratched the back of his head. "It'd also be nice if you, I mean, if you wanted to... to... stick around for a while longer."

Sweat prickled Antonio's armpits as the silence dragged on while Juanita's impassive stare drilled into him.

"Alright then," she said at last, standing.

Antonio's heart leapt in his chest. "So... you're staying?"

"How can I leave when I haven't forgiven you yet? Or when there are murdering outlaws threatening our family?"

And she left Antonio feeling like he was melting into a puddle on the ground.

Chapter 22

Rivals

"I think I'm getting better," Cassidy says, slidin' the scrambled piles of batter onto our plates. I guess it were s'posed to be pancakes.

"Sure you are," I say, reachin' fer the sugar.

Megan takes her helpin' without a word. There's tension 'tween her an' Cassidy. The two rarely speak, but neither do they break into fights anymore.

"This is real good," I say. To be honest, once the pancakes're covered in sugar they taste fine.

"Thank you." Cassidy smiles.

"This is the best thing you've cooked yet. Don't you think so, Megan?"

Megan grunts again an' shoves 'nother scrambled pancake in her mouth unner her mask.

No one speaks fer a while, all of us busy eatin'.

"I want a washing machine," Cassidy says.

"What's that?" I ask.

"It's a tub on legs. You turn a handle and it helps wash clothes. It's easier than scrubbing clothes against a board."

"No," Megan says firmly. "We ain't made of money."

The tone of her voice makes me sit back in ma chair. It's on the edge of shoutin'. Megan must be inna sour mood today if she's already this angry.

"You're not the one washing your greasy, bloody clothes." Cassidy's lookin' at Megan with fierce eyes. "If you did your own washing, you'd understand what a pain in the backside it is."

Megan slams her hand down on the table. The plates jump in the air an' clank back down. "I said no, an' I mean no!" she shouts. "You're our hostage an' ma brother's fancy. Your opinion don't count fer squat. An' you'll do what you're told to do, 'less you want a bullet in your brain."

Heat rushes to ma face as Megan an' Cassidy glare at each other fer a minute, both lookin' ready to spring 'cross the table at the other. But Cassidy looks away an' Megan's shoulders relax. Cassidy's eyes're full of hurt an' threatenin' tears. I should open ma mouth now, I should say summit to lighten the mood, to deny Megan's words, or back up Cassidy, but I jest sit there, too scared of Megan's anger to speak. An' I hate maself fer it – fer ma cowardice an' fer not bein' able to deny the truth in Megan's words.

"Brother," Megan says, "Git ready to go."

Feelin' sick, I nod.

Megan knocks her plate an' fork to the floor. The fork bounces, but the plate shatters. Megan strides outta the room without a word.

Cassidy goes to pick up the broken plate, but I git there first. I pull down ma mask.

"Let me," I say.

"Why didn't you stand up for me?" she hisses.

"I'm sorry. It's jest that—"

"What? It's just what, Cole? You said – you said that I would have a say on how things are run in this house."

"Yeah, I did—"

"But you haven't told Megan that, have you?" Her balled hands press into the floor. A tear lands 'tween 'em.

"Cassidy..."

"Why did you let her walk all over me like that? I feel so humiliated."

Her cheeks're wet an' her eyes've started turnin' red. I wanna reach out an' wipe away the tears, to lay ma palm 'gainst her face, but ma hands hang at ma sides. Then Cassidy sits back.

"You're going to have to start standing up to her," she says, her voice soft an' low.

"There ain't no point. Megan never listens to me."

"If she doesn't listen to her own brother, then who is she going to listen to?"

Then Cassidy reaches out an' takes ma hand in hers. The heat of our connection burns ma skin, an' a bolt of lightnin' runs up ma arm as she gives ma hand a gentle squeeze. Fer a long time, neither of us move, then Cassidy pulls away. I'm already wonderin' if I imagined the whole thing, but the lingerin' warmth of her skin tells me it happened.

"One day," Cassidy says, "she'll go too far and she'll take you with her. Then you'll regret not stopping things sooner." She looks at me an' I've never sin so much emotion in one pair of eyes. "Please, Cole, talk to her."

We begin the bank robbery like any job. We ride into town an' hitch the horses outside the saloon, but when we go inside to pay fer their care, Megan orders a whisky. Instead of drinkin' it at the bar, she takes it upstairs an' drinks it lookin' out a window down at the bank. I stand next to her, waitin' fer her to finish. When she does, she slams the glass down, puts on her hat an' storms out the upstairs door.

"Come on, brother!" she calls. I scramble after her down the wooden outside staircase.

It'd taken us a while to work out how we were gonna transform from two regular folks into the Blood Twins. In the end we decided to wear low-brimmed hats an' have our masks slung 'round our necks, ready to pull up.

We stand in the queue at the bank. I look 'round the room fer anythin' or anyone that could cause trouble. The plan's fer me to grab a hostage while Megan gits the folk 'hind the counter to give her the money.

The room's small, with the counter opposite the entrance that stretches from one side of the room to the other. There's a lattice wooden screen on top 'hind which stand three bank clerks. There's a door at the end of the counter, an' 'nother in the wall 'hind it. They've very likely got guns 'hind there. We've jest gotta hope we can git the room unner control 'fore they can reach fer 'em, then hope the hostage stops 'em from firin' 'em 'til we've gotten away.

There's a table to the left of the room an' a bench. Oil lights hang from the walls an' there ain't any windows.

Four spaces in front of us in the queue is a mother an' her little girl. The little girl's carryin' a rag doll an' is holdin' onto her ma's skirts. I glance at Megan, an' I pray she ain't gonna choose the little girl as the hostage. It'd be jest the sorta thing she'd do.

The ma an' her little girl leave the bank. I breathe a sigh of relief. The little girl stares at us on passin'. She tries to see unner ma hat. I pull the rim lower.

Megan nudges me with her elbow. I look at her an' she nods at a gentlemen who's dressed in fine clothes, an' is writin' summit at the table at the side of the room. He's a lot older 'n me, an' stronger built too.

I nod back an' walk over to the gentleman. He's got his

back to me, so I tap him on the shoulder.

"Excuse me, sir," I say, keepin' ma voice an' hat low, "have you a match? I seem to've run out."

The gentleman looks a little surprised by ma request, but he pats his pockets. "I think I have some in here somewhere... Ah, here you go." He takes a box of matches out from the inside of his jacket, an' holds 'em out to me.

"That's mighty kinda you," I say, an' knock the box outta his hand. With ma other, I press ma pistol to the side of his head, then pull ma handkerchief over ma face.

"Nobody move!" I holler. Everyone looks 'round at us. Eyes widen. Megan – her face now covered – takes out Florence an' Smithy. She fires two shots into the ceilin'. Sumone screams.

"Git to the sides of the room, now!" she barks. "Do as we say or the old man's brains'll be on the floor."

The gentleman stiffens – from either bein' called old or from the threat I can't tell.

The other folks move to the sides of the room. Megan orders 'em to sit on their hands. It'd be safer to search 'em fer weapons, but we need to git outta here as fast as we can, an' Megan can't take her attention off the bank clerks fer too long.

She pulls a large sack from inside her coat an' throws it through the small gap between the counter an' the wooden screen where the clerks usually pass money.

"Fill it up," she says, pointin' her pistols at him. "An' be quick 'bout it!"

The clerk does as she bids. Megan shoots the lock outta the door in the wooden screen an' goes 'hind the counter to make sure he ain't gonna sneak away an' raise the alarm.

I glance 'round the room. All the customers're doin' as Megan told 'em to. Most're lookin' at their feet. There's a woman in the corner sobbin' quietly onto her husband's shoulder. One young man's glarin' at Megan with nuthin' short of pure hatred. I keep ma eye on him. He looks like the type to do summit stupid.

"Are you the Blood Twins?" the hostage asks. The fearful silence that ripples 'round the room can't be missed. I swallow.

"Yeah," I say.

"Oh. Marvellous. In that case, could I ask you to do me a favour?"

I look from the back of the gentleman's head to where the barrel of ma gun's pressed to the side of his skull. Is this man crazy?

"Brother!" Megan's head snaps 'round. "Shut him up."

I warn't gonna answer the gentleman's question, but I clench ma jaw.

"Listen," the hostage says, "I'm a reporter. I work for *The Arizona Gazette*. An interview with the Blood Twins would be a front-page smash. If you could co-operate with me, I'll promise that I'll give you a share of what I make from the article."

Is this man's head screwed on loose?

I shake ma head. "No can do, sir. Sorry."

The gentleman opens his mouth to say summit else, an' the bank doors flies open. Sumone lets off a fearful whimper as a group of people enter the room. Ma heart sinks as I recognise two of the women from the attack on The Sleepin' Racoon.

The Reckoners.

All of 'em look jest as surprised to see us we are to see 'em.

"What the hell are you two doin' here?" the woman named Annie says.

"Brother," Megan hisses, "why didn't you bar the door?"

'Cause I'm kinda busy with a hostage.

"What the fuck are you doin' on our turf?" 'nother woman says. She's the same colourin' as Megan, but her red hair's cropped close to her skull.

"This ain't your fuckin' turf," Megan spits. "We were here first. This place belongs to the Blood Twins, so you can clear out."

"I don't see any signs of this bein' your turf," the red-haired woman says.

"Blood Twins don't need to have signs," Megan hisses. "Our reputation is enough."

She swings her guns 'round an' points 'em at me. Megan fires an' ma hostage jerks. He crumples to the floor, blood gushin' from the wound in his neck. He gargles as blood floods his throat, chokin' him.

Ma stomach turns cold.

The man gives a final gurglin' gasp an' then falls still.

His dead eyes bore into mine.

Ma breath quickens. Ma chest pulls tight.

Shots ring out 'hind me.

Then all hell breaks loose as all sides fire at each other.

I dive 'hind an overturned table. Megan's crouched 'hind a table on the opposite side of the room. She's pressed 'gainst the wall, her eyes dartin' right an' left.

The gang're shootin' from the door, the clerks from the back of the room, an' me an' Megan're in the middle of it.

I fire a bullet at the gang an' then 'nother at the clerks who've joined the fightin'. The room's quickly fillin' with smoke an' several bullets bite into ma table, splinterin' the wood. Customers're screamin'. I can hear 'em runnin' 'round the room, lookin' fer a way to escape.

Sumone moves at the back of the room. At first I think it's a clerk makin' a dash fer the front door, but it's the young man who'd bin glarin' at Megan earlier. He's headin' straight fer ma sis, with a pistol in his hand.

I don't think.

I shoot him in the chest.

His pistol falls from his hand as he hits the floor.

Screams erupt in the room.

The back of ma throat burns.

Four.

Flames lick the walls.

The walls of the bank disappear an' I'm inside a church.

Jesus on his cross glares down at me.

Ma knees are weak. Ma body burns from the heat of the fire engulfin' the room.

Please.

No.

I don't wanna be back here.

Please.

Anywhere but here.

Then an explosion of pain hits ma left arm, makin' me cry out.

The church an' the fire disappear, an' I'm back in the bank.

I clutch the new pain in ma arm. Ma hand comes away bloodied. Ma chest heaves.

I grit ma teeth an' fire two more bullets at the bank entrance.

Megan appears beside me. She's ruffled but unbloodied.

"They git you?" she asks.

"Yeah."

She spits. "We need to git outta here 'fore the smoke clears. We'll git 'hind the counter an' head out the back. We go on three. One... two... three!"

Megan darts out from 'hind the table, runnin' fer the door at the end of the counter. I shove ma gun in ma belt an' follow. All three clerks're dead 'hind it. Megan leads me into a store room. There's a door on the other side, but the red-haired woman's standin' 'tween us an' it, her gun pointed at us.

She fires. I brace maself, waitin' fer the bullet, but I feel no pain. Has she missed?

Megan groans.

I glance left an' ma blood freezes.

Megan's doubled over, her hand pressed to her side. Blood's tricklin' through her fingers an' soakin' her shirt. Even as she gasps fer air she raises her pistol at The Reckoner. She holds it there an' then collapses.

The pistol hits the floor along with its owner.

The woman turns her gun on me.

Chapter 23

Pursuit

"Is that helping?"

Antonio pulled his head away from the wall. He rubbed his eyes. They hurt. Even after he pulled his hands away his vision was still blurry.

"No," Antonio said.

Juanita shut the bedroom door behind her. "Well, I mean I think it helps if you can see the map in order to track what you're hunting."

Antonio sighed and stepped away from the wall. Juanita stood beside him.

"I can't see anything new," Antonio admitted. "It's just one big blur."

Juanita rubbed his back. "You'll get there, but for now perhaps it's best that you take a break."

Antonio nodded and sat down on his bed. His eyes were drawn back to the map, so he covered his face with his hands. The bed shifted as Juanita sat beside him.

"You know that conversation we were having on the back porch?" Juanita said.

Antonio quickly shifted through the memories of their discussion the morning after The Reckoners attacked the saloon. What immediately came to mind was Juanita lounging on the decking with her face turned up to the sun. He pushed that memory aside and quickly searched for the one he knew Juanita wanted to talk about. Then he remembered.

"About the fact that you hate me?" he said.

Juanita snorted. "I don't hate you. I did once, during that first year after you left. I was going through so much and I needed you there to talk to. The fact that you abandoned me made it all worse. But after a while I did forgive you. Until I saw you again the other night, and then it all just came flooding back."

"The forgiveness?" Antonio asked hopefully.

"The anger," Juanita said. Antonio uncovered his face in time to see a small smile flit at the edge of her mouth. But it disappeared far too quickly. "I'm going to need time, Toni. In order to find that forgiveness again."

"I'm not expecting you to forgive me in a few days," Antonio said. "I know what I did to you was unforgivable, and hearing that you've already been able to forgive me once... Well, it makes me happy, and just having you here again with me makes me even happier."

"I'm happy being back with you, too."

They smiled at each other.

"Sheriff! Sheriff, you here?"

Juanita and Antonio looked at each other.

"Dean?" Antonio asked and Juanita nodded.

They went downstairs and found Dean out the back. His face was red and sweating.

"They just left," he said. "Cole and Megan. They're headin' east."

"Thank you," Antonio said. "We'd better get going."

"Where's your deputy?" Dean asked.

Antonio shrugged. "No idea."

"You can't go after 'em on your own. I'll—"

"I'll be going with him," Juanita said. She met Antonio's eye. "Get the horses ready. I'll get the guns and water."

"I'm still happy to come along, if you want me to," Dean offered.

"Don't worry," Antonio said. "Juanita and I can handle this."

"She seems like a great woman," Dean said.

Antonio smiled. "Yes, she is."

They left a few minutes later, heading first to the Hayes's house on the edge of the town and then picking up their horses' tracks from there. Antonio stopped his horse outside the property fence. The house was small and shoddy. Someone had tried caring for it, but either didn't have the funds or the knowledge to do it properly. Antonio noticed that one of the windows on the ground floor was boarded over.

"Want to see if Miss Scarborough's in there?" Juanita asked.

Antonio hesitated. "No," he said. "Let's go after the twins first. After we've captured them, we can check the house to see if Cassidy's there. Bringing those two down is our priority."

So they kicked their horses into a gallop and made off across the desert, Juanita riding on Antonio's right.

The Blood Twins' tracks finished at Faircliff, a medium-sized town Antonio remembered reading somewhere had been a centre for copper mining in the area. If that was still the case, there wasn't any sign of it. Many of the houses they passed were empty, abandoned by workers who had left once the mine had closed. The general store's shelves were dusty and sparse. The streets were quiet. Antonio gave the town another week before it was forsaken like so many old mining towns in the west.

They had slowed their horses as they entered the town. Antonio ensured his sheriff star was clearly on display as they passed through. The sight of a Mexican and a Native American woman on horseback was certain to get some people riled up. But to his relief, aside from a few prolonged stares, no one gave them any trouble.

The horse tracks got harder to find once they entered the town, but Juanita pointed out that the Blood Twins would need somewhere safe to tie them that wasn't far away from the bank. So they headed towards the building and found a saloon, outside of which were two horses – one with a coat of dark sorrel and the other a light dun colour.

"Are those theirs?" Juanita asked.

"I don't know. I've never seen them before, but both of them are breathing hard enough to make me think they've just run through the desert."

"Do you think there's a back entrance?" Antonio asked.

"There always is."

They hitched their horses alongside Cole's and Megan's at the drinking trough and moved around the side of the saloon. A wooden staircase was fixed to the back wall of the building. Juanita and Antonio crouched close by and kept their eyes on the door at the top.

A minute passed. Megan appeared dressed in her usual clothes with a black mask around her neck.

"Come on, brother!" she snapped. A moment later, Cole appeared, stuffing his mask into his pocket. He hurried after his sister.

"They're not wearing the Blood Twins' red clothes," Antonio said. "But those masks look familiar."

"So, they are the Blood Twins?" Juanita said, pulling

her rifle from the holster on her back.

"Yes," Antonio said. "Yes, I think they are. Let's watch what they do next." Antonio's hand rested on his pistol as they moved towards the bank. They stopped a little way away behind the corner of another building.

"What's the plan?" Juanita asked.

"I'm not sure," Antonio admitted. "There'll be people inside, and knowing the Blood Twins, they'll use them as hostages. Perhaps we should wait until they come out with the gold and then arrest them. But I don't like the idea of leaving them in there with all those people..."

"So we storm the place and take them out before they notice us."

Antonio bit his bottom lip. He didn't like that idea either. The Blood Twins were quick to shoot. If they surprised them, it would end up with the loss of civilian life, or perhaps his or Juanita's.

Antonio scanned the landscape and saw a group moving around the side of the bank.

"Oh, blazes," he said under his breath. Juanita saw them a second later and laughed. "Don't," Antonio said, groaning.

"But what a coincidence," she said, as five of The Reckoners went inside the bank. The rest of them stayed outside the door, guns drawn. Tu, Xin Lorenzo, Mei and Rou were with them, standing unarmed and pressed against the side of the building. "What now?"

"Retreat," Antonio said. "If the Blood Twins get out, we'll ambush them at their horses."

They turned to retreat around the side of the building and came face to face with Alejandro. He smiled down at them, his arms folded across his chest.

"Fancy seeing you here, Toni," he said. "It seems we might be after the same thing."

Chapter 24

Goodbye Friend

I stare down at Megan's body, ma heart thumpin' in ma ears.

It takes a second fer the cold shock to turn to burnin' rage. It starts in ma stomach an' spreads out to ma limbs. Ma hands itch 'wards ma gun belt.

"Nuthin' personal," the woman says an' pulls the trigger.

I spin. I've moved too late. As I do I hear a click but no sound of a gunshot.

The gun ain't fired.

Ma bullet takes the woman in the chest while she's still grimacin' at her empty cylinder.

She falls to the floor, eyes wide with shock, chest heavin' with her last breaths.

It don't take her long to fall still.

The rage subsides an' the cold shock comes back.

Vomit burns the back of ma throat.

Five.

That's five folks I've killed now.

How many times've I sworn to never hold a pistol again? How many times've I broken ma promise? How many times will I break it again? If only I were stronger an' told Megan long ago that I don't want any part in this, then maybe—

Megan groans on the floor. I swallow ma feelin's.

Cole, toughen up.

I pick Megan up along with her gun – she'll never fergive me if I leave it 'hind – an' stagger out the buildin' carryin' her. Ma left arm screams.

The saloon we'd tied the horses outside ain't far from the bank. I listen out but don't hear anyone followin' us.

I struggle 'cross town. Megan's heavy an' ma left arm's screamin' at me, the bullet lodged in there's pressin' 'gainst ma flesh. Ma legs tremble with every step, but I keep movin'.

The horses come into sight. At our appearance they whinny, an' they jostle at the smell of blood.

"Easy, girls," I whisper. "Easy now."

I tie Hattie an' Rosie togither. I sling Megan over Rosie's saddle an' pull maself up. I sit Megan up so she's in front of me an' wrap an arm 'round her. I take up the reins with the other.

"Don't die on me, Megan," I whisper while I reload ma gun.

"Cole..." Her voice's faint, but it's there.

"Megan, keep talkin' to me. Don't pass out." I stick ma gun back in ma belt an' urge Rosie into a canter. We rush outta the town an' into the desert. Ma hands soon become slick with Megan's blood, but I keep hold of her.

Blood's pumpin' in ma ears. An' I still have a burnin' pit of rage in ma stomach.

A mile into the desert a gun sounds an' a bullet

whizzes by ma head. I glance 'hind. Two horses're quickly gainin' on us.

I shoot, but miss. I loose 'nother bullet. The man on the right tumbles from his horse. I fire at the man on the left, but ma shot's off again.

I turn back fer a second to check Rosie's still headin' in the right direction, an' then the ground 'neath us seems to give way. The world twists 'round me. I sprawl in the dirt. Dazed, I lay in the dust fer a few moments, starin' at the sky. Then I sit up an' look 'round. Megan's beside me, blood soakin' her shirt an' pants. She ain't movin' at all.

Why'd we fall from the horses?

Then I see Hattie.

She's snortin' an' whinin', strugglin' to stand. Her left back leg's gotta bloody hole through it. Two more of her legs're bent at wrong angles.

'Nother shot sounds. The remainin' gang member advances quickly, a smug smile on his face. I fire ma pistol. The bullet hits his horse. He goes down screamin', crushed beneath his steed.

I look over at Rosie, who's up, seemingly unhurt. She walks over to her sis an' nudges Hattie's face with her nose, makin' soft snorts.

There ain't no hope fer Hattie. She can't git back to the house on three broken legs, an' even if she did there's only a slim chance her legs'll set right. She'll never run again.

But we need to git home. Megan's life depends on me bein' strong an' actin' fast. The gang's still after us. I don't have time to be scared.

I untie the rope that holds the two horses togither, an' lead Rosie away so she don't see what I'm gonna do next. I wish sumone would do the same fer me.

I kneel beside Hattie an' stroke her nose. She's stopped thrashin' an' is quiet, but there's pain in her eyes. There's a lump in the back of ma throat.

"It's all right, Hattie," I say, tryin' to keep ma voice

calm, but it shakes. A tear falls onto Hattie's nose an' I sniff. "It's all right, girl. Ain't nuthin' to be scared of."

Slowly, I bring ma pistol 'round an' hold the barrel to Hattie's forehead. I breathe inna shudderin' breath. Ma hands're shakin', but I will 'em to be calm. I can't mess this up.

"Goodbye, friend."

An' I pull the trigger.

Chapter 25

Resolution

"Alejandro," Antonio said, trying to make his voice as light as possible. "What are you all doing here?"

Alejandro snorted. "I think that much is clear. We're topping up our funds."

Antonio inclined his head towards the bank doors. "You do realise there's already a pair in there who are thinking the same thing?"

"Really? Oh well, Annie and Hart'll deal with them."

"Since when are you on first-name terms with the gang that took our family home and are keeping them hostage?" He glanced at Tu, Xin Lorenzo, Mei and Rou. Mei noticed him looking. She said something and the others raised their heads. Antonio turned his head away.

Alejandro's lips curled at the edges. "Since they gave me the opportunity to get the one thing I truly want." Antonio caught the faintest flicker of movement as

Alejandro reached for his pistol. Juanita raised her rifle.

"You've grown, Ale," Juanita said. Alejandro's eyes slid over to Juanita. For a few moments he stared at her, his brow furrowed. Antonio could almost see the gears turning in his brain, and then the moment the gears connected.

"J—"

"Juanita," Juanita said quickly. "It's nice to see you again. Although, I never would have thought you'd get so tall."

Alejandro smiled. "Apparently my grandfather was quite the giant. But I never thought I'd see you again. We all gave you up for dead, along with this one." He nodded at Antonio. "A shame that the rumours weren't true." He looked at Antonio and Antonio saw a gleam of murderous intent behind his eyes. An intense cold gripped Antonio's stomach. "Where have you been?"

"Oh, here and there," Juanita said.

"You look good."

Juanita smiled and held her rifle higher. "Thanks. How's the hand?"

Alejandro looked down at his bandage-wrapped hand and let out a loud barking laugh. "So that was you. We did wonder who that cloaked stranger was. When did you get to be such a good shot?"

"I hate to break up the reunion." Clint appeared at Alejandro's side. His arm snaked around the taller man's shoulders and he leaned on him like an old friend. It sent a shiver of revulsion through Antonio. "But I think we've met 'fore. Helena's sheriff, right? What the hell are you doin' out here?"

Antonio straightened his spine, extending himself to his full short height. "Juanita and I are here on matters of the law," he said. "There are two outlaws inside that bank that we're here to catch."

"Don't you worry 'bout those two," Clint said. "Let us deal with 'em. The sooner we wipe out the Blood Twins, the better. An' I'm sure you're jest as eager to see 'em gone as we are."

"Of course," Antonio said. "But this is a matter for the law. They're wanted criminals."

"Like us?" Clint's eyes gleamed with the challenge. It took all of Antonio's willpower to remain silent. At last, Clint patted Alejandro's shoulder. "Alejandro tells me that you used to belong to this little family. Ran away after sum poor kid drowned. Tragic. Real tragic."

"That poor kid was my little brother," Alejandro growled, pushing Clint's arm off his shoulder.

Clint held up his hands. "Sorry. Geeze. Sensitive much?"

Alejandro's fists clenched, and Antonio got the feeling whatever truce Alejandro had cut with The Reckoners was perhaps less stable than it first appeared to be.

"Your family hassa real history with tragedy, don't it?" Clint said.

Juanita frowned. "What's that supposed to mean?"

"You know—" Clint waved his hand "—that story 'bout those family members of yours that got murdered durin' the gold rush. Hadda load of gold stolen from 'em 'fore they was killed by that English man?"

"Yeah..." Antonio said. Beside him Juanita stood taller, and he knew she was thinking the same thing as him – how odd it was that Dean should come to them interested in this story just to have it brought up a few days later.

"Quite the tale, ain't it? Surprised you folks never went after the stolen gold. Stupid of you, really. You could've bin livin' like kings instead of in squalor in that rundown desert fort of yours."

"It's a story," Juanita said. "Nothing more than a family legend."

"Oh," Clint said, "it's very real. An' we're gonna find that gold."

"How?" she asked.

"By goin' after the man who stole it from your family in the first place."

"But we don't know who that is."

"We do," Alejandro said. "The adults just never told us his name."

"Who is it?" Antonio snapped.

"Helena's most well-to-do miner." Clint smiled. "A one Mr Benjamin Scarborough."

The floor dropped from under Antonio's feet. He had to dig the toes of his boots into the ground to convince himself that it was still there.

"You must be mistaken," he said.

"Oh, no," Clint said.

"Then it's someone with the same name."

"I can assure you it's the very same. Your employer used sum of that gold to set up his minin' company. Now we're out to git the rest of it back from him. At the moment, we're jest killin' time 'til he returns. Once we git our hands on him... Well." Clint smiled. "We'll ensure he tells us where it is."

Antonio's legs trembled. He felt weak. He wanted to sit down, but the only place was in the dust. He couldn't believe it. Mr Scarborough wasn't that kind of man. He'd taken Antonio under his wing – introduced him to important people in New York, allowed him to be friends with Cassidy and had made him Helena's sheriff. Sure, there were a lot of sides to him that Antonio had seen that made him uncomfortable, but never had he thought that Mr Scarborough was a murderer. If he really was a murderer.

Perhaps Antonio should confirm the story before he passed judgement. In the end, Mr Scarborough had helped him, and Alejandro and Clint weren't the most reliable of sources.

"I think when you get to the end of this particular rainbow," Antonio said, "that you'll find no gold there."

Clint opened his mouth to answer, but gunfire started inside the bank, followed by a siren of screams. There was the sound of breaking glass, and then silence. The doors of the bank opened and a group of The Reckoners walked out.

"So?" he asked.

"Hart an' the twins are still in there," Annie called. Seeing Antonio and Juanita she paused, along with the other members of the gang. "What're they doin' here?"

"Jest passin' through," Clint said. "Ain't that right, Sheriff?"

"Sure," Juanita said. She caught Antonio's eye and her look told him to keep quiet. Antonio gave her a small nod in return. "And now you'll let us be on our way, right?"

Two lines appeared between Annie's eyes as her mouth set into a hard line. Antonio had a feeling letting them go was the last thing Annie wanted to do, but she made no objection when Clint said, "Of course. Now, off you run. Let this be the last time we run into each other fer sum time, yeah?"

"I don't think my stomach could take the sight of your face again," Antonio said.

Clint snorted. "I don't think ma stomach could take the stench of your self-righteousness again."

The sound of a gunshot came from somewhere close by. Everyone froze, eyes fixed on the bank. Then came a second one. Annie signalled for two of the gang to go round the back of the building. Sweat beaded on Antonio's palms, which he pressed to the sides of his pants. He wanted to run inside the bank, to find out what the hell was going on, but with all these guns around and the tense atmosphere between him and the gang, he was too afraid to make a sudden movement. And as Juanita seemed to think the best way of getting out of this was to fake disinterest, he would follow her lead. A while later, the others returned with Annie. All three were pale, and

Annie's face was streaked with tears.

"They killed Hart," she spat, her voice venomous. "The twins. They shot her in the chest. Ike an' Sam are goin' after 'em."

Antonio breathed out a long breath as he pressed his hands against the outside of his pants. So the Blood Twins had survived the robbery. He glanced at Clint. Rage had eclipsed his features and his eyes became two burning wicks.

"After 'em!" Clint bellowed. "Everyone on horseback, now!"

The gang did what they were told, ushering Antonio's family onto the horses along with them. Antonio's heart sank as he watched them ride away. Alejandro hesitated for a moment, the murderous intent shining out bright from his eyes, but then he looked at Clint's expression and jumped onto a horse.

"See you soon, Toni," he said, as he kicked his horse into a gallop.

Then it was Clint, Annie, Antonio and Juanita left outside the bank. Annie sobbed while Clint's eyes bore holes into the ground. He shook with rage.

"What do we do with her body?" Annie asked.

"I'll take it back," Clint said. "Go with the others. I'll meet you at the fort."

Annie left. Juanita and Antonio stood staring at Clint.

"You can still give this up," Antonio said. "Free my family. Go somewhere new. Start afresh."

"No." Clint's voice was soft and quiet. "It's too late fer that. We chose this life. We'll see it through to the end."

"Then this will not be the last time you see me," Antonio said.

Clint grunted. "You're not the first sheriff who has tried to destroy The Reckoners. An' you won't be the last."

Then he strode into the bank. Juanita grabbed Antonio's arm.

"Let's move away," she said, dragging him around the side of another building. They stayed there, hidden around the corner but watching the bank. Clint came out carrying the limp body of a woman with red hair. He rode away with her.

"Let's take a look inside," Juanita said. Numb, Antonio followed her into the bank, where they found the floor covered with bodies and the walls peppered with bullet holes. For a long time, Antonio and Juanita looked at the scene in silence. Antonio's stomach churned.

"They did this," he said. "The Blood Twins. The Reckoners."

"Yes," Juanita said, her voice wavering. "We can't let this go on, Toni."

"I know." Antonio took a deep breath and almost gagged on the stench of iron in the room. He covered his mouth with his hand. Juanita grabbed his arm and led him outside. She rubbed his back while he threw up. He was vaguely aware of the townsfolk approaching the bank, feeling safe enough to come out of their homes now that the shooting had stopped. He leant against the side of the building.

"Sheriff?" It was the town Reverend. Underneath his sunburn, his skin was pale. His hands shook around the bible he clutched to his chest. "What's goin' on?"

"There's been a bank robbery," Antonio said. He knew he should stand up. He knew he should put on a show of strength for the dozens of people watching him and not sit on the ground beside a puddle of his own vomit, but right now he didn't give a damn. "A lot of people have been killed. Can you send the doctor over? And your sheriff?"

"T-there's no sheriff here," the Reverend said, "but I'll fetch the doctor r-right away." He turned towards the bank, crossed himself and muttered a prayer under his breath, and then hurried off. The rest of the town folk hung around the building, whispering among themselves, every one of them curious but unwilling to go inside. In the sky a red-tailed hawk let out a piercing cry as it circled their heads.

"We're going to have to take The Reckoners out," Antonio said. "It's my duty as sheriff, I can't let them continue like this. And if they're after Mr Scarborough... I owe him, Juanita. If what Clint said is true... If he really did murder my great-uncle and all those people... But it's thanks to him that I'm back here – that I survived New York at all. He'll be back in Arizona any day now. I can't allow him to come to harm."

"We shouldn't be doing this for your employer, Toni," Juanita said. "They've taken our home. They've murdered our family and brainwashed Alejandro. I would have assumed you cared more about our family than the man that murdered your great-uncle."

"I do care!" Antonio snapped. "Of course I care! It's just that..."

It's just that he felt sick every time he thought of home, and the idea of going back there made his hands shake. He couldn't go back. Couldn't face the consequences for what he had done.

Juanita's hand clasped his. "We'll work it out."

"We?"

Juanita gave Antonio an exasperated look.

"Do you really think I'm going to leave you to sort this mess out? It's not like your deputy's going to help you. But at least we know for sure that Cole and Megan Hayes are the Blood Twins. If they survive the gang's pursuit, we can arrest them when we get back to Helena. At least that will be one problem solved."

"Yes," Antonio said. "That is one less problem."

But even as he said the words, an idea began to form in his mind. An idea that would likely create a whole new host of problems but was the only way he could see ending another one.

Chapter 26

Prayin'

Cassidy's workin' outside as I approach the house. Her sleeves're rolled up to her elbows an' she's unbuttoned the top of her blouse. She waves but stops when Rosie pulls up. She stands there, pale-faced, unsure what to do while I struggle to git down without droppin' Megan.

"Help me!" I say. The words come out sharper 'n I want 'em to, but Cassidy runs over an' holds Megan while I git down. I need Cassidy's help gittin' ma sis into the house. By the time we've got her on the kitchen table we're both covered in her blood.

As I step back, it ain't Megan lyin' on that table, but Pa. All a sudden I'm back in that night, standin' over Pa's body while Megan storms from the room, Pa's lips're movin' as he says summit to me, an' then his hands grip mine inna last show of strength. What'd he said 'fore his hands'd seized mine?

"Cole? Cole!" Cassidy callin' ma name pulls me back to the present. Pa fades away an' it's Megan's body back on the table again. "What happened?" she asks.

"That gang jumped us again – the same one that came into the saloon the other night." I wipe the sweat from ma face. "I need to git Dr Fallon. Can you watch over her while I'm gone?"

"Of course." Cassidy's gaze drifts to ma left arm an' her eyes widen.

"It's fine," I say, even though ma arm feels like it's on fire. "I'm fine."

I need to go. I need to go now, but I'm so exhausted an' I don't wanna leave Megan. But Cassidy can't go into town without riskin' bein' recognised. So I hafta do it.

"All right," I say. Then Dean walks into the kitchen.

"Howdy," he says, takin' off his hat. "Came by to say hi." His eyes focus on Cassidy, an' then flick 'wards Megan lyin' on the table. "What happened?"

"Megan's hurt!" I blurt out. "She needs a doc. Couldja... couldja run fer Dr Fallon? Take Rosie if you need to."

"I'll be right back."

Without 'nother look at Cassidy or Megan, Dean leaves the house.

Ma legs give away an' I sink down on the kitchen floor.

"Who was that?" Cassidy asks. She's scratchin' her arm an' glancin' at where Dean were standin' a moment ago.

"Dean," I say.

"Didn't he work for my father?"

"Yeah."

"Do you think he recognised me?"

"I hope not." But I've a bad feelin' in ma stomach that he has. Dean knew Cassidy growin' up. She's changed in the last few years, but not enough that she's unrecognisable from the girl she'd once bin.

"Let's get Megan upstairs before the doctor gets here,"

Cassidy says.

I nod but stay on the floor. It ain't 'til Cassidy holds out a hand fer me to take that I find the strength to stand with her help.

Once Megan's in bed, I rip a long strip of cotton from her bed sheet an' tie it 'round her middle, liftin' her shirt to do so. The blood's almost stopped flowin', but I tie the strip as tight as I can to stop anymore from escapin'. I hold ma hand over her mouth. I can't feel her breath or see her chest movin'. She's so pale, yet summit tells me she's still alive.

Ma whole body hurts an' ma left arm's burnin'. I hafta to git the bullet taken out.

I kneel by Megan's bedside an' I lay ma head on ma arms on her mattress. There must be summit I can do to help her, but I don't know what it is. Ma eyelids droop – all the panic leaks outta me, lettin' weariness take over.

"Sis," I whisper. "Don't leave me. Please, not yet. I ain't ready."

Ma hands slip into prayer. "Gawd, I know you must be sick of hearin' this from me, but I'm sorry. I'm sorry fer killin' that woman. I'm sorry fer all the other deaths I've caused. I pray that you welcome her an' the other three into your kingdom. I ain't expectin' fergiveness, but..."

I take a breath.

"I know we ain't the best of folk, but Megan's a good person. I know that unner all that hate there's a gentle soul. If you let her live then I swear we'll become honest folk. No more guns, no more stealin'. No more killin'. We'll settle down. I swear on ma parents' graves."

I cross maself, reach fer Megan's hand an' fall asleep.

Chapter 27

Stalling

Jason waited for them outside the sheriff's office, sitting on the porch, smoking. A heavy sense of dread settled over Antonio as his deputy watched them approach the building, his eyes swivelling from Antonio to Juanita.

"Well, howdy," he said, as they dismounted. "Was wonderin' where you'd got to, Sheriff."

"I was tracking some outlaws in another town," Antonio said.

"And you didn't think to ask your faithful deputy fer help?"

"You weren't around, so I asked someone who was. Juanita, this is my deputy, Jason."

Juanita met Antonio's eye and gave him a look of disbelief. Antonio raised his eyebrows back at her, signalling his agreement.

"You're very tall fer a woman," Jason remarked.

Hot anger flashed through Antonio's body. He opened his mouth to make a retort, but Juanita said, "Yes, I am." As though she was gliding on ice, she walked over to Jason and held out a hand to him, like a debutant at a ball. "Thank you for the compliment."

They stared at each other for a few moments, Juanita looking down at Jason, who kept puffing on his cigar. At last, he took Juanita's hand and kissed it.

"You're welcome, darlin'." Jason threw his cigar in the dirt and stood up. "I'm guessin' from the glum look on our sheriff's face that your excursion warn't a success."

"No," Antonio said. "It wasn't."

"Ah, well, ain't that a shame? There's plenty of other work to be gittin' on with. This town ain't gonna protect itself."

"Like you would know anything about it," Antonio muttered. He went to put the horses away.

Walking up the stairs, Antonio heard Juanita playing her guitar inside his room. Leaning his head against his door, he listened to her pluck out a calming tune and the gentle scrape of her callused fingers sliding across the strings. He waited until she had finished the song and opened the door. With the guitar still resting on her legs, Juanita raised her head to look at him. Low afternoon light streamed through the window, falling across her body. Antonio felt himself reaching for the doorframe as the force of her beauty knocked into him.

"You don't play anymore, do you?" Juanita asked, turning her gaze towards Antonio's guitar case leaning against the corner of the room. "I haven't seen you pick it up."

Antonio released the doorframe. "I'm too busy to play," he said.

Juanita snorted. "I remember you playing while you waited for the rice to cook, or sitting against a tree after you'd finished hanging the washing. You always found time to play."

"Yeah, well... I had less responsibilities back then."

"Hmm," Juanita said and put down her guitar. "Well, anyway, we need to talk about how we're going to rescue our family."

Antonio took a deep breath and sat beside her. "Yes. We do."

"I was thinking," she said, "there's no way of success unless we have more firepower. There's only two of us and... What? Fifteen? Twenty of The Reckoners."

"The newspaper reports said there are sixteen of them," Antonio said.

"You going to round up a posse?"

Antonio paused. "No," he said. "After what The Reckoners did at the Racoon, I don't want to put the civilians of this town in anymore danger, or risk the formation of a vigilante group. Anyway, this is a family matter."

"Then what about Dean? He seems capable and willing to help if there's something in it for him."

"I don't think we'll need a whole host of people to make this work," Antonio said. "I think four should be enough."

"So us, Dean and...?"

"I don't think we should ask Dean."

Juanita raised her eyebrows. "Then who should we ask?" Antonio bit his bottom lip, which caused Juanita to raise her eyebrows further. "I don't like that look. Come on, Toni. Spit it out."

Antonio took a breath, and Jason's voice bellowed from downstairs.

"Sheriff! Mr Carson's here to see you."

"One second," Antonio said and backed out onto the landing. Switching to English, he shouted "Send him up!" down the stairs.

"What do I look like?" came Jason's reply. "A damn

secretary?"

"You're my damn deputy!" Antonio snapped. "And you do what I tell you to. Now send him up!"

The silence that followed Antonio's words was so acute he felt it ring in his ears.

"All right, all right. Keep your panties on." There followed a few muffled voices, and then Dean appeared at the bottom of the stairs.

"Afternoon, Sheriff," he said.

"Afternoon, Dean. Come on up."

The three of them gathered in Antonio's room, Juanita on Antonio's bed, Antonio leaning against the door and Dean standing in front of the tracking map. Dean took a good look at it for a while and made an approving noise.

"Bin hard at work, I see," he said.

"Always," Juanita said.

"Well, you'll be able to take that thing down soon. I've jest come back from the Hayes's. Bin waitin' 'round their house all day an' saw Cole come back onna single horse. Paid 'em a friendly neighbourhood visit, an' found Megan bleedin' out on the table. Ran to git her a doctor, an' then came straight here afterwards. Now's a good time to go arrest 'em."

There was a pause during which time Antonio felt all eyes turn on him.

"They've also gotta young lady with 'em who looks an awful lot like Miss Cassidy Scarborough," Dean added.

"Is that so?" Antonio said. "That's quite a coincidence, since Miss Scarborough's in New York right now."

"Yes," Dean said. "That is quite a coincidence, then. She were her spittin' image. Do you want me to come with you to arrest 'em? Act as an extra gun?"

"No," Antonio said. "No, thank you. Juanita and I can deal with this."

"Suit yourself, but I'm lookin' ferward to seein' those two 'hind bars."

"Don't worry," Antonio said, "we'll be paying them a visit shortly."

Dean wished them luck and left.

"Why are we stalling?" Juanita asked. "Let's arrest them now."

Antonio walked across the room until he was standing in front of the map. He scanned the articles he already knew by heart and traced the string to the locations he had visited. All these weeks of hard work and he was about to throw it all away.

He heard Juanita cross the room and stand close behind him – so close he knew that if he leant back he would fall against her. "What's going through your head?" she asked.

"I have a plan," Antonio said, "and I don't think anyone is going to like it."

Chapter 28

Truce

Megan's still asleep.

She ain't opened her eyes once in three days. Not to demand food, or to shout at me, or to swear vengeance 'gainst The Reckoners. She jest keeps sleepin'.

"She's gotta slim chance of pullin' through," Dr Fallon told me. "The bullet didn't touch any of her organs, but it went deep an' she's lost a lot of blood. But she's a strong healthy woman, so her chances of survival are high. She'll need good food, plenty of rest, an' you'll need to change her bandages daily an' keep the wound clean. Do the same fer that arm of yours. I'll be back inna few days to check in on her, but if you find signs of infection in the wound 'fore, come find me."

We did what he told us to, changin' Megan's bandages, cleanin' the wound. There ain't no signs of infection an' when the doctor came back he looked pleased at how it's healin'. But he's jest as concerned as we are 'bout the fact Megan still ain't opened her eyes.

"We hafta let her wake up on her own," he told me on the third day. "If we force her awake, it'll do more damage 'n good."

So I stayed by Megan's bedside, watchin' over her durin' the day an' sleepin' near her at night, ready to be there when she finally wakes up. She's paler 'n I've ever sin her, an' looks like one wrong move might shatter her. I cry often sittin' by her side.

Cassidy comes in an' stands beside me.

We watch Megan in silence fer a while. "She'll wake up soon," Cassidy says. "There's no way something small like a bullet will keep your sister down for long. Remember that time she crashed into that fence when we were children – broke the panel clean in two. But she just picked herself back up and kept on running."

I smile at the memory. "Yeah. Pa took her to the doctor the next day – turned out she'd cracked a coupla ribs. Didn't bother her one bit though."

"What was the name of that game she made up? The one where you had to barrel into the cactus..."

"Cactus catch me?"

Cassidy laughs an' the sound lifts ma spirits. "That was the one. Did you ever play that in the end?"

"Megan tried to with sum of the boys from school... but they wouldn't play with her 'cause she were a girl."

We lapse into silence again listenin' to Megan's steady breathin'.

"You didn't mind spending time with me," Cassidy says. "Even though I'm a girl."

"I much preferred the games we played," I say, "compared to what the rest of the boys used to play. Yours were always so calmin', even if I were awful at makin' conversation at parties."

Cassidy smiles. "My toys always used to moan when

they heard you were coming to tea again. 'He's no fun and has no gossip,' they used to tell me. 'But he's good-mannered and has a good heart. Unlike that wild sister of his. She never even comes to tea.'"

I laugh. "Megan never had the patience fer those types of games."

"No," Cassidy says. "She always likes to be on the move, doesn't she?"

"All those times we made you play outside with us, instead of playin' with your dolls you... you didn't hate it, didja?"

"No, Cole. I didn't hate it. I was glad for your company. Truly, I was. Without the two of you I..." Cassidy takes a deep breath. "Well, I wouldn't have had anyone. I used to look forward to you coming over every day once you finished school."

"An' I," I blurt out. I wanna look at her, but I'm very aware of the heat spreadin' through ma cheeks. I don't want Cassidy to see the true feelin' in ma expression, so I keep ma eyes on the floor. "I used to look ferward to seein' you every day."

Those words should be enough. I should be satisfied with jest tellin' Cassidy that, but more words are risin' up ma throat, threatenin' to spill out. I need to tell her. I need to say that fer all those years she were away, I looked ferward to the day I saw her again, an' now I look ferward to spendin' every day with her. 'Cause I love her. I've loved her since we were children, an' I pray every night that she might love me back, even though a lady like her can never love sumone like me.

But jest as I open ma mouth, summit touches ma shoulder. Thinkin' it's a creature dropped from the ceilin', I brush it away an' find maself touchin' Cassidy's hand.

I freeze.

I should snatch ma hand away.

I should apologise.

But I don't. I let ma fingers brush over the smooth skin on the back of her hand, an' then down. Cassidy's fingers part an' lift, an' our hands slot togither like they were made fer each other—

There's a knock on the door.

Cassidy an' me jump away from each other. Heat rushes to ma cheeks as we look at each other, but Cassidy don't look at all flustered.

"Dean?" Cassidy asks.

"I guess so," I say, 'cause who else can it be.

"I'd better hide," Cassidy says. As she moves 'wards the door, I go to the window in Megan's bedroom, which looks out at the front of the house. All ma insides drop.

"It's the sheriff," I whisper.

Cassidy reappears in Megan's doorway. "The sheriff?"

I nod an' grip the edge of the windowsill as ma heart pounds faster 'n a horse's hooves.

"What do I do?" I whisper.

"Answer the door," Cassidy says inna level voice that calms ma nerves. "Find out why he's here. Until you do there's no sense in panicking."

"What should I tell him 'bout Megan?"

Cassidy licks her lips as her eyes dart from Megan lyin' in the bed to the window.

"Tell him... Tell him that she got into a bar brawl. I think that's believable after what happened the other night."

"All right." I take 'nother deep breath an' then go downstairs. By the front door I almost turn 'round an' go back upstairs. Ma heartbeat's in ma ears. I take hold of the doorhandle an' push it open.

The door creaks open, revealin' the sheriff an' a tall Indian woman. Ma eyes dart from the rifle on her back to the pistols on the sheriff's hips. Ma hips suddenly are very light an' I remember ma pistol lyin' on the floor unner ma bed.

"Morning, Cole," the sheriff says.

"Mornin', Sheriff Valdez," I say. A bead of sweat runs 'tween ma shoulder blades. "What can I do fer you?"

"This is Juanita," he says, introducin' the woman beside him. We nod at each other. "I have a proposition for you and your sister... Can we come in?"

Even though a sick feelin's brewin' in ma stomach, I nod an' step aside, allowin' the sheriff an' the woman inside. With the parlour in disarray from bein' turned into Cassidy's bedroom, I lead 'em through to the kitchen. The sheriff pulls a chair out fer the woman to sit in, but continues to stand, as do I, as near the door as I can.

Sweat trickles down ma face as silence radiates 'round the room.

At last the sheriff clears his throat. "I think I should start by laying my cards on the table," he said. "But when I do, I must ask you not to be alarmed, and not to speak until I have finished my full proposition. Is that agreeable?"

I nod, not trustin' ma voice.

"All right. Where is Miss Cassidy Scarborough?"

I blink. "What?" I ask.

"I know you have her – that you took her hostage on that train."

I shake ma head. "No. No, we... I don't know what you're—"

"Cole," the sheriff says, "I know you and your sister are the Blood Twins."

A nettin' of bright white light fills ma vision. Ma back hits the wall an' I slide down to the floor.

Through the roarin' in ma head, I hear Juanita ask, "Did he faint?"

"I think so."

"I'm fine," I say, still sittin' on the floor. I can't move. Can't look away from ma boots. All ma limbs've turned to wood. I swallow down the burnin' feelin' in the back of ma throat. "I think... I might stay down here. Jest—" I drop ma voice "—don't talk 'bout Cassidy so loud. Not with ma sis around."

A line appears between Sheriff Valdez's eyes. "Is she safe, Cole?"

I nod. "She's hidin' in the house. She saw you comin' an' hid. Please, don't take her back to her pa. She don't wanna go."

A strange expression crosses the sheriff's face, but he composes himself quick. "All right. So... despite what we know, we haven't come to arrest you."

"You haven't?" I squeak.

"No. We haven't. We've come to propose a truce, because we have a common enemy."

"Enemy?" I mumble.

"Yes. The band of outlaws who came to the Racoon the other night. Who shot your sister three days ago while you were robbing a bank. I know you want that gang off your territory, and I've got a personal bone to pick with them. But Juanita and I can't deal with them by ourselves. So I'm proposing that we team up."

"Team up?"

"Yes, join forces. Just temporarily until the gang are dealt with."

Ma head's whirrin' so loud. It's all too much.

The sheriff knows.

He knows.

How does he know? What has he discovered to make him think that we're the Blood Twins?

An' what am I gonna do 'bout his proposition?

Should I go fer it? True, it would be a good means to an end – we could protect ourselves from arrest an' git rid of that band of invaders. But, what are we gonna do once the gang're taken care of an' we hafta go back to bein' enemies? How're Megan an' me gonna keep livin' now that sumone knows we're the Blood Twins?

An' what will Megan want me to do?

But what if Megan never wakes up?

That dark thought leaves me feelin' shaken but also makes up ma mind. 'Cause if it's jest me then I need to protect ma sis, more 'n ever. I need to create a world where it's safe fer her when she does wake up.

An' if that means gittin' rid of that gang, an' the sheriff an' his assistant, then I'll do that.

I stand up to announce ma decision, but Juanita looks up. Upstairs I hear arguin' voices. Sheriff Valdez notices where we're both lookin' an' rotates his head so his uncovered ear's turned up. Then Megan's voice shouts out loud 'n clear: "I'm fuckin' fine, you hear me. Git your hands off me!"

I scramble 'wards the stairs. Megan emerges from her bedroom. She's standin', but is paler 'n milk an' is leanin' over to one side, her hand on her wound.

"You shouldn't be up," I say.

"Shut up, Cole. I heard every word of that damn conversation an' you can tell that bastard he can go fuck that truce of his."

The sheriff appears 'hind me. "I thought it would be an amicable situation for the both of us," he says.

Megan's eyes flash an' her fingers twitch 'wards her hips, which're thankfully gunless.

"We don't need your help takin' those bastards down," she says. "We can do it without your help."

"That bullet wound in your side says something different," the sheriff says.

If emotions could show 'emselves, Megan would've burst into flames. Even though her anger ain't directed at me, I still cower 'gainst the wall at the intensity of it.

"The Blood Twins ain't in need of help," she spits. "Now git out."

"You realise the moment we leave this house we'll be enemies?" Sheriff Valdez says.

"We've bin enemies all the time you've bin in this house, so you'd best watch your backs as you walk away."

Fer what feels like an age, Megan an' the sheriff glare at each other down the stairs. Finally Sheriff Valdez turns away.

"You'd best be ready," he says.

I run up the stairs an' put ma arms 'round Megan's back. I expect her to fight me off, but she slumps 'gainst me an' doesn't struggle as I lead her back to her bed. Cassidy, who's hoverin' outta sight inside Megan's bedroom, steps ferward to help me.

Once we've got Megan into bed, Cassidy grabs me by the elbow an' drags me to the window. Ma face flushes at the feelin' of her hand pressed into ma skin. Her grip's stronger 'n I thought it would be.

"Cole," she says inna low voice, "talk to Megan. Git her to agree to the truce."

Cassidy runs outta the room an' clatters down the stairs.

Chapter 29

Rescue

"Now what?"

Juanita and Antonio stood a little way away from the Hayes house. Shielding his eyes from the sun, Antonio looked back at the wooden structure for signs of movement.

"We go back to the office," he said, "and we get ready to storm the house tonight. If it's a fight they want, it's a fight they'll get. But we'll do it carefully – our priority will be to rescue Cassidy. I guess that is who Megan shouted at upstairs."

"Someone's in there – other than the siblings." Antonio gave her a look. "I could hear another set of footsteps above us before Megan came downstairs," Juanita added.

"I do envy your hearing sometimes," Antonio said.

Juanita smiled but quickly frowned when a figure came running out of the Hayes house. They were wearing a skirt so couldn't have been Cole, but they were the wrong shape to be Megan. It wasn't until they were a little closer that Antonio recognised her.

"Cassidy!" he whispered and ran towards her. "Thank God," he cried, switching to English. He opened his arms and she threw herself into them. They had never hugged before. They had never been without an escort, but Antonio had wanted to embrace her some days. She always looked like she needed comfort.

They clung to each other, Cassidy's face pressed into his shoulder. They drew apart. Antonio gave her face a quick scan. Apart from a long scab on her cheek there was no sign of harm. Antonio's back teeth pressed together as he realised the wound was a bullet graze.

"You're safe," he croaked.

"Safe enough," Cassidy said.

"What happened to your face? Did the sister shoot at you? If that brother has laid a hand—"

"I'm fine." Cassidy grabbed Antonio's hand and squeezed it. "Really. It's just a graze. It's good to see you again, Antonio."

The insistent look Cassidy gave him was enough for Antonio to relax his jaw.

"I've been searching for you," he said. "I knew when the Blood Twins robbed that train they had taken a hostage. I followed the tracks and found the carriage they'd cut loose with your luggage inside, and when your father messaged to say that you were on your way... I knew the worse had happened. Why in the blazes were you on the train past Barren Post anyway?"

"Trying to escape to Los Angeles." The sad smile on Cassidy's face broke Antonio's heart. "But I only got myself captured again."

"We only learnt that the Hayes siblings were the Blood Twins the other day."

"We?"

Cassidy looked behind Antonio to where Juanita stood, patiently waiting. Antonio stepped aside and introduced them. He didn't miss the hint of confusion in Cassidy's eyes. If Juanita saw it, she didn't let it show.

"I'm so relieved you're all right," he said to Cassidy. "When I realised it was you the Blood Twins had taken hostage, I feared the worst. Your father's also worried sick about you. I've put off telling him what happened, but you can come back to the office with us now, and we can send him a message together."

"I need to stay here," Cassidy said.

Antonio's shock must have shown on his face, because Cassidy took his hands again.

"I can't let Megan know who I am," she said. "She's got a vendetta against my father, because he killed her and Cole's father. If she finds out who I am... she'll use me against him."

"Then that's more the reason to get you away from here," Antonio pointed out.

"As long as my identity is kept a secret from Megan, I'm safe. And... there's the fact that I don't want to go back to my father."

A guilty cramp seized Antonio's stomach as he recalled everything he had seen in New York, the longing look in Cassidy's eyes as she watched him from the window walk away from the house and the almost constant grip of Mr Scarborough's hand on her shoulder.

Antonio didn't move. Cassidy gave his hands one last squeeze and let them drop.

"Was it so awful for you, in that house with your pa?" Antonio asked.

Cassidy paused. "I don't miss him," she said. "Isn't that terrible? What sort of daughter doesn't miss their father?"

Antonio understood. He didn't miss his father, despite the very few years they had had together. "You should still send a message to him. Even if it's to let him know you've arrived. I can bring you straight back here—"

"No," Cassidy said, "because you won't let me come back, will you?" Antonio cleared his throat. Cassidy kicked a dust cloud over his boots. "Thought not," she said. "But I agree – he does need to be sent a message. So you have my permission to send him one on my behalf. Just let him know that I've arrived safely. Say I was too busy sorting out the house to send him a message. That should keep him at bay."

"I still don't like leaving you here," Antonio said, his eyes shifting back towards the Hayes house. "The sister doesn't seem like the most rational person."

"Don't worry about me," Cassidy said. "Cole will keep me safe. But, could you do me a favour? Can you hold off taking any action on the Blood Twins? Cole's going to talk to Megan again. I know he'll get her to agree to your truce."

"I can't hold off forever," Antonio said. "Those two have to be brought to justice. If you knew what they'd done, you would feel the same."

"I know what they've done," Cassidy said, her voice quiet. "And I agree with you. They need to answer for their crimes, but could you give them a little more time? Just a few more days."

As he opened his mouth to reply, Juanita said, "The brother's coming."

Cole ran towards them from the house.

Chapter 30

Agreement

"That sneaky sunvabitch," Megan curses. She twirls Florence an' Smithy, spinnin' 'em 'round her fingers. "How dare he come here an' spout that shit. In our own home. How the hell did he know anyway we're the Blood Twins?"

"I don't know," I say. "He didn't say how he knew."

Megan pulls out Florence's cylinder, spins it an' snaps it back in. "Lucky guess, then. A shame. I didn't want it to come to this."

"Come to what?" I ask, dread growin' in ma stomach.

Megan gives me a witherin' look. "Well, now that sumone knows who we are, we're gonna hafta leave Helena."

Cold creeps over ma limbs. "Leave Helena?" I repeat.

"Yes, Cole! We can't stay here now. It's either that or we kill the sheriff an' his companion an' hope they haven't told anyone else. Actually—" Megan smiles as she spins

Florence's cylinder "—I think I prefer that idea."

"But what if we didn't do either," I say.

Even though I ain't lookin' at Megan, I can feel the intensity of her gaze on me.

"An' what you propose we do?" she asks.

I struggle to pull the words up from within me, scared of what Megan'll do when I say 'em. "I think we should accept the sheriff's offer," I say at last.

"Are you outta your mind!" Megan hollers, makin' me wince. "They're the enemy, Cole! They wanna string us up! We either need to put 'em in the ground or die tryin'. There ain't no way we're teamin' up with 'em."

"I know," I say.

I wanna disappear into the floor. I hate arguin' with Megan – hate arguin' of any sort – but Cassidy's asked me to do this an' she's right. I need to git Megan to agree to the truce, otherwise we ain't gonna survive what comes next. The only hope we've got of gittin' rid of those outlaws is by teamin' up with sumone, an' if that sumone hassa be the sheriff then so be it.

"But he's right," I say. "We can't git rid of that gang on our own. There's too many of 'em an' they're too well armed. We need help. An'... don't you wanna keep Pa's memory alive?"

It's a low blow. A super low blow, but it changes Megan's expression. Her resolve falters at the mention of Pa.

"An' how can we do that when we can't rob no more 'cause that gang's blockin' us at every turn?" I press on. "How're we meant to earn a livin' when they're stoppin' us from stealin'? Surely, it's best that we git rid of 'em as quick as possible?"

"I don't want it to be him, though," Megan mutters.

"Neither do I," I say, "but there ain't 'nother option, sis."

Fer ages Megan keeps silent, keepin' her gaze on

Florence an' Smithy. I can almost see the cogs rotatin' in her head. At last, she twirls the guns 'round her fingers.

"All right," she says. "We'll accept his deal, *but* tell him the moment the final outlaw in that gang drops dead, we're enemies 'gain."

"I'll tell him," I say,

Megan sighs. "Well, guess there ain't no point wearin' our masks 'round Miss Priss anymore."

I almost trip over maself to git out the room 'fore I can work out what Megan means by that comment.

Downstairs, I'm surprised to find the front door open an' Sheriff Valdez an' his friend standin' a little way away from the house. But sumone's standin' with 'em. I freeze in the doorway, squintin' at the third figure.

Ma stomach drops. It's Cassidy.

I run 'wards 'em.

"Cassidy!" I shout.

They watch me approach. Cassidy must see the panic on ma face, 'cause she takes ma arm an' grips it tight.

"It's all right, Cole," she says. "Antonio and I know each other – we met in New York. He won't let anyone know I'm here, or tell Megan who I am."

"Although I should drag you off to the jailhouse right now for kidnapping," Sheriff Valdez says. His voice's measured, but there's a dangerous flash in his eyes. He's pissed. Real pissed at us fer kidnappin' Cassidy. Gawd, it's not like I can blame him 'cause I'd feel the same.

"But Cassidy has persuaded me to let her stay here," he continues. "Rest assured, though, I will not hesitate to put a bullet in anyone who hurts her."

"Rest assured that I'd do the same," I say.

Ma shoulders ache as ma gaze locks with Sheriff Valdez's, but of course I'm the one who looks away first. Once I do, Cassidy lets go of ma arm.

"I talked to ma sis," I say. "She's agreed to the truce, on the condition that once the final member of The

Reckoners falls we will go back to bein' enemies."

"I'm happy with those terms," Sheriff Valdez says. "I should let you know that I have an agreement with my benefactor to get rid of the Blood Twins, so once our truce has ended it will become my goal to take you two in."

"Benefactor?" I ask. "Who's that?"

There's a pause in which Sheriff Valdez's eyes flick to Cassidy, who's frozen with tense shoulders.

"Mr Benjamin Scarborough," Sheriff Valdez says.

Ma mouth's suddenly very dry.

"Mr Scarborough?" I repeat.

Sheriff Valdez nods. "He's coming back to Helena and wants the two of you cleaned out before he gets here."

"You never told me your pa were comin' back," I say to Cassidy.

She doesn't meet ma eyes. "I thought it was obvious he was coming since I'm here. The only reason I was allowed to come back was because he was as well. I persuaded him to let me come back early to get the house ready."

I press the palms of ma hands 'gainst ma pants. They're sweatin'.

"Don't let Megan know Mr Scarborough's comin' back," I say. "She wants nuthin' more 'n to..." I glance at Cassidy, who's turned her back to me. I swallow. "She wants nuthin' more 'n to take her revenge on him."

"Because Mr Scarborough killed your father."

I nod. Where did the sheriff learn that?

Sheriff Valdez sighs an' sticks his thumbs through his belt. "You've got quite the web of lies here."

"And I have a feeling that they haven't stopped growing," Juanita adds.

Summit cold sinks to the bottom of ma stomach. It's hard to disagree with the statement.

"Back in the house," I say, "you said you'd a personal bone to pick with The Reckoners. What kinda personal bone?"

The sheriff looks the most nervous I've ever sin him. After a coupla moments of internal struggle, he says, "They've taken over my home. Murdered members of my family, and others remain in danger while The Reckoners stay there."

I swallow. "That's real personal."

Antonio nods. "I know. And I know it's a lot to ask you and Megan to help me fix it, but I wouldn't be asking you if I wasn't desperate. But they've hurt you as much as they've hurt me. So—" the sheriff sticks out his hand to me "—shall we make the deal official?"

It feels dishonest that the sheriff didn't tell us his real reason fer wantin' to take out The Reckoners, but at the same time I can't blame him fer holdin' back the information. 'Specially since Megan's involved. An' I wanna help him. I know the sickenin' desperation that comes with wantin' to save your family.

I spit on ma palm. He spits in his an' we shake hands.

"Megan'll need sum time to recover," I say, "'fore we make a move."

"All right," Sheriff Valdez says. "But we can't wait around forever."

"Megan won't wanna," I say. "I'll let you know when we're ready."

With one final nod to each other, Cassidy an' me head back 'wards the house while Sheriff Valdez an' Juanita walk the other way. Once the front door's closed, I let out a long breath.

"You've made the right choice," Cassidy says.

"I don't think I hadda choice," I say.

Chapter 31

Change of Plans

Juanita wouldn't look at Antonio as they walked back to town. Her disappointment rolled off her in waves.

"You don't approve of this plan," he said, as they stepped onto the town's main street. "Do you?"

"No," Juanita replied. "I don't, but I can understand why you're doing it. And why this situation is too personal to find help elsewhere. In the end it kills several birds with one stone – we rescue our family, take down The Reckoners and keep an eye on the Blood Twins before we can arrest them. But I don't trust those siblings – especially the sister. She's a loose cannon, Toni."

"She'll comply if it means the Blood Twins get their territory back."

"She'll be the first to turn on us once the truce is done. She might even turn on us before."

"And that's why we have each other – so we always

have someone to watch our back." He hoped Juanita would look at him then, but she kept her eyes on the road, her jaw set.

"And what about Miss Scarborough?" she said. "Whose side do you think she's on?"

"I'm not sure," Antonio admitted. The thought made his stomach clench. "But I have a feeling it's whatever side Cole Hayes is on."

"And she's Mr Scarborough's daughter?" Juanita asked.

"Yes. I spent a lot of time with Cassidy in New York. Her father rarely let her leave the house, and when he did allow it, he never let her out of his sight."

"Why?" Juanita asked.

"Don't know," Antonio said. "But Cassidy told me once he sometimes wakes up screaming from bad nightmares. Like he's afraid someone's after him."

"Well," Juanita said, "if you murder three men and take their gold, then I guess you'd be paranoid that there might be someone coming after you."

Dean walked into the sheriff's office as Antonio was writing his reply to Mr Scarborough. Antonio stopped scratching his head, laid down his pencil and took a deep breath.

"Howdy," Dean said, taking off his hat.

"Morning," Antonio replied. "I have a feeling I know what you've come to talk to me about."

"Yes," Dean said. "You see, I dropped by the Hayes house this mornin' an' to ma surprise found that Cole an' Megan were still there, an' not in your cells. What're you playin' at, Sheriff?"

Antonio put his hands on the desk. "There's been a change of plan."

Dean frowned. "What sorta change?"

"The band of outlaws that attacked The Racoon the other night, the Blood Twins and I share the same desire to eradicate. Juanita and I can't deal with them ourselves, and there are reasons why I can't ask for help from another sheriff, so we've made a deal with Cole and Megan – a truce until this band of outlaws are dealt with."

Dean's frown deepened. "You can't be serious," he said. "I've handed the Blood Twins to you practically onna plate an' you're gonna let 'em go?"

"We're not letting them go. Just... working with them until we've sorted out our common problem. Once the problem's solved, we'll take them into custody. Now that you've told us who they are, they won't be able to hide." Dean's expression did not relax. In fact, the colouring of his skin deepened towards an angry red. He stood up. "I haven't told them that it was you who revealed their identities to us, so as far as they're aware you're innocent in this situation. We can always use that against them if necessary to aid their capture."

"Sheriff," Dean said, "with all due respect, this ain't good enough. Those two should be 'hind bars now."

"And they will be, I promise." In an effort to be appear relaxed, Antonio leaned against the side of his desk. "Dean, can I ask why you're so determined to see the back of the Blood Twins? You know everything I know about the gold. That was our deal."

"It doesn't matter." Dean put his hat back on. "Thanks fer the information on the gold."

"I hope you find it useful," Antonio said. "And I'm sorry it wasn't more." A thought flitted into Antonio's head – a reminder that he hadn't told Dean what Alejandro had told him about Mr Scarborough. That he had been the one to steal the gold. Guilt niggled at Antonio, telling him that he should tell Dean that information, that it was only fair to. But a nervous feeling slithered in Antonio's gut, and he knew that telling Dean would only put Mr Scarborough in further danger. Even if the man had murdered his great-uncle, Antonio still owed him.

Dean tipped his hat. "Best of luck, Sheriff."

Dean shut the office door behind him. Juanita appeared at the bottom of the stairs.

"I heard everything," she said. "Are you all right?"

Antonio sighed and ran a hand down his face. "I have a feeling," he said, "I might have just made a new enemy."

Chapter 32

Confession

I take Rosie fer a ride.

It's bin too long since she's hadda chance to stretch her legs. Truth be told, ever since Hattie's death ridin's bin the last thing I wanna do. I want little to do with Rosie. I barely see her or talk to her like I used to. When it were jest me an' Megan livin' alone I told the horses everythin'. I told 'em all ma secrets an' worries when I felt like I'd burdened Gawd with too much.

Now lookin' at Rosie I feel guilty. Guilty that I failed to keep her sis alive. That I killed her sis so mine could live. Since Megan's recovery I'd finally sin how sad Rosie's bin lookin', how she runs 'round her small paddock, desperate fer a chance to stretch her legs.

We fly through the desert, dodgin' cactuses, jumpin' over rocks an' feelin' freer 'n we've done inna long time. Rosie snorts an' I whoop.

Rosie starts to tire an' I slow down. Ma left arm's also startin' to hurt from holdin' the reins. We trot through the heat. I look back at the trail of hoof prints in the sand.

Back at the house, Cassidy's outside scrubbin' clothes 'gainst a washboard. She waves as I pull Rosie into the yard. A wide smile breaks 'cross ma face as I wave back. Cassidy's let her hair loose, her sleeves're pushed up to her elbows an' she's opened the top button of her shirt. Ma heart feels like it's gonna burst.

An' I ain't sure how much longer I can keep ma feelin's hidden from her. But fer now I need to brush an' water Rosie.

Part way through fillin' up the water trough, I hear the gunshots from inside the house. Both Cassidy an' me freeze, our hearts poundin' in time.

Then 'nother cracks across the land an' Cassidy whispers, "Cole, what's going on?"

"I'll check it out." Takin' ma gun from its holster, I go inside. A third shot sounds, confirmin' ma fears that the shots're comin' from Megan's room. As I run up the stairs, I pull the pistol's hammer down. Has the sheriff come back to arrest us? Or has the gang sumhow found out where we live?

There's only one way to find out.

I open Megan's door an' charge inside, ma pistol held out in front of me.

I find Megan lyin' on her bed, Florence an' Smithy in her hands. She's pointin' 'em at the wall. There are three bullet holes in it near the floor.

"What're you doin'?" I ask, lowerin' ma pistol.

"Bloody mice've bin scratchin' an' squeakin' all night. Gittin' sick of 'em."

I hear a scramble of claws on the floor an' Megan fires. A little grey furry body runs along the bottom of the wall. Megan fires 'gain. The shot hits home an' the body explodes, leavin' a red star on the floor. I turn away, feelin' sick.

"There were no need to shoot it," I mutter.

"This is ma home," Megan points out. "Therefore, it's trespassin'. It got what were comin' to it." Megan lays Florence an' Smithy on her bedside table. She smiles at the pistol in ma hand. "It's good to see ma brother's ready to protect me."

I click the hammer back. As I return it to its holster, Megan sits up an' swings her legs over the side of the bed. Thinkin' she wants to use the chamber pot, I kneel down an' pull it out from unner the bed fer her, but instead she starts movin' 'wards her bedroom door.

"Megan," I say, "it's too soon fer you to git up. The doc said it'll be—"

"I don't care what the doc says," Megan spits, pressin' a hand 'gainst her side while she shuffles ferward. "While we're sat here, those bandits are sweepin' all over our territory, erasin' the Blood Twins, likely crowin' 'bout how they've beaten us. Well, I'll pay 'em back – I'll pay 'em back tenfold fer this hole in ma side."

As Megan reaches 'wards the door handle, she cries out an' crumples to the floor. I reach fer her, but she slaps ma hand away.

"I'm *fine*, Cole." She takes her hand away from her side an' there's blood on her palm. I open ma mouth to tell her to go back to bed, but in that same moment ma hand throbs from where she hit me, so I keep ma mouth shut.

At last, Megan stands an' begins shufflin' downstairs, one hand grippin' the handrail tight.

"Where the hell is that useless sheriff?" she says. "He's too slow. We need to start movin' 'gainst that gang now. What kinda man hesitates 'fore goin' to rescue his family?"

I'd bin hesitant to tell Megan that the sheriff's real reason fer wantin' to git rid of The Reckoners were 'cause his family were bein' held hostage by the gang, but in the end I did 'cause I knew the truth were gonna come out at sum point. I expected her to be delighted – to see it as a bargainin' chip she could use 'gainst him – but instead I were surprised at the lack of reaction it got outta her. Perhaps when it came to matters of family, ma sis warn't as heartless as folk thought her to be.

"He said he would give you sum time to heal," I say. "There ain't much we can do while you're still injured."

"I ain't injured! This little scratch ain't gonna stop me from doin' nuthin'. An' if that self-righteous sheriff thinks he can use it as an excuse not to git up off his ass, then he's got 'nother thin' comin'. I will not sit here while that gang pisses all over our territory."

Cassidy comes in from outside as we enter the kitchen. She peers 'round the side of the front door, checkin' fer danger. Seein' Megan an' me in the kitchen she comes inside.

"You shouldn't be up," she says to Megan. "The doctor said—"

"I don't care what—"

"The doctor said," Cassidy almost hollers, "that it will be months until you are fully healed. You cannot get out of bed after only a few days."

"You're fergittin' yourself, Miss Priss," Megan hisses. "Your job here is to wash ma clothes an' cook ma food. It ain't to stick your nose into matters that don't concern you. So shut the hell up."

The two of 'em glower at each other fer a few moments, both refusin' to look away. Then finally Cassidy says, "Fine. Kill yourself. See if I care." An' leaves the room.

"Megan," I say. "I think you should rest."

"Not you too," Megan snaps. "I'm fuckin' fine, Cole. It's nuthin' serious."

"But it's hurtin' you," I say. "So you should rest."

I pull out a kitchen chair an' Megan allows herself to

sit in it. I don't miss her sigh of relief. I change Megan's bandages an' then go to find Cassidy.

Night's fallin' along with the temperature. Cassidy's figure stands out as a sharp silhouette 'gainst the streaks of yellows, oranges an' reds painted 'cross the sky. She sits on the upturned wash bucket, her back straight.

"Why don't you ever stand up fer me?" she asks, as I crouch in the dust beside her. "You know I'm right. I can see it on your face. But you never say anything."

"I'm sorry," I say.

"No, you're not!" Cassidy snaps. Then she sighs an' tips her head back to the sky. "Are you afraid of her?" she asks.

I think 'bout the moment by the river. Ma whole body turns cold as I remember the snarl on Megan's face 'hind her gun barrels.

"Sumtimes," I admit.

"You shouldn't be afraid of your own family," Cassidy says.

"Megan's jest Megan," I say. "She don't mean no harm."

Cassidy laughs. She laughs so hard she clutches her stomach.

"Oh, Cole," she says. "You really need to open your eyes or she's going to drag you over the edge of a cliff."

This conversation's makin' me uncomfortable, so I don't reply.

"You need to stand up to her, Cole," Cassidy continues. "Don't let her ruin your life."

"She ain't," I say. "Ma life's wherever Megan is."

"Fine," Cassidy says. She stands up. "If that's how you feel."

"But," I say, also standin'. "I also want ma life to be wherever you are, Cassidy."

Cassidy stops an' slowly turns 'round. The light's so low now that her face's cast in shadow. Not bein' able to see her expression helps me finally git the next words out.

"I-I love you, Cassidy."

Ma heart hammers in ma chest as ma words hang in the air 'tween us. As the silence drags on the hammerin' gits stronger, so strong I'm sure ma heart's gonna burst through ma ribs. Ma knuckles shine white as ma hands grip each other, fingers twistin' harder as I wait fer Cassidy to give her answer.

Instead Cassidy closes the gap 'tween us an' takes ma face in her hands. As I'm suckin' inna breath of shock, she pulls me down so her lips can reach mine.

Fer the first second I'm so surprised I stand frozen. Then the flush of heat that courses through ma body knocks all other emotions from ma head, apart from the desire to be as close to Cassidy as I can.

Ma arms circle her waist an' I pull her tight 'gainst me. I always thought kissin' Cassidy'd be soft, like pressin' ma lips to a cloud, but her lips are solid an' real. They move 'gainst mine inna way I don't know how to match but enjoy the feelin' of anyhow.

Cassidy's arms fall to ma shoulders an' her hands lock 'hind ma neck. Ma arms drop from her waist an' slide down the back of her dress. A shiver runs through Cassidy that sends a vibration through me. As one, she jumps an' I catch her. We stay standin' fer a few moments, her legs locked 'round ma waist, ma hands holdin' her up, then we teeter backwards an' fall in the dust.

We gasp in surprise, breakin' the kiss. Then we're laughin' into each other's shoulders.

"That surprised me," Cassidy says.

"You surprised me," I say. Ma hands splay 'gainst the back of her dress. Should I remove 'em so Cassidy can move off ma lap? But her fingers are threadin' through ma hair as she presses the tip of her nose to mine, so I pull her closer instead.

"Nice surprise?" she asks.

"The best. But—" I swallow "—should we be doin' this? We ain't married. This ain't—"

Cassidy's kiss stops all thoughts in ma head.

"I think God will turn a blind eye to this one," she murmurs 'gainst ma lips.

She presses her body to mine an' I hold her as tight as I can 'gainst me. Sumhow her hands are up the back of ma shirt, an' her skirt rucked 'round her hips.

Gawd, I hope you'll fergive me fer this one.

At last we pause fer air.

"Run away with me," Cassidy whispers. "Let's find a house somewhere in Los Angeles – somewhere on the edge of town where you can have land to start your own ranch. I can join the suffrage movement in the city."

"That sounds like a dream," I murmur.

Cassidy smiles. It pulls at the freckles on her cheeks. All a sudden I have the urge to kiss every one of 'em.

"I always knew my knight in shining armour would rescue me." Cassidy sighs an' presses her face into ma neck. "Let's leave tonight. Now. To start our new life together – free of my father. Free of Megan."

Ma hands that'd bin tracin' a waterfall up an' down her back still. I swallow. "I can't leave Megan now. I promised Pa I'd take care of her."

The air 'tween us that'd bin hotter 'n the sun a moment ago is now frigid. Cassidy moves off me, pullin' her skirt back down. I stand an' adjust ma clothes.

"You have to leave her, Cole," Cassidy says. "She's going to get the both of you killed."

"That's more the reason fer me to stay with her. I need to be there to protect her wherever she decides to go. At least, to do as little as I can to protect her."

"Do you want to die, Cole?"

I blink. "Course I don't, but I will if it means keepin' ma promise to Pa."

"But you love *me*!" Cassidy protests. "You said so."

"An' I do—"

"Then run away with me. Live for me. If you give up Megan and come with me, neither of us will ever be lonely again." She grasps ma hands so tight that it hurts where she squeezes ma knuckles togither. Her eyes are wide as they stare up into mine. "You're *my* knight, Cole. You're meant to rescue me."

I wish I could be.

I wish so much that I could be Cassidy's knight – wish I could've gone to New York an' whisked her away outta her bedroom window like she always dreamed.

But I ain't no knight.

I'm one half of the Blood Twins.

I'm Cole Hayes.

An' I made a promise to ma pa that I'd protect Megan – a promise that I ain't gonna break even if it means damnin' ma soul fer eternity.

I can't be the man that Cassidy wants me to be.

Gently, I prise her hands away an' step back. The hurt in her eyes makes summit crack in ma chest.

"I'm sorry, Cassidy," I say. "I can't run away with you, but I unnerstand if you wanna leave now. I'll make up sum excuse to tell Megan, to make sure she won't come after you."

I walk away, thinkin' Cassidy's gonna want sum space.

"I thought you loved me!" she shouts.

I stop.

"I do," I say. "I do love you. More 'n anythin'."

"Liar," she hisses.

Anger I didn't think I were capable of feelin' 'wards Cassidy flares through me. "Well, you ain't said it back."

"What?"

Only the top edge of the sun's 'bove the horizon now. Our shadows are stretched thin on the ground.

"You ain't said you love me back," I say. "You say you wanna run away with me – to be with me forever – but you ain't said that you love me."

"I know what happened at the church."

Ma stomach twists.

"I read about it in the newspapers," she continues, "while I was in New York. I read how you shut all those people inside and burnt them alive." Cassidy's mouth twists into summit that I never thought I'd see on her face. "You burnt a whole church full of innocent people," she says. "Tell me, Cole, how could I possibly love someone who would do something like that?"

Then she gits up an' leaves me alone 'neath a blanket of stars.

I do the only thing I can think of doin' in that moment.

I fall to ma knees an' pray.

"Gawd?" I whisper, squeezin' ma eyes closed an' ma fingers togither. The words hang in the air, suspended onna thread of desperation as I wait fer Gawd to give me His answer, but He remains silent as ever.

"Gawd?" I ask 'gain. Ma voice catches an' all a sudden I'm sobbin'. "Gawd," I choak. "Gawd... I..."

Kneelin' in the dirt with ma stomach crampin' I try to find the words, but what can I ask Him when all this is ma own doin'? What good can fergiveness do when the one who I want fergiveness from the most is down here on Earth?

Curlin' into a ball, I press ma forehead 'gainst ma knees where ma prayin' turns to beggin'.

I beg Him fer His fergiveness.

I beg Him fer Cassidy's fergiveness.

Fer the souls of all those folks who died in the church that day.

Fer the courage to do what is right.

I don't hear the footsteps comin' 'wards me.

I don't know there's sumone standin' over me.

Not 'til the rifle barrel slams into the side of ma head an' I black out.

Chapter 33

Play

"Are you coming to bed at all tonight?"

Antonio looked up from his desk at where Juanita stood at the bottom of the stairs. The light from the lantern on his desk illuminated her concerned features.

"Soon," he said.

"That's what you said an hour ago."

Antonio blinked. "It's been an hour?"

Juanita sighed. "You work too hard," she said and disappeared up the stairs, leaving that all-too-familiar feeling of guilt swirling in Antonio's stomach.

Exhaling, he dragged his hands over his face and stood up. His eyes were sore from scouring old newspapers. Helena's previous sheriff had hoarded copies of *The Arizona Gazette*. Even though Antonio knew The Reckoners were from California, he still wanted to check if there were any reports of them in old copies of the gazette.

Perhaps Juanita was right. Perhaps he did work too hard.

As he climbed the stairs, he heard Juanita plucking a tune on her guitar. He recognized the song – it was an old Chinese folksong that Auntie Ju had always sung while steaming bao. Juanita didn't sing along as she plucked the notes, but Antonio could hear Auntie Ju's voice singing along to the tune. He slumped against the wall at the top of the stairs and held back his tears. The last note faded into the air.

"Why don't you play anymore?" Juanita asked.

"I can't," Antonio said.

"Can't tell me? Or can't play?"

"Both? I... I don't know really." He walked over to the doorway. Sitting on his bed, Juanita held her own guitar between her legs, but Antonio's stood against the wall in the corner of the room. The longer Antonio stared at it, the stronger the feeling of sickness got in his stomach, but he found he could not tear his eyes away from it. He wasn't able to until Juanita grabbed him by the arm and pulled him to his bed.

"Sit," she said, pushing him onto the mattress. She grabbed his guitar and pressed it into his hands. "Try," she said.

But the guitar felt like a dead body in Antonio's hands. He had bought it in New York, having left his in California when he ran away. The hollow wood and strings of that guitar had once seemed to vibrate in his hands every time he touched it, but he'd never played this one. He'd only wanted to lay it to rest.

"I can't," he choked out.

"Play," she commanded, then pulled her own guitar back between her legs. Antonio knew the song from the first note she plucked. He knew it would be the one she'd pick. They'd played it so many times together, sitting on the roof of the fortress in the hot sun, or huddled under the awning in the pouring rain. They'd worked on it for months, trying to match each other's rhythm, until the day they'd played it through effortlessly together. Antonio could still remember the way Juanita's face lit up on that day. As he did, his fingers twitched, mapping out the notes on his leg as he would on the fretboard.

"Play," Juanita whispered.

Antonio pulled his guitar against him and played.

At first his fingers were stiff, tripping over the notes that had once flowed effortlessly. Thirteen years of disuse had left them soft, so every press of the string stung his fingers where calluses had once protected them. But after the first verse and chorus, it all came back.

They fell into step once more, like two dancing partners, their fingers keeping time with each other as the melody flowed between them. He made a dozen mistakes, but unlike before when she would have berated him, Juanita allowed him to keep playing.

As the last note hung in the air, Antonio's dam burst and he dissolved into a flood of tears. Juanita pulled his guitar away and wrapped her arms around his chest. He pressed his face into her shoulder.

"I'm sorry," she said, once his shoulders had stopped shaking. "I shouldn't have pushed you."

"No," Antonio said, "I'm glad you did. I would never have picked it up again otherwise." The tips of Juanita's fingers traced Antonio's spine. He relaxed into her, enjoyed the sensation. "Every time I looked at that instrument I remembered the fort, the family meals, the desert sunsets, the hours we spent playing together... And also the guilt that's followed me around ever since I ran away – because of what I allowed to happen."

"It was an accident," Juanita said. "You weren't the only one there that day. All of us share in the guilt for Elìas's death."

"But I was put in charge. I insisted we go to the lake."

"You were eight years old, Toni. You shouldn't have

been given that much responsibility."

"I think that's what really drove me to become a sheriff." The words tumbled out of Antonio's mouth like a rockslide. It was a thought he had never voiced to himself, let alone anyone else. "Before it was just a childhood dream, but then it became a way to make amends for what I had done. To prove something to myself." Antonio looked down at the guitar. "This guitar was a constant reminder of what I had done, although the sight of it is too much to bear sometimes."

"Then let's put it away," Juanita said. "You never have to pick it up again."

Juanita reached for Antonio's guitar, but Antonio grabbed her hand and pressed it to his chest. "I want to, though," he said, threading her fingers through his. "And I will try, because whenever I play I also think of you."

He wasn't sure which one of them leaned in first, or if they did it at the same time, but their mouths met in a kiss that left Antonio's lips tingling.

"Does that mean you've forgiven me?" Antonio asked.

Juanita grinned. "Nearly," she said. "It still hurts, but my desire for you is stronger."

Grinning as well, Antonio leaned in to kiss her again.

"You know," Juanita said when they drew apart. Her voice dropped to a whisper. "I'm also scared of going home."

Antonio's brow furrowed. "Why?"

"Because I'm..." She gestured to her body. "I'm not the same person I was when I left. I'm worried... I'm worried they won't understand. I'm worried... that they'll turn me away. Tell me never to come back."

"Didn't you tell anyone else in the family who you really are?" Juanita shook her head. Antonio wrapped an arm around her shoulders and she leaned against him. "Neither of us are the same person we were when we left," he said. "Hopefully, they'll accept the new versions of us. If not... Well... We'll work it out together."

A gunshot ripped the air.

Antonio grabbed Juanita and pushed her to the ground. They lay still, both listening out for signs of movement downstairs.

"Anything?" Antonio whispered.

Juanita shook her head. "I think—" she began, but a voice shouted from outside.

"Sheriff! Sheeeerriiffff! Let us in, you sunvabitch!"

"Is that?" Antonio asked.

Juanita nodded. "The sister."

They looked outside. Two figures stood in the street outside the office. The only light Antonio had to make them out by was from the moon, but he now knew Megan Hayes's silhouette anywhere. At first he assumed that the second figure was the brother, then he noticed they wore a skirt and a shawl over their head.

Cassidy.

Megan raised her pistol and fired another shot. "Sheriff! Git out here!"

"Is she declaring war?" Juanita asked.

"Not sure," Antonio said. "Stay here and cover me. I'll go down and see what she wants."

Antonio unlocked the front door and Megan barged through it.

"What the hell took you so long?" she demanded. "Ma brother's life is in danger an' you can't be bothered to answer the damn door!"

"What do you mean?" Antonio asked, as she collapsed against his desk. She held a hand to her wounded side.

"Cole's been kidnapped," Cassidy said, stepping through the door after Megan. Once she'd shut it behind her, she removed her shawl from her head. At that same moment, Juanita appeared at the top of the stairs, rifle in hand. Antonio caught her eye and it was enough to make her lower it. "We were outside together and then... I went in, but when I came back out he was being dragged away by some people."

"What did these people look like?"

"Oh, come on, Sheriff," Megan snapped. "We all know who they were – that intrudin' good fer nuthin' gang that's bin shittin' all over our territory."

"I couldn't see them clearly," Cassidy admitted. "It was dark and they were far away from the house. But one of them was very tall."

Antonio sighed and ran a hand down his face. "I'm sure that's them."

"How did they know where to find Cole?" Cassidy asked. "I didn't think they knew."

"They don't," Antonio said. "At least I didn't think they did. They must have found out somehow."

"It doesn't matter how they found out," Megan said. "What matters is gittin' ma brother back. You." She pointed at Antonio. "You know where they are, right?"

For a moment, Antonio paused. Then he nodded. "Yes. I know where they'll be keeping him."

"Then let's go get him back."

Chapter 34

Kidnapped

Ma head hurts.

That's the first thought that comes to me as I wake.

The second is that ma arms an' legs ache. I try to move 'em, but they're stuck.

I open ma eyes. I'm in an empty small room with stone walls, tied to a chair. There's wooden shutters closed over the only window, but 'hind 'em I can glimpse bright hot sunshine.

What happened?

I remember talkin' to Cassidy outside. I remember... her tellin' me she can never love me back, an' then cryin' in the dirt, an' then... a pain in the side of ma head.

Sumone musta knocked me out an' taken me captive. But who?

Ma answer comes later when the door opens an' in they walk. The moment I see 'em, I knew I shoulda guessed.

"Good mornin', Cole," says the leader of The Reckoners. 'Hind him is a small group of people standin' in the hallway – sum of whom I recognise from the attack on The Sleepin' Raccoon an' the bank. "Or should I say, good afternoon. You've bin asleep the whole day."

Megan woulda made sum smart comment back at 'em, but I keep ma mouth shut. This situation ain't lookin' good.

"You're not very talkative, are you?" the man says. "Unlike your sis. 'Less that bullet Hart put in her gut shut her up?"

His words send a cold shiver up ma spine.

They know.

They know Megan an' me're the Blood Twins.

'Course they do. It's why they kidnapped me.

But how? How do they know?

Did the sheriff tell 'em? Has he sold us out? Were his truce all a lie?

"All right, then." The man crouches down on the floor in front of me. "I'll cut to the chase. Where's the gold?"

I blink. "What gold?"

"The gold your father stole."

"Ma pa didn't steal any gold," I say. But as the words leave ma mouth, summit niggles at the back of ma head. A memory: words whispered to me when the air were thick with the smell of blood. But the memory disappears as quick as it comes, leavin' me inna state of confusion. 'Cause Pa hadn't stolen any gold. He'd robbed stage coaches, stores an' folk's houses, takin' all the dollars they had so we could eat. But he'd never come home with any gold.

"He did," the man says, his eyes refusin' to look away from mine. "He stole a fortune of gold from Mr Benjamin Scarborough, who in turn stole it from the folks he found it with, an' murdered 'em fer it."

I don't unnerstand.

This don't make any sense.

Pa hadn't stolen any gold, an' Mr Scarborough ain't murdered no one. Yes, he'd shot at Pa, but that were 'cause he'd bin protectin' his house an' his family. But murdered folk in cold blood? No, I can't see that.

The confusion must be showin' on ma face, 'cause ma captor says, "Still don't believe me? All right." He sits on the floor, cross-legged. "Lemme tell you a story 'bout four prospectors an' a trove of lost Spanish gold."

Chapter 35

Revelation

When Antonio first came to Helena, he never would've thought he would find himself in this situation – riding out into the desert alongside Juanita, Cassidy Scarborough and one half of the Blood Twins. On a mission to rescue the other half. Even as they rode, he kept pinching himself to check he wasn't asleep. But each time he did, the scene before him remained as clear as ever.

There weren't enough horses to go between them, so Megan and Juanita rode alone, while Cassidy rode with Antonio, sitting behind him and gripping onto his shirt as they galloped through the desert.

It was a two-day ride from Helena to Antonio's family fort near Martinez Lake on the California border. It was a ride Antonio could have done alone in a day, but after an hour or so of riding it was obvious the other two horses did not have the same endurance, and also that Antonio's horse would not manage his usual speed with two riders instead of one.

So when it got too dark to see, they set up camp under a rocky outcrop. To save space for water and to travel light they had left without cooking equipment, so dinner was hard biscuits, dried meat and fruit.

On the journey, barely a word passed between them. The anger radiating off Megan was palpable, Cassidy was tense with nerves and Juanita watched Megan like a firework that was about to run out of fuse. Antonio just felt sick with exhaustion.

They sat around the campfire, each chewing silently on their food. Cassidy said, "I don't understand how The Reckoners knew Cole is one of the Blood Twins. I can't work it out."

"It don't matter how they found out," Megan said around a mouthful of jerky. Antonio didn't miss the sickly pallor of her skin, or the way she leaned to one side. With that side wound, she shouldn't be riding – not that anything said by anyone would make her stop.

Cassidy pulled her blanket closer around her shoulders to ward off the cooler desert night air. "But aren't you interested how? It's not like they know you as Cole and Megan Hayes. How could they have—"

"It don't matter how," Megan repeated, louder this time. "All that matters is that we git him back alive."

"And if you don't?" Juanita asked. She had her rifle laid across her lap, her hand resting near the trigger.

Megan gave her a one-eyed glance. Her gaze flickered from Juanita's face, down to her rifle and back again.

"Then I'll have ma revenge," she said.

"Why did they take him?" Cassidy asked. From the way she sat with her shoulders hunched, staring into the heart of the fire, Antonio thought she almost looked guilty. Was she the reason The Reckoners had known where to find Cole? Antonio dismissed the idea immediately. He was

certain there was nothing romantic between Cassidy and
Cole, but it was obvious she cared for him.

"Likely to lure Megan into a trap. They're trying to get
rid of the Blood... Twins..."

Antonio's voice trailed off as a thought came into his
head. It was just a flicker of an idea, like the flare of a
poorly caught match before it burnt out.

"You don't sound very convinced," Juanita said.

Biting his lip, Antonio held up a finger, struggling to
hold onto the thought. Because something was starting to
slot into place. Something that meant this messy web
Antonio had found himself in stretched wider than he
could have imagined.

"Megan," he said, "do you know anything about some
lost gold?"

Leaning back, Megan spread out her palms. "Would I
be sittin' here in these threadbare clothes an' livin' inna
little house in the middle of the desert if I did? No. I ain't
heard of nuthin' 'bout any lost gold."

Antonio frowned and said, "Hmm," because that was
not the answer he had been expecting.

"But you think she should?" Cassidy prompted.

Antonio caught Juanita's eye. She shrugged.

"Our family has a legend," he said, "about some lost
Spanish gold that my great-uncle found when he was
prospecting in California. Apparently, he and three other
men found it together, but one of the men turned on the
others, killed them and took the gold for himself."

It took all of Antonio's willpower not to look at Cassidy
as he said these words.

"An' you think those outlaws took ma brother 'cause
they think he knows summit 'bout this gold?" Megan
asked, her eyebrows raised.

"Yes."

"Why?"

"Call it a hunch."

Megan paused for a moment, and then said, "Our pa used to tell us a story – 'bout our grandpappy comin' over from England fer the gold rush. He died without findin' any gold, but Pa said our grandma used to say that he found summit. But it'd bin stolen from him 'fore he were murdered."

"It matches up!" Cassidy cried. "Antonio, do you know who the other three men were?" Her cheeks were flushed, either from excitement at this revelation or from the heat of the fire – Antonio couldn't tell.

"One was a man from China – he was the grandfather of some of my family," Antonio explained. "My great-uncle, who was from Mexico, and another from England."

"The men from England – do you know their names?"

"Just one of them."

"So." Cassidy leaned forward, eyes shining. "What is it?"

"Not Hayes," Antonio almost said, but at the last moment he stopped himself, because Cassidy deserved to know. He didn't want her to suffer, but keeping her in the dark about her father's past felt crueller. So he said, "Benjamin Scarborough. He was the man who killed the other three and took the gold."

The change on Cassidy's face was immediate.

Her expression dropped and the blush drained from her skin.

Antonio's eyes darted towards Megan, searching for any suspicion in her expression. They couldn't risk Megan finding out Cassidy's true identity. Not now, but Megan was staring into the heart of the fire.

Cassidy must have had the same thought, because she whispered, "How awful. How could... How could... someone kill all those people?"

On the other side of the campfire, Megan laughed.

"Why does that not surprise me in the slightest?" She slapped her knee. "That bastard would shoot his own family for a pile of gold." Cassidy kept very still, her hands balled into fists on the tops of her thighs.

"And if we're working on the case of presumption," Juanita said, "it seems to me your grandfather might have been one of the three forty-niners that found the lost gold."

"An' were shot fer it." Megan spat into the fire. "First ma grandpappy an' then ma pa. Sounds like I git to take ma revenge twice on Mr Benjamin Scarborough."

"So The Reckoners think Cole knows something about the lost gold," Juanita said. "But how did they know Cole and Megan's grandfather was the second person from England?"

"Not sure," Antonio admitted. "Unless they were able to make a match from the family stories."

But even he didn't believe his own words. There was a missing thread in this messy web. And he wanted to end this conversation for Cassidy's sake.

As if reading his thoughts, Cassidy stood up and said, "I'm just going to take a turn before bed."

"I'll come with you," Antonio said, also standing.

"Be sure not to step on any rattlers," Megan called after them. "I hear they bite real bad."

Antonio followed Cassidy away from the camp.

"She's insufferable!" Cassidy spat. "I hope she gets bitten by a snake during the night. That would be one less problem to deal with!" Suddenly, she stopped and stuffed the knuckles of her right hand into her mouth. "I can't believe I just said that. I didn't mean it."

"You did," Antonio said.

"Cole would be distraught if she died," Cassidy said. "He loves her. More than anything."

They stood together with their backs to the camp, staring out into the dark desert.

"Is it true?" Cassidy asked. "What you said about my father?"

"Yes," Antonio said. "It's true." She sniffed and he offered her his handkerchief. Cassidy took it but just clutched it in her hand while she cried.

"You must hate me," she gasped.

"Of course I don't hate you."

"Then you hate my father."

"Your father believed in me." The sheriff star was cold beneath Antonio's fingers. "He gave me the job I'd always wanted – a job I never would have gotten otherwise."

Cassidy blew her nose and wiped her eyes on her sleeve. "Did you seek us out in New York? Were you looking for him to revenge your great-uncle?"

"No," Antonio said firmly. "I only found out about your father's involvement recently. Meeting you was by chance."

"What a chance." Antonio heard the smile in Cassidy's voice and smiled as well.

"Was coming home what you were hoping for?" Antonio asked. Cassidy laughed, but it was too hard, on the verge of being hysterical. Antonio winced. "Sorry. That was poorly put."

Still gasping for breath, Cassidy wiped her face again. "No. No, it hasn't been what I expected at all. But—" she took a deep breath "—I was right. Here is home. Not New York. But I knew that."

"Don't miss your friends?"

Cassidy guffawed, which surprised Antonio. New York Cassidy would never have made that sound, or unbuttoned the top of her shirt, or pushed her sleeves up, or worn her hair loose. He preferred this version of Cassidy. She seemed happier. Freer. He just hoped when her father got back that she would remain this version of herself. If she was allowed to stay.

"Those phonies," she said. "They only hung around me to please their parents. They weren't my real friends. You're my only real friend. You, and... Cole, I guess." There was an uncomfortable pause. "How have you found coming back?" Cassidy asked.

Antonio ran a hand down his face and found himself laughing in the same hard manner as Cassidy. Then Cassidy was laughing too, and they were laughing together in the desert.

"I don't think I'm home yet," Antonio said at last. "But I will be soon."

Chapter 36

Recollection

They'd started untyin' me at least.

They'd begun on what they called small torture – pressin' the ends of their hot cigars 'gainst ma bare skin, pushin' splinters unner ma nails an' hittin' me 'cross the face with wet clothes. Then they moved onto what they called medium torture – pushin' hot knives 'gainst ma skin, starvin' me, denyin' me sleep, or jest hittin' me over an' over while they kept askin', "Where's the gold? Where did your father hide the gold?"

I sob. I plead. I beg. I pray.

I hear 'em laughin' one time, sayin' they thought the Blood Twins'd be tougher 'n this. Pa's voice comes an' goes in ma head – *Cole, toughen up* – but even that's not enough to stop me from beggin' to make the pain stop.

An' no matter how many times I tell 'em I don't know where the gold is, they do not believe me.

How can I know when Pa never mentioned any gold?

I don't unnerstand why these folks think I know where it is.

I jest want 'em to stop.

I want the pain to stop an' then to go home to Megan an' Cassidy an' Rosie.

What can I do to make 'em stop?

I lose count of the days. The light that shines from 'hind the shutters gives me sum idea of what time of day it is, but time blurs into one continuous repeat: Wake up, git tied to the chair, bleed an' scream an' cry, black out. Wake up an' repeat.

Durin' one of the long dark nights, I try thinkin' 'bout Cassidy to lift ma spirits. But I jest end up feelin' guilty as I realise how she musta bin feelin' all that time we kept her locked in the parlour. 'Cause what she were feelin' back then – the fear, the shame, an' the constant tension – is what I'm feelin' now. How could I do summit like that to her?

Too wracked with guilt, I didn't sleep that night.

The first time there's a change is when I wake to the sound of voices.

The skin 'round ma eyes is swollen an' crusted with blood, so I open 'em slow. Ma room's dark, but there's light in the corridor outside, illuminatin' the figures of the two men standin' in the open door. I recognise one of 'em as the gang leader. The figure next to him's the same height, an' is familiar sumhow. But I can't git ma eyes fully open, an' I'm already startin' to lose consciousness. I can hear the two men talkin', but their voices sound like they're comin' from 'cross the other side of a canyon.

"... doesn't know," the leader says, who I now know is named Clint. "This is a waste of our time."

"He knows," says the second man, his voice sendin' 'nother jolt of recognition through me. "Keep tryin'. He'll remember soon enough."

How can I remember summit I don't know? I think an' slip back into unconsciousness.

Ma body jolts awake.

I sit up gaspin', ice cold water runnin' down ma face.

"Rise an' shine," Clint sings.

I crawl away, but two hands grab me unner the arms an' lift me off the floor. Ma wet clothes cling to me as they bind ma arms to ma sides an' tie ma feet togither. I should fight back. I should try to git away, but ma body an' mind hurts too much.

I jest want this to stop.

Perhaps if I keep silent they'll make it stop.

Even if it means I'll never see Megan or Cassidy 'gain, I want this to stop.

Not wantin' to see the way they're gonna make me hurt today, I close ma eyes an' pray silently, beggin' once 'gain fer His fergiveness. I need it more today 'n ever.

"Have you remembered yet?" Clint asks.

I shake ma head an' squeeze ma eyes shut.

He sighs. "All right then. String him up."

They loop the end of the long rope trailin' from ma bound feet over a roof beam, an' pull me into the air.

Gawd, fergive these men fer they do not know what they do. Fergive me fer ma sins. Fergive ma sis as well an' watch over her when I am gone. Protect her as I have bin unable to do – like I promised Pa I'd do on his death bed.

A tall man enters carryin' a deep bucket of water. He places it on the ground unner ma head.

"Last chance," Clint says. "Tell me where the gold is."

I begin to say, "I don't—" but they release the end of the rope holdin' me over the beam an' I plummet 'wards the bucket of water. Ma forehead hits the edge. I barely register the pain then ma head's enveloped. It burns ma nostrils, it fills ma mouth, soaks down ma throat an' crushes ma chest. I thrash, tryin' to tip the bucket over, tryin' to escape to git air, but no matter how much I thrash I stay in the water.

Then jest as I'm gonna drown, they pull me up.

I cough an' gasp. Ma vision's blurry an' a little dark 'round the edges, but I can still see Clint's face as he leans close to me.

"Final warnin', Cole," he says. "I grow tired of this game. Tell me where the gold is."

"Please," I sob. "Please. I don't know. Please. Please. I swear. I don't. Please. Please."

Clint tuts. He raises his hand.

"Pa," I say. "Pa, I'm sorry. I'm sorry. I tried. I really did, Pa. I'm sorry I'm so wea—"

The rope slackens. I fall 'wards the bucket.

Then I'm back in our kitchen at home, Pa slumped 'gainst the table, one of his hands in mine as I sit on the floor beside him. In the background, I can hear Dean calmin' Megan down while she rages, but then Pa's voice breaks through. He'd spoken to me in that moment. I remember now, an' 'though I'd heard the words he'd said, I never registered 'em.

But they come to me now.

They break through the memory, like the clearin' of the fog from a window.

'Cause in that moment, Pa'd said, "Listen, Cole. I've stolen sum gold from Mr Scarborough, an' I've hidden it. A lotta gold, an' I want you to go find it. Remember that lake we found that spring – the one in those caves? It's there. At the bottom of the water. Cole? Cole?"

Then he'd grabbed ma hands.

But the rest of the memory that'd always bin so clear to me were now jest hazy.

"Wait!" I shout.

But the water enters ma mouth 'gain. I thrash harder 'n the first time, harder 'n a caught fish on dry land.

They didn't hear me.

I'm gonna die.

They didn't hear me an' I'm gonna die. I'm gonna break ma promise to Pa. I'm gonna leave Megan an' Cassidy. I don't wanna die. Gawd, please. I don't wann—

Air floods ma lungs. I pull in great deep breaths. Ma throat burns, but I manage to croak, "I've remembered! I've remembered. I know where the gold is!"

The air feels very still, an' even though I can't see very well, I know all gazes in the room are turned to me. Clint's pale eyes bore into mine. He crouches 'fore me.

"Where?" he asks.

Chapter 37

Storming the Fortress

"It hasn't changed at all," Antonio said.

Cassidy leaned out from behind him and looked at the fortress on the edge of the lake. It was a large pale stone rectangular structure, with a high outer wall, two towers and a wooden gate. Antonio's grandparents along with Hu's grandmother and both sets of their then small families found the fortress and made it their own after the murder of Antonio's great-uncle and Hu's grandfather. What the building lacked in style, it made up for in the decorations that the generations of families had adorned it with. Papel picado, climbing plants and wind chimes covered the walls, while the ground around the fort was littered with red paper lanterns, mosaic flower pots, potted cactuses, stone dragons and mini pagodas. Although the plants looked like they needed some care.

"So Cole's in there sumwhere?" Megan said, eyeing the

building.

"Sure is," Juanita said.

"You two got any plans fer gittin' him out?"

Antonio caught Juanita's eye. "One or two."

"Huh," Megan said, rubbing her side. She was squinting against the bright sun, but Antonio thought that might be hiding her pained grimace. "Me too. See here?" She held up her left gun. "This is plan one, an' this." She held up her right gun. "This is plan two."

"Our plans involve a little more talking," Juanita said.

"I always let Florence an' Smithy do the talkin'."

"Are you for real?" Juanita said. "You've named your guns?"

"All the best outlaws name their guns."

"All the stupid ones, you mean."

"Stop it. Both of you," Antonio said.

Juanita shrugged, while Megan stuck her guns back into their holsters.

"No one tells me what to do," she said. "An' if it means goin' in there with both ma guns blazin', that's what I'll do."

"This is our home," Antonio said. "Let us handle this."

"An' that's ma brother in there." Megan's gaze met Antonio's. His body core chilled at the full force of the rage behind her eyes. "An' if I find one hair on his head outta place, I'll burn that place to the ground."

Cassidy's grip tightened on Antonio's shirt. He placed his hand over hers and gave them a light squeeze.

"All right then," he said. "Let's go say howdy."

The gates of the fortress were firmly shut, but someone sat in the squat open tower to the right of the gate, rifle in hand, watching their approach. Juanita gave Antonio a side-eye. Antonio knew she disapproved of his plan. The Reckoners had already proved they weren't open to reasoning with, but Antonio was willing to try to avoid bloodshed.

"Good morning," Antonio called up to the figure in the tower. He waited for them to say good morning back, but it never came. "I want to speak to Clint. Is he here?"

For a long time the silence stretched on. Then a glob of spit landed on the ground between the front hooves of Antonio's horse. "Fuck off."

"Waste of fuckin' time," Megan muttered.

Juanita sighed. "It's no use, Toni."

"Hold on. Let me keep trying," he whispered. He raised his voice again. "My name is Antonio Valdez. I'm the sheriff of Helena, Arizona. This is my family home. You are holding my family hostage, and you also recently kidnapped an acquaintance of mine – a Mr Cole Hayes. I would like to negotiate for their release."

"Release ma brother, you sunvabitch!" Megan yelled. Antonio winced and Cassidy renewed her grip on his shirt. She was tense against his back.

"The command of a sheriff ain't worth a nut out here," said a voice from the top of the wall. "In fact, sheriffs that're stupid enough to show their faces 'round here tend to git 'emselves shot."

"I could say the same for outlaws," Antonio called back, "but we're all reasonable people here. Why don't we work something out? You want the gold. I want my family, acquaintance and home returned safe and sound. How about you call Clint here and we—"

The shot bit the dust next to Antonio's horse. Antonio clung on and gripped the reins as the horse shrieked and reared. Cassidy's arms around his waist squeezed all the air from his lungs. Megan fired her pistols up at the tower.

"Fine," Juanita said, wheeling her horse around. "Then we'll take him by force."

Another shot rang over Antonio's head. Ducking, he kicked the horse into action and they galloped around the side of the fortress towards the west wall.

On one of those boredom days that only occurred during childhood, Antonio and Juanita had found the hidden passage in the west wall. It was very small – small enough that it had been a squeeze for Antonio to get through when he was a child. When Juanita had proposed the plan of using the passage to get into the fortress, he worried that it would be too small for them, or that someone else had bricked it up.

But after a little scrambling, they found it – a piece of stone that was thinner than the rest of them. Antonio pushed the wall several times to find the place that made the fake stone swing up to reveal a short passage. On the other side was the back of a fireplace. Being slight of build, Juanita got through easily by folding down her tall frame. Even though Antonio turned himself sideways, he still needed Juanita to pull him the rest of the way. Cassidy slipped right through, and it took a bit of wiggling, cursing and pulling to get Megan through.

They were in a small stone room on the side of the courtyard that took up the centre of the fort. As Antonio beheld the room on the other side of the fireplace, memories of his childhood assaulted him. A vase of dried flowers he had picked with Ai; a frayed sombrero hanging on the wall that had been his grandfather's; a painted scroll from China that Auntie Zhu claimed had been in her family for ten generations; a withered bonsai Auntie Ju had killed years ago but refused to throw away.

The sound of the clanging warning bell and the shouts of "Intruders! Intruders!" from the watchtower brought Antonio back to himself.

A shot from Juanita's rifle cracked across the courtyard and the bell and the lookout fell silent. Juanita ducked back into the room, a grim expression on her face.

"Stay here," Antonio told a wide-eyed Cassidy, who nodded. Antonio looked for Megan and found her already gone from the room.

"She's halfway across the courtyard," Juanita said.

"Why the blazes can't she stick to the plan?"

"To be honest, we didn't have a plan," Juanita pointed out.

"She'll end up hurting our family."

"Or killing any Reckoners she comes across on her way to finding her brother. We need to concentrate on rescuing our family, which we need to be quick about to ensure Megan doesn't come across them first. Now. Where are they going to be?"

Antonio sighed and ran a hand down his face. It came away covered in dust and sweat.

"Somewhere away from the gate. Somewhere hard to escape from. One of the buildings on the ramparts? The storage room on the west side is big enough."

"Let's start there, then."

"Cover me while I go across the courtyard."

Juanita raised her Winchester rifle to her shoulder. "Yes, Sheriff."

Cassidy touched Antonio's shoulder. "Good luck," she said.

He flashed her a reassuring smile, raised his pistol and headed for the door out into the courtyard. It was clear. Antonio scanned the ramparts, but there was no movement. Just as he was about to set foot outside, he heard a gunshot at the far end of the courtyard, in the direction where Megan had disappeared. Then a series of gunshots sounded down the far end. The exchange lasted for about a minute and then the guns fell silent. Antonio waited for a sign of movement, but none came. He wasn't sure if that was a good or bad sign.

Taking a deep breath, he moved into the courtyard. Halfway across, a gunshot cracked the air and a bullet struck the ground near his left foot in a spray of dirt. Antonio ducked and ran for the wide wooden ladder on the other side of the courtyard, weaving as best as he could as bullets continued to bite the dust near him. He dived behind the ladder and peered between the rungs. Two figures stood on the ramparts on top of the building he had exited, their guns pointed at him.

Antonio rested his pistol on a rung and fired three times. The figure on the left fell. The moment of triumph was brief. The second figure's next shot hit one of the ladder rungs. The wood shattered, spraying Antonio with splinters. Antonio staggered back, a hand raised over his eyes. A second shot reminded him to drop to the floor and make himself as small as possible. Something sharp dug into his cheek.

A bullet hit the floor near his foot. Antonio rolled away and stood up. Opening his eyes, he raised his pistol to locate the target. But just as he sighted them, a shot split the air. The figure crumpled to the ground. Juanita lowered her smoking rifle and waved at Antonio across the courtyard. Antonio waved back to let her know he was unhurt. He yanked the splinter from his cheek. Blood ran down his face and dripped onto his shirt.

"All right?" Juanita asked.

"Fine," Antonio said.

They ascended the ladder onto the ramparts. There was the renewed sound of gunfire from the southern side of the fort. Antonio guessed Megan's troubles weren't quite over yet.

The door to the building on top of the ramparts opened and a Reckoner stepped out. Antonio's heart kicked in his chest as the gang member's eyes widened. Antonio raised his pistol, but before he could fire Juanita's bullet took the Reckoner in the chest. The gang member fell back and lay still.

Both of them stayed still, waiting for anyone else to emerge from the building, but no one did. The southern side of the courtyard had fallen silent once again.

"Perhaps that's the last of them," Antonio half mused, half prayed.

"Let's hope so," Juanita said.

They pulled the Reckoner's body away from the door. Antonio reached for the latch but then stopped.

This was it.

His chest tightened. He felt sick.

He couldn't do this.

He should never have come back.

He should turn around right now and run back to Helena because coming here was a mistake. No one on the other side of that door was going to want anything to do with him, even if he so desperately wanted everything to do with them.

Juanita's hand wrapped around his own and squeezed. "Go on," she whispered. Antonio took a deep breath and pushed the door open—

—and screamed as something flat and hard slammed into his face. His nose crunched.

Reeling backwards, he covered his nose with one hand while the other held his gun out before him. Not that he could see who he was pointing it at, as he was squeezing his eyes shut from the pain cracking across his face.

"Antonio?"

Slowly, Antonio opened his eyes. White lights met him at first, but they quickly faded to reveal a woman standing in front of him, gripping a frying pan. She had more grey streaks in her hair and more lines on her face than the last time he had seen her, but Antonio's heart still let out the same pang at the sight of her. He lowered his gun.

"Mother," he whispered.

The frying pan hit the ground with a clang. Antonio let out a gasp as her arms closed around him and pulled him into an enveloping hug.

"My baby," she cried. "My baby."

Antonio's gun fell from his hand as he wrapped his arms around his mother and pressed his face into her shaking shoulder. Antonio held her tight as her tears soaked his shirt and as his own tears stained her dress.

"Is that Antonio?"

"I thought he was dead?"

Raising his face, Antonio saw the room filled with makeshift beds and members of his family. Some he had known all his life, and some small ones he didn't know. His breath caught at the sight of them. It put into context how long he had been away. Unsurprisingly, it was Auntie Ju and Uncle Andrés who had just spoken.

"I'm not dead," Antonio said.

Antonio and his mother broke apart. She reached up and pressed her hands against the sides of his face. Antonio knew his eyes were shining as much as his mother's.

"Sorry about your nose," she said.

Antonio laughed, which sent a fresh wave of pain across his face. "It's fine," he said. "If my son returned home after disappearing for thirteen years, I'd probably hit them in the face with a frying pan."

His mother's eyes slid over to Juanita. Antonio tensed, waiting for his mother's reaction.

"Hi, Auntie Valentina," Juanita said. "You haven't met Juanita yet."

"No," Antonio's mother said. "I haven't, but it's so good to have you home."

Antonio heard the air squeezed from Juanita's lungs as his mother wrapped her in a tight embrace. Juanita laughed and wrapped her arms around the small woman, ducking her head and pressing her face into the older woman's neck.

"Did you kill all those sons of bitches?" Auntie Ju asked in Cantonese.

"At least the ones we came across," Antonio replied in the same language. "How many are in the fort?"

"Not sure. Never saw them together in one place."

"I assume this isn't all the family?" Antonio said,

nodding at the full room.

"No. They're keeping the other half somewhere on the south side," Uncle Andrés said.

"Shit," Antonio said. Juanita was out the room before he was. They ran the ramparts together, heading towards the direction Megan had gone.

"I can hear voices," Juanita said. "Shouting."

A series of gunshots rang out before screaming started. Antonio gritted his teeth and pumped his legs as fast as he could. As they clattered down one of the ladders, a stream of people poured out into the courtyard. Megan pursued them, guns drawn.

"Megan!" Antonio shouted as Juanita raised her rifle. Megan turned her guns on them. Antonio raised his hands. Megan's eyes were wild, her chest heaving, her hand shaking.

"Megan," he said, as calmly as he could. "Megan, hold your fire. Now, what's going on?"

"What's goin' on?" Megan repeated, her voice low and dangerous. "What's goin' on?" she hissed. "What's goin' on is that your fuckin' family have killed ma brother! So I'm gonna kill every last one of 'em!"

"My family had nothing to do with it," Antonio said. "We will go after the rest of The Reckoners later. For now, let's see what we can do for Cole."

Acting braver than he felt, Antonio turned his back on Megan and strode into the building. In the first room he found the bodies of two dead Reckoners. He found another in the second room. Then in the third, he found Cassidy cradling Cole's head on her lap, tears streaking down her face. Antonio took a deep breath and forced himself to look down at Cole.

He sucked in a breath.

"Is he going to be all right?" she asked.

It took far too long for Antonio to find the pulse on Cole's neck and once he did it was faint. But it was there.

Antonio wasn't sure how with the state Cole's body was in.

"I'll get Auntie Zhu to look after him," he said. "There's nothing that woman can't cure. That's if we can stop Megan from shooting her first."

Chapter 38

New Deal

Sumone's pressin' a cold cloth to ma head, soothin' ma achin' body an' flushed face.

I sigh an' the cloth draws back.

"Cole?"

I open ma eye – jest one 'cause the other's so swollen it won't budge. I'm layin' onna bed inna small but brightly painted stone room. The shutters over the windows are open, but it's dark outside. Cassidy stares down at me, a drippin' cloth clutched in her hand.

"Oh," she says. "You woke up. Thank God."

She stands up an' crosses to the door.

"Antonio!" Cassidy calls out the door. "He's awake." She smiles an' crosses back to her seat by ma bed. "We were all so afraid you wouldn't wake up."

Is she a dream? Am I still strapped to that chair in that dark room, waitin' fer those men to torture me again?

Cassidy must see summit on ma face, 'cause she squeezes ma hand.

"I'm here, Cole."

The feelin' of her hand on mine an' the sound of her sweet voice makes summit crack inside me. I nod again, but this time tears spill from ma eyes.

Then the memory of our last conversation comes back to me an' all the joy at findin' her beside me drains outta me. I wish I could die right here.

I never thought I'd be glad to see the sheriff, but when Sheriff Valdez enters the room a wave of relief so strong passes through me I almost reach out to grab his hand as he approaches ma bedside. Juanita comes in after him an' leans in the doorway, Cassidy standin' beside her. There's no sign of Megan.

"Good to see you're awake," he says. "We were very worried about you."

"When didja all git here?" I croak.

"This morning," Sheriff Valdez says, takin' the seat Cassidy'd bin occupin'. His nose's swollen an' red, an' bent slightly to one side, like he's bin punched. "But Clint and a lot of the gang are missing. I don't suppose you know where they've gone?"

I lick ma dry lips. Cassidy must notice, 'cause she comes over with a glass of water.

"Thanks," I croak as I take it from her. Ma throat an' lips hurt a lot less once I've drained it. "They've gone to a cave system, jest outside of Helena."

"Why?" Sheriff Valdez asks.

"To git the gold ma pa hid there – at the bottom of a lake."

"The gold your grandfather found in the gold rush, along with Benjamin Scarborough?"

I nod. "That's what that fella told me. He said..." I glance at Cassidy but quickly look away.

"Go on," she whispers.

"He said that Mr Scarborough murdered ma grandpa an' the two other men to git the gold. An' that ma pa stole the gold from Mr Scarborough an' hid it."

Sheriff Valdez an' Juanita exchange a look. "So that's why they kidnapped you," Sheriff Valdez says. "But how did they know your father stole the gold from Mr Scarborough?"

The sheriff's question catches me off guard, 'cause I haven't thought 'bout that. How did they known Pa'd stolen the gold from Mr Scarborough when Megan an' me hadn't known?

"I don't know," I say.

"And did you know all this time where the gold was?"

"No. Well, I guess, sorta. I'd forgotten. Pa told me 'fore he died, but I didn't remember that he'd done so 'til... Well, 'til yesterday."

"Can you show us where the gold is?"

Megan says, "An' why should we?"

I don't miss the sheriff's eyeroll as he looks 'wards the door where Megan's leanin'.

"Because we made a deal," he reminds her.

"No," she says, stickin' her thumbs through her belt. "We made a deal to work togither 'til The Reckoners were taken care of. Nuthin' were said 'bout any gold. This changes everythin', 'cause by rights that gold belongs to me an' Cole."

Juanita scoffs an' Sheriff Valdez's eyebrows rise.

"Our grandpappy found it," Megan says, "an' then our pa stole it back from the man who took it from him. So by rights it's ours."

"Your grandfather wasn't the only one who found it," Cassidy points out. "By rights, it equally belongs to you and Cole, Antonio's family and m—" Ma heart jumps in ma chest, but at the last moment Cassidy catches herself an' says, "And Mr Scarborough."

"That murderin' sunvabitch don't git a say in this,"

Megan spits. "He had the gold an' he lost it. It's mine an' Cole's now."

"It won't be if The Reckoners get there first," Sheriff Valdez points out. "And they've got a good day's head start on us. The situation has not changed. If you and Cole go after the gold alone, you will have to deal with a whole gang by yourselves, and looking at the state both of you are in I don't think that's going to end well."

Megan straightens with a scowl.

"If you want a shot at getting that gold," Sheriff Valdez continues, "then continue to work with Juanita and I. We'll take care of The Reckoners together, and the prize of the gold at the end will just be an added bonus for the victor. So, Cole, can you show us where the gold is?"

I glance at Megan, who's givin' the sheriff one of her mean stares, but Florence an' Smithy are still in their holsters, so I nod in agreement.

"Good. Get some rest tonight. We'll set out first thing in the morning." There's a moment's pause. Sheriff Valdez reaches out an' pats me on the shoulder. "I'm glad you're all right."

I jest nod, not wantin' to speak.

Sheriff Valdez an' Juanita leave the room. Cassidy looks like she's gonna stay, but when Megan doesn't move, she goes, closin' the door 'hind her.

The moment we're alone, Megan seems to grow smaller.

"Are you all right?" she asks. "Truly?"

"I'll be fine," I say, forcin' a smile. "Truly."

"Good," she says.

"How's your side?"

"Holdin' up. Hurts a bit after all the ridin'." She reaches fer her shirt to check the wound but then changes her mind an' drops it. Ma stomach twists at the sight of the blood on the inside of the material.

"Perhaps you should change the bandages," I say.

Megan nods. Fer sumone who injures others almost onna daily basis, Megan's never bin great at lookin' after her own wounds. "Didja ride here on Rosie?"

"Yes. She's out the back with the other horses."

I nod an' a little jump of excitement runs through me at the idea of seein' Rosie again.

Megan stands in the middle of the room, chewin' on her bottom lip like she wants to say summit more. But then she turns 'wards the door.

"Megan," I say, ma throat dry, "didja kill anyone today? When you were tryin' to rescue me?"

Any traces of meekness disappear from Megan's expression. "'Course I did," she says. "Ain't no sunvabitch allowed to hurt ma brother an' git away with it."

I slump back 'gainst the pillows. "Then it's broken," I say, starin' at the ceilin'.

"What's broken?"

"Ma promise to Gawd. The one I made to Him to save your life after you got shot at the bank." I take a deep breath, feelin' a wetness 'hind ma eyes. "I promised Him that we'd give up our life as the Blood Twins."

"Cole," Megan says, her voice heavy with irritation, "don't be dumb. There ain't no man in the sky that saved ma life that day. It were thanks to the doctor an' ma body. It ain't got nuthin' to do with a promise you made to sumone that don't exist."

"But—"

"Cole," she says, her voice dangerously low, "there ain't no one who's gonna stop me from livin' the life that I want."

She leaves me on ma own to reckon with what I've done.

I were a fool. A desperate fool to believe that Megan'd change her ways.

Now it'll only be a matter of time 'fore He casts His judgement down upon us.

Chapter 39

Welcome Home

It wasn't evident to Antonio how big the family had grown until everyone sat down for dinner, squeezed onto two tables outside in the courtyard. Those who had been children when he left were now adults with small children of their own. Several teenagers who he had never met introduced themselves to Antonio. There were a few external newcomers who had married into the family, and also some who had left for various reasons. Although apparently none of them had run away in the dead of night – something that Auntie Ju told him with a snide side-eye that made Antonio squirm.

But when he sat down to eat and heard the mix of Spanish and Cantonese conversation around him, the final tension left his shoulders. He was finally home – a place he didn't have to pretend to be anyone else, a place where he fitted like a tile in a mosaic.

Cassidy sat next to Antonio, looking very confused. She eyed the mixture of Mexican and Chinese cuisine on the table with suspicion. Antonio had to pile food into her bowl to get her to touch any of it. Cole was still in bed, and Megan had disappeared somewhere.

"So, your name is Juanita now?"

Juanita's smile was so tight that it almost reached her ears. He couldn't blame her, given the number of times her family had already asked her that question. Especially Uncle Andrés, who had asked three times. Antonio would have refused to keep answering it by now, but Juanita kept smiling and playing the saint.

"Yes," she said, again. "My name is now Juanita."

"Right." Uncle Andrés and Auntie Thomasina exchanged a look. "And you're wearing woman's clothes now?"

"That's because I am a woman," Juanita said, helping herself to another tamale.

"Right," Uncle Andrés said again. There followed another exchange between him and Auntie Thomasina. As soon he opened his mouth again, Antonio started to say something to interrupt, but his mother got there first.

"I've never thought about how lucky I am," she said, "to have been born into my body. I don't think any of us stop to consider how lucky we are to have been born into our bodies until we meet someone who makes us understand that." She reached out across the table and took Juanita's hand. "God works in mysterious ways. He throws us many trials in life to overcome, but He will always support us in overcoming them. As we should all be doing for each other. And I am so blessed to have my daughter back with me, looking more like herself than she has ever done."

Juanita's bottom lip trembled as she gripped Antonio's mother's hand.

"Thank you," she said. "But please don't think of me as

being unlucky. I know who I am. It was hard at the start. I felt so alone, but after years of travelling and meeting other people, I understood there were more people out there like me. They helped me understand myself." She looked at Uncle Andrés and Auntie Thomasina. "And I became stronger because of it. I know myself. And no one can make me doubt myself."

Antonio's mother's eyes shined. "I didn't think of you as being unlucky. Not for a moment."

Antonio's eyes grew wet and he had to look away to stop the tears from spilling over. Uncle Andrés and Auntie Thomasina glanced at each other again, but they looked a touch more sheepish than they had done before.

"You're still too skinny, though," Auntie Ju said, switching the conversation to Cantonese. "You were always too skinny. Antonio, put some more food on her plate. You could also do with eating some more."

"I've got some old clothes that I haven't worn in years," Auntie Zhu said to Juanita. "They don't fit me anymore and Fen doesn't want them, but you're welcome to them if you want."

"You won't want them," Fen muttered and then quickly raised her rice bowl to her face as Auntie Zhu shot her a look.

"Thank you," Juanita said. "I would love to have them."

"Would you like a new Chinese name?" Auntie Zhu asked. "J— I mean, it was the same as your old name."

"I would love one," Juanita said. "Could you think of some for me to pick out?"

Auntie Zhu patted Juanita's hand. "Your aunties and I will have a think. It'll be easier to name you now we know who you are."

"I hope that doesn't work against me," Juanita said, with a smile. But Auntie Zhu just nodded gravely. Antonio raised his bowl to hide his laugh at the look on Juanita's face.

"It's been boring around here without you and Toni," Mei said. "I've missed the two of you. It'll be so much more fun now that you're back."

"Yes," Auntie Thomasina said, clapping her hands, obviously delighted to have a safe topic to talk about. "We've missed your guitar duets, and your chicken mole, J — Juanita. No one's been able to recreate your recipe."

"Now that gang is gone and Antonio and Juanita have come home," Auntie Zhu said, "we can be a family again."

"Not all the gang members are dead," Mei pointed out. "And Alejandro is not here."

"I did notice their leader is not here," Antonio said.

"They left yesterday," Antonio's mother said. "For once not taking half of us with them as hostages. Didn't say where they were going."

"We know. We're going to go after them, and we're going to bring Alejandro back. I..." Taking a deep breath, Antonio raised his head to meet Auntie Thomasina's eyes across the table. "I promise to bring him back alive. I'm sorry I wasn't able to do the same for Elìas."

Silence followed Antonio's words. The pounding of his heart grew louder as he waited for his aunt's response.

At last she said, "What happened wasn't your fault. I told Elìas before you left to stick close to everyone and not to stray too far away. But—" she sniffed and swiped her fingers under her eyes "—he was a stubborn boy. We should have sent someone with you. We put too much responsibility on your shoulders."

A weight lifted from Antonio's shoulders. He ducked his head and reached for the cross around his neck, whispering a silent prayer. His eyes grew damp again. On either side of him, Juanita and his mother placed their hands on his back.

"But," Auntie Thomasina added, her voice cracking, "if you could bring Alejandro back alive, I would be so grateful. He's lost his way, and I know it's not too late for him to see sense."

"I'll do my best," Antonio promised.

"Where did you say Ai, Hu and Silvana are buried?" Uncle Yufei asked.

"In the churchyard in Helena," Antonio said. "I hope you don't mind. I wanted them buried somewhere I knew they would be safe."

"No," Auntie Silvia said. "It's better that they're together."

There was a moment of silence as everyone bowed their heads and thought about their lost family members. Auntie Silvia wiped a tear away and Uncle Yufei put an arm around her shoulder. Antonio swallowed the lump in his throat and crossed himself.

"Now that Antonio and Juanita are back," Auntie Zhu said, "we can finally be a family again. You two have plenty to catch up on."

"We can't stay," Antonio said.

Silence radiated around the table. Mei dropped her fork.

"What?" she asked.

"I can't speak for Juanita, but I have a job." Antonio touched the star on his left breast. "I'm needed in Helena."

"But you'll be staying here for a few days?" Auntie Thomasina said.

Antonio shook his head. "We'll be leaving tomorrow morning. I would leave tonight, but Cole's condition is too bad to travel. The Reckoners already have a head start."

"Just stay tonight," Antonio's mother said, "and we'll work out the rest later."

"I've made up your old room," Antonio's mother said, pushing the bedroom door open.

A wave of nostalgia hit Antonio as the door swung open. The murals on the stone walls Juanita and he had painted over the years, the two single beds pushed up against opposite walls, their small shared chest of drawers scarred from years of being kept in a room with two adventurous children, and their collection of makeshift toys on wobbly shelves.

"The bed looks smaller than I remember," Antonio said, throwing his pack onto his bed.

"I don't think I'll fit into mine anymore." Juanita stretched out on her bed. The ends of her feet stuck out over the end.

"The monsters will get you if you sleep like that," Antonio said. To his surprise, Juanita's expression grew uncomfortable. "Seriously? You still believe there are monsters lurking under your bed?"

"Of course not," she said, but she sat up and drew her feet back onto the mattress.

"I keep meaning to ask you." Antonio's mother tapped the bandage over Antonio's ear. "What's this about?"

"Oh." Antonio pulled the bandage away to show his whole ear beneath. "Nothing. Just something I wear to make it easier for people to understand."

"Well," his mother said, "make sure you change it. It's looking grubby."

"Yes, Mother."

"I'll pack some spare bandages for you before you go. What time are you leaving tomorrow?"

"As soon as it gets light," Antonio replied.

"I'll try to be awake but come see me if I'm not, all right?"

Before Antonio could nod, his mother's arms wrapped around him and crushed him to her. He felt her make a gesture behind his back, and soon Juanita's long arms were around the both of them.

"I'm so glad you found each other again," Antonio's mother said. Drawing back, she placed a hand on each of their cheeks. "Take care of one another," she said. "I love you both, and whatever you decide to do, I will support you every step of the way."

With a final squeeze, she wished them goodnight and left the room.

"Guess we'd better get some sleep," Antonio said.

Even though the two of them had slept in the same room for the past few days, and had slept in there together more times than Antonio could count, the atmosphere felt different. Charged, like the desert before a thunderstorm.

Choosing to ignore it, Antonio turned his back on Juanita to give her some privacy while he also removed his jacket and boots. And heard the scrape of wood against stone. He turned and saw Juanita pulling her bed across the room towards his.

"Give me a hand?" she asked.

Antonio stared at her. "What are you—"

"Shush! Just help me."

With his heart beating hard in his chest, Antonio helped Juanita push her bed next to his. Then she turned her back to him and continued to strip off her outer layers like nothing had happened. Antonio's fingers trembled as he unbuttoned his jacket.

"We don't have to do anything," Juanita said. Her words were followed by the sound of heavy fabric dropping to the ground, which made Antonio freeze. "I just want to be near you while we sleep."

"Worried about the monsters?" Antonio managed to croak out. He laughed at the indignant noise Juanita made.

Antonio got into bed first while Juanita blew out the candle. Every hair on Antonio's body raised as he heard her slide into bed. He hadn't been planning on going anywhere near her – he knew he should stick to his side of the bed and let her stay on hers for the sake of protecting both of their virtues. But hearing the rustle of her movin' across the sheets and the approaching warmth of her body, he couldn't help but reach out.

Juanita slid into his arms and nestled against his body like a missing puzzle piece.

They both sighed and Antonio thought he might die from happiness.

"How you feeling?" she asked.

Antonio paused. "Relieved, I guess. That apart from getting hit in the face with a frying pan, they didn't set upon me in revenge."

Juanita snorted. "They were never going to hurt you. I told you, everyone knew it was an accident."

A wave of grief washed over Antonio, bringing tears to his eyes. He sniffed. "It made me realise. I wish... I wish I hadn't stayed away for so long. I've missed out on so much."

Juanita pulled one of Antonio's hands up to her mouth and kissed his knuckles.

"Do you want to talk about it?" she asked.

Antonio sighed. The hairs on the back of Juanita's neck tickled his nose. "Not tonight. Tonight I need to rest. But I will take you up on that offer."

"Anytime."

"How are you feeling?"

Juanita sucked in a deep breath and released it slowly. "Relieved, also. When Uncle Andrés and Auntie Thomasina wouldn't shut up I... I thought the worst was about to happen. But when everyone changed their tune, I almost burst into tears I was so relieved."

"There was no need for Uncle Andrés and Auntie Thomasina to be so invasive."

"They've always been that way, though. Guess if anyone was going to give me trouble it would have been those two." She sighed again. "At least we know we can come home again, now."

"Yeah. If we survive tomorrow, that is."

"We'll survive and we'll bring Alejandro home. Even if we have to knock some sense into him in order to do it."

Antonio paused. "Is it wrong that the idea of doing that makes me feel happy?"

"He did try to kill you. I think that's a justified emotion."

Antonio yawned. "Guess we'd better get some rest, then."

"Yes. Good idea. Night."

"Night."

They fell asleep to the sound of crickets chirruping outside their window.

Chapter 40

Truth

The door of ma room opens. Half asleep, I crack open ma eyes. Cassidy stands frozen in the doorway.

"Sorry," she whispers. "I should have realised you'd be asleep. I'll leave you in peace."

"No," I say, strugglin' to sit up. "No, it's all right. I— Ah!" A tearin' pain rips through ma side. Then Cassidy's there beside me.

"It's all right," Cassidy says, lowerin' me back down onto the mattress. "I've got you."

I'm in so much pain I don't register Cassidy's hand on ma arm or how close she is 'til she steps back from me.

"Are you going to be able to ride tomorrow?" Cassidy asks, sittin' down in the seat beside the bed.

"I'll hafta," I say. "We've wasted enough time thanks to me."

"Have you had anything to eat?"

"Yes. Sheriff Valdez's ma bought me summit."

"She's nice."

"Yeah. She is."

"The food was rather strange, though," Cassidy blurts out. "And I couldn't understand half of what they were talking about at dinner. I was rather hoping I could come in here and have some normal conversation."

"Well," I say, "I warn't sure if you wanted to talk to me... Not after our last conversation."

Cassidy shifts uneasily in her seat. "I've replayed it so many times. I said and did some awful things. I'm sorry. I... I shouldn't have said what I did about the church, but I wanted to hurt you. Because you hurt me by pushing me away."

"It's fine. I too said sum awful things."

"No," Cassidy protests. "No, you didn't. I knew how you felt about me, but I... I used you." She lets out a breath. "I realise that now. At the time I was so desperate to get away – from Helena, from Megan, from Father's estate – that I didn't consider I might hurt you."

"What woulda happened," I ask, "if we'd run away togither that night? Wouldja've stayed with me? Or wouldja've jest used me to git to Los Angeles?"

Cassidy rubs her dress fabric between her fingers. She doesn't meet ma eyes as she says, "I don't know. I... I thought about you every day for the past six years, imagining the day I would see you again, but..."

"I've changed," I say.

Cassidy nods. "I think it was the idea of you that I loved. I... I liked you when we were kids, but... when I was in New York I blew it all out of proportion. It was..." She sobs. "It was easier to believe that someone was going to come save me than to save myself." Furiously, she swipes her fingers unnerneath her eyes. "Which is so stupid because how can I ever go into politics to help people if I can't help myself?"

I avert ma eyes so she can compose herself. Once Cassidy stops sobbin', I swallow an' say, "The church. Do you... do you believe that me an' Megan'd do summit like that?"

Cassidy sniffs. "Not you. I can't believe you could do anything like that. But Megan... yes... I think she could."

"Do you wanna hear our take of what happened? 'Bout what really happened?"

Cassidy nods.

"Truth is it were an accident." I swallow. "'Though accident don't seem like a big enough word to describe that day.

"We'd only bin robbin' fer a few months when Megan told me we were gonna rob a church. I didn't wanna go. I hated the idea of robbin' a church, but you know how me an' Megan are. I can't go 'gainst summit she wants to do.

"We snuck into the church 'fore anyone else were there an' hid unner the altar. Halfway through the service we jumped out. Megan held her gun 'gainst the Reverend's head, while I took guns an' money off the congregation. We took all the silver we could find." I shiver. "I felt Gawd's eyes on me the whole time.

"When we left the church, we blocked the entrance from the outside, so we'd have time to git away without anyone followin' us. We got on our horses an' rode away."

I glance at Cassidy an' me love what I see in her eyes. Relief. Relief that we hadn't done what she feared we had.

"Then when we were a little outside the town, I glanced back. I don't know why I did. It were like sumone pulled a string on the back of ma head.

"An' I saw the smoke.

"It warn't a lotta smoke, only a thin snake of it, but it were comin' from the church.

"It musta bin sum sorta accident. Sumone musta knocked over a candle. But they were all locked in there.

All the children an' their mas an' pas. All of 'em burnin' to death.

"I wanted to help. I wanted to ride back an' free 'em, but Megan said no. She said we shouldn't help 'em – that they'd got 'emselves into that mess an' they should git 'emselves outta it.

"But I ignored her. I turned Hattie 'round an' rode back to town.

"Most of the townfolk'd bin in the church fer the service, but a few of 'em hadn't. They were dressed in dusty travellin' clothes, so I guessed they'd bin passin' through an'd come runnin' when they'd sin the smoke. We struggled to unlock the door togither.

"By the time I'd arrived back to the town the smoke'd gotten thicker. The fire were gittin' fiercer, spreadin' quick through the church an' roarin' out the windows an' roof. I heard the first screams.

"The door wouldn't open. While we were strugglin' summit broke through one of the windows. It warn't 'til it started screamin' did I realise it were a person. They rolled on the ground, but the flames wouldn't go out. They screamed 'til they stop movin'.

"By the time we got the door open, the smoke were seepin' outta the buildin' an' creatin' a fog 'round the outside. The plume of smoke musta've bin sin fer miles 'round.

"Only five folk came outta that church. Their clothes were black an' they were coughin' an' chokin' with wide bloodshot eyes. It were the looks on their faces I'll never fergit. It were like they'd sin the gate to hell.

"I fled the scene as fast as I could. The folk who survived didn't recognize me, but I couldn't stay there. There were nuthin' I could do. I rode back to Megan. She were in the same spot I'd left her, starin' at the town an' the plume of smoke risin' from the church. She said nuthin' to me. Jest punched me."

Cassidy covers her mouth.

"Afterwards she gave me a lecture, remindin' me why we were doin' this, how this were what Pa woulda wanted. She said this needed to be done whatever the cost. An' even though she were shoutin' at me that whole time, I could see how upset she were by what'd jest happened. I know she didn't like me helpin' those folk, but she also hated herself fer not helpin'."

"She's so proud," Cassidy murmurs.

I breathe out. "I guess she is. She's never spoken 'bout that day again, but I know she feels jest as bad 'bout it as I do."

"Do you ever think about it?"

I laugh. It sounds wrong. Too high. "All the time. I dream 'bout it. An' I... ma head keeps takin' me back to that day when things git too intense an' when I smell smoke. I ain't stepped foot inside a church since that day, 'cause whenever I see one... it's always on fire an' shrouded in screams. It's Gawd's way of punishin' me fer that day. It's His way of tellin' me I ain't fit to set foot inside His house again."

I wait fer Cassidy to speak. Ma chest feels heavy an' ma head hurts. Should I've told her? Perhaps sumthin's are better left buried. Then two arms wrap gently 'round ma neck. Strands of long auburn hair fall 'cross ma face.

"Accidents happen," Cassidy says in ma ear. "It wasn't your fault the church caught fire. Yes, you barred their escape, but you went back to help them. You cared about those people." Cassidy takes ma head in her hands an' lifts ma eyes to hers. "You tried. That's all God asks you to do in a situation like that. And you said something made you look back at the church. I think that was God. I think he turned your head to see that smoke so you could run back and help those people."

Choked with emotion, all I can do is nod.

"Thanks, Cassidy."

"Cole," Cassidy says, "if you hate being a bandit so much, then why do you do it?"

"'Cause Megan says it's what Pa woulda wanted – we're carryin' on his legacy. Doin' what he wanted us to do."

"But do you think this is what he really would have wanted? It isn't what I think he wanted you to do."

"No," I say. "I don't think it's what he wanted either, but I made a promise to him that I'd look after Megan 'til she were settled. So as long as she wants to do this, I hafta do it too."

"Have you told her what you think?"

"No. I don't think she'd unnerstand."

"You want to know what I think?"

"Always."

Cassidy gives me a coy smile. "I think you should try talking to her. Just give it a go and see what she says."

"Sure," I say, jest to settle Cassidy's mind. "I'll talk to her." Wantin' to turn this conversation quickly around, I said, "Once we've found the gold, will you go to Los Angeles?"

"Yes," Cassidy said. "At least, I won't be going back to my father."

"Don't you miss him at all?"

"No. Not really." Cassidy stares at her clasped hands in her lap. "Truthfully," she says, "I don't want to see him again, Cole. Being with you and Megan has made me realise how... wrong my life was before. When I lived in Helena, I knew that something was off about the way he treated me – not allowing me out past the house perimeter, and not allowing me to go to school like you and Megan did. But after we moved to New York, I realised how paranoid he was that someone would take me away from him." Cassidy sniffs an' wipes her eyes on the back of her sleeve. I wanna reach out an' touch her hand, but I keep ma arms by ma side. "Guess I know why now. Murdering three people to rob them of the gold you promised to split would make anyone paranoid. Guess he thought their ghosts were after him."

"Or their families," I say.

Cassidy laughs. "Yes. I guess between you and Megan, and Antonio's and Juanita's family there are a lot of people after Father's head."

"I won't let Megan harm you," I say, "or your pa. I promise."

Cassidy's hands squeeze mine. "Thank you, Cole."

We sit like that fer a while, listenin' to the crickets chirrupin' outside the window. I'm so at peace in that moment, I drift offta sleep again, but I force ma eyes to stay open. I wanna enjoy this moment fer as long as it lasts, 'cause this could be the last moment Cassidy an' me have like this togither.

"I was so lonely in New York," Cassidy whispers in the low light. "I missed you."

"I missed you," I say. "I would've written, but..."

But I couldn't write an' Cassidy's pa'd left no address. An' what sorta man writes to the daughter of the man his pa'd jest robbed?

"I thought about writing to you," Cassidy says. "I even put pen to paper a few times, but every time I did this huge well of guilt overtook me, because my father killed your father. I couldn't imagine a scenario where you wanted to hear from me. What sort of man wants to get a letter from the daughter of the man who killed his father... and also his grandfather?"

"I would've wanted to hear from you," I say, which makes Cassidy bite her bottom lip. I can tell she's doin' her best to hold back the tears. I give her hand a squeeze an' she takes a deep breath.

As the silence between us drags on, the weight on ma chest grows heavier. I know what Cassidy wants me to do an' what she wants me to say, but I can't give her what she wants.

There's no future fer the two of us, even if I love her an' even if a small part of her still loves me.

Not while ma promise to Pa still stands.

Chapter 41

Ecstasy of Gold

Antonio said goodbye to his family as the top curve of the sun broke the horizon, washing the sky orange and the desert purple. Most of the family were still asleep when Antonio, Juanita, Cassidy, Cole and Megan packed up their things, saddled the horses and gathered outside the fortress gates, but Antonio's mother, Auntie Zhu, Mei, Fen and Uncle Andrés woke before the dawn to see them off.

The tears in the backs of Antonio's eyes grew in volume with each hug he exchanged and goodbye he said. Fen clapped him on the back as they drew apart and said, "At least you said goodbye this time," which sent a sickening wave of guilt through him. It must have shown on his face, because Fen muttered, "Jeez, it was a joke, Toni."

After their hug, Uncle Andrés clapped a hand to Antonio's shoulder. "Don't be a stranger, Toni," he said.

Antonio could only nod, too choked for words.

His mother clung to him with a desperation that bruised Antonio's ribs, but it was her wet sniff and the feeling of her tears against his cheek that finally cracked him. She pressed her forehead to his. They stayed like that for longer than they had time for, neither speaking. They didn't need to. Antonio could feel his mother's heart breaking all over again, and he knew she could see the tears on his face. She brushed her fingers across his cheeks.

"Sorry again about your nose," she said at last.

"It'll heal," Antonio replied. "I'll come back when I'm handsome again."

"You'll always be handsome," she said.

At last they mounted the horses. It took both Juanita and Megan to get a very pale Cole into the saddle. He was in no fit state to be riding, but without him they wouldn't be able to find the gold. Megan mounted behind him and wrapped a secure, almost protective arm around her brother. Antonio hoped he didn't pass out on the ride.

As they set off everyone – apart from Megan – turned and waved goodbye to the small figures standing in front of the fort. They soon lowered their arms, but Antonio didn't stop glancing back until the fort had been swallowed by the horizon.

"Is this the place?"

"Yes," Cole said.

Antonio stared up at the ledge twenty feet above them.

"How the blazes do we get up there?" he asked.

"We climb," Megan said, getting down from her horse. Without her support Cole swayed, but Megan caught him before he could fall. Antonio was surprised Megan could act with such tenderness towards someone.

"You'd better stay here, Cole," Antonio said.

"No," Cole said. Megan helped him down to the

ground, where he leaned heavily on her. Antonio hadn't missed the moments on the ride where Cole had fallen asleep. "I'm comin' with you. There's a network of caves at the back that you'll need me to navigate."

"Can't Megan show us the way?" Antonio asked. "You're really in no fit state to be going anywhere."

"If ma brother says he's fine," Megan snapped, "then he's fine. Stop gripin' like an old woman an' let's git climbin'."

Antonio decided that perhaps he had spoken too soon about Megan's tenderness. He got down from his horse and helped Cassidy down. Juanita was already at the bottom of the rockface, her rifle slung across her back, looking up at the ledge above her.

Antonio scanned the landscape.

"Is there another way into the cave?" he asked.

"Not that I know of," Cole replied. "Why?"

"If The Reckoners are already here," Antonio said, "I expected to see their horses."

"Perhaps someone stole them," Cassidy suggested. "Or they ran away."

"Or perhaps they've already found the gold an' left," Megan said. She spat on the ground an' touched the handles of her guns. "'Though I'm hopin' that ain't the case."

"I guess we'll find out," Antonio said. Looking up at the rockface he clapped his hands together. "Right. Let's get going."

Juanita scaled the rockface like a spider, then extended her long arms down and helped the rest of them over the ledge. Megan grunted in pain as she stretched her side muscles and pulled herself up. She leaned against the cave wall with a hand pressed to her side afterwards. Cassidy took the longest to climb up. Despite his injuries, Cole came down and gave her a boost when she got stuck. His face twisted in pain as he hauled himself over the ledge a second time. Once he was on it, Antonio headed to the back of the cave, where the floor sloped down towards a letterbox opening to the cave system.

"How far is it from here to the lake?" Antonio asked.

"Not far," Cole said. "A coupla minutes, perhaps."

But they had only stepped through the letterbox opening when they heard the gunshots ahead. Antonio, Juanita and Megan drew their guns, while Cole moved in front of Cassidy.

"I'll lead the way," Antonio whispered. "Cole, direct me."

In a line they moved through the caves of grooved undulating red stone. There were enough parts of the ceiling open to the sky for them not to use lanterns. If Antonio wasn't so worried about what they would find up ahead, he would have stopped to admire the beauty of his surroundings. As it was, he was focused on the noises echoing in the tunnels.

They reached a point where the cave started to narrow again. Cole pointed ahead at the second letterbox opening and said, "It's jest through there."

"Juanita," Antonio said, "up front with me. Megan, Cole, you come next." He looked at Cassidy, who was very pale. "You, stay here. Do you have a gun, Cole?"

Cole shook his head. Juanita said, "Here," and pulled her pistol from her belt. She handed him her ammo belt, which Cole strapped across his chest.

"Remember," Antonio said, "let me talk to Alejandro. The rest are fair game."

"An' I told you I don't take orders from you," Megan said, checking her revolver barrel. She spun it around and snapped it back into place. "That gold is ours, Sheriff. An' Cole an' I will do anythin' to git it."

"Remember that we have a deal," Antonio said, his voice low.

"Yes, to 'deal' with those bastards, warn't it? So let's

go deal with 'em."

With that, Megan dashed through the narrow gap. Cole gave Antonio and Juanita one last apologetic look and chased after his sister.

"Come on," Juanita said and followed them through.

Antonio sighed. Cassidy looked very nervous. "Stay here," he repeated and got a nod in reply.

Moving as fast as he could, Antonio squeezed through the gap and came out in a large flooded cave. A bay of sand swept around the edge in a crescent moon shape, while the rest of it was flooded. Tunnels branched off the cave, disappearing into the dark. The only light illuminating the space came from the lanterns dotted around on the sand. Between two of the lanterns he saw something catch the light. Something small and round.

A coin.

So they had already found the gold.

But where was it?

Antonio scanned the cave, but the reasons for the earlier gunshots remained unclear. Two members of The Reckoners were stood at one of the tunnel entrances only a couple of metres away from Antonio, Juanita, Cole and Megan, their guns drawn. Then he saw the two bodies floating face down in the lake, both dead.

Had someone in the gang turned traitor on the rest of them and taken the gold for themselves? Or had one half of the group turned on the other?

The two gang members nearby had their backs turned to them, unaware of the four people who had just entered the cave. Antonio made to give the order for the others to sneak up on them and knock them out, but Megan raised her guns.

The first figure slammed into the cave wall as a bullet took him in the chest. He crumpled to the floor. The second screamed as another one took him in the gut.

"Two down." Megan sneered.

Juanita was about to say something, then her head snapped around. Antonio caught the outline of the shadowy figure in the entrance to one of the tunnels. A bullet grazed past his face as a gunshot cracked around the cave. Antonio dived to the ground. Juanita raised her rifle and fired. There was a cry and something heavy hit the lake water.

"I hope that wasn't Ale," she whispered.

Antonio rested his hand on hers, gave it a squeeze and moved away. The crack of a gunshot startled him. The Blood Twins were firing at four more Reckoners. Three fell to Megan's guns, while Cole seemed to be holding off firing. Then Megan's guns clicked with the tell-tale sound of empty cylinders and Cole snapped out of his daze and fired. The fourth man fell with a hand to his neck, choking on the bullet lodged in his throat. Cole's face grew drawn and pale while his sister thumped him on the back.

Antonio stepped forward.

"Clint!" he bellowed. His voice bounced back at him from the stone cave walls as he shouted in all directions. "Clint! Come out and talk to me!"

There followed silence, only interrupted by someone's low moans to the side of the cave.

"Someone's coming," Juanita whispered.

It took a while and a lot of head turning for Antonio to pick up the approaching footsteps. Unsure which tunnel they were down, Antonio glanced at Juanita, but from the look she gave him, he guessed she was also having difficulty deciding. Slowly, the two of them moved towards each other until they stood back-to-back. Megan and Cole also shifted closer to each other. Between the four of them they had all directions of the cave covered.

The footsteps stopped their approach.

Antonio waited for the figure to speak, but they remained silent. "We have you surrounded, Clint," he said. "If you and the rest of your gang surrender, we will give you a fair trial."

Clint's voice came back soft and echoey, so distorted that Antonio couldn't make out the words.

"You'll have to speak up," he called back. "The echo in these caves is playing havoc with my hearing."

Clint raised his voice. "An' if we don't?"

"Then we'll ensure you never leave this cave," Antonio said.

"Tell me," Clint said, "how you findin' bein' Helena's sheriff? Do you feel fulfilled? Wanted? Appreciated? At the end of the day, do you go to bed feelin' happy? Or do you feel hollow? Empty? Frustrated at the lack of appreciation folk's are showin' you fer workin' your hardest, 'cause you haven't saved the town in sum glorious gunfight that day? But instead have spent it collectin' their tax money?"

Antonio paused. A resonance hummed through him in response to Clint's words. But as soon as he felt it, he shook it off. He wasn't going to fall for Clint's tricks. Even if he heard a ring of truth in them.

"If you have a chip on your shoulder about your job, save it for someone else," Antonio said. "I'm proud to be a sheriff. And I can't blame the people of Helena for being thankless when they didn't vote me into the office. But I go to bed every night knowing I've done the best I can for them."

Clint's laugh echoed around the cave. "Well, ain't you a self-righteous bastard. You were right, Ale. This one's all yours."

Antonio's stomach dropped. He opened his mouth to call out, but his voice was silenced as a gunshot split the air. Juanita jerked against his back, pushing Antonio forward. Antonio grabbed her to keep her upright. Juanita clenched her teeth, a hand pressed against her shoulder.

"He got me," she snarled.

"Ale," Antonio hissed and raised his gun. Alejandro stood in a tunnel above him, sighting at him down the barrel of his gun. Antonio's finger moved to his pistol trigger. As it brushed the curved metal, his hand stopped.

In Ale's eyes there was no such hesitation.

A gunshot echoed around the cave.

Alejandro jerked backwards. His gun clattered to the floor. As Ale crumpled to the ground, Megan twirled her smoking pistol.

"One more to go," she said and ran toward the nearest tunnel, grabbing a lantern off the sand on her way.

"Sorry," Cole said to Antonio and took off after his sister, leaving Juanita and Antonio in the cave. Antonio knew he should go after them, but his feet felt heavy, like they'd been encased in ice.

"Go." Juanita's voice broke the spell on him. Antonio dropped to the floor, but she pushed him away. "Go," she ordered. "I'll deal with the wound and check on Ale."

"Is he dead?" Antonio whispered.

"We don't know yet," Juanita told him, putting a hand on his chest.

Antonio swallowed. He didn't want Ale to be dead. He wanted to make amends with him. To keep his promise to Aunt Thomasina and bring Ale home. Or at least try. God, the man had tried to murder him, but he understood the anger that was flowing through him. And he would regret not having the chance to talk to Ale one more time.

"Go," Juanita said. She pushed Antonio away from her.

Antonio took off running into the nearest tunnel.

Chapter 42

Standoff

Six.

That's six folks I've killed now.

The number keeps runnin' through ma head as I take off after Megan down the tunnels. I wanna pray. I wanna ask Gawd fer fergiveness once more, even though he must be sick of hearin' ma excuses, but I need to keep up with Megan. Hafta keep ma promise to Pa. Can't break that one like I've broken the one to Him. I don't unnerstand how Megan can move so fast with that wound in her side. I try to keep up with her, but today ma body aches so bad from the bruises an' half-closed wounds I can barely walk without gaspin' fer breath. I wanna call out – wanna ask her to wait – but I'm scared to shout in case I lead Clint to where I am.

Fer what seems like ages, I wander the caves, Juanita's gun held out in front of me, finger restin' on the trigger, while ma heart pounds in ma ears as I turn every corner, strainin' to hear the sound of approachin' footsteps.

Jest as I come to a dead end, a gunshot echoes 'round the caves. I jump an' swing 'round, but there's no one 'hind me. Frozen, I listen out fer the sound of voices, but none come. Did Megan fire that shot? Is she all right?

Unstickin' ma feet from the floor, I backtrack into the tunnel.

An' almost walk into sumone.

Both of us jump back, raisin' our guns.

Then I see it's Sheriff Valdez. I lower ma arm an' slump 'gainst the cave wall. The sheriff exhales as he lowers his, a lantern swingin' in his other hand.

"Did you hear that gunshot?" he asks.

I nod. "Megan ran ahead an' I lost her."

"It sounded close so she can't be far. Come on."

He leads the way through the dark tunnel, the light from our lanterns castin' ghostly shadows on the walls. We take several twists an' turns an' catch sight of a shadow movin' ahead of us. It's Clint. He must see us out the corner of his eye, 'cause he stops runnin'.

"Clint!" Sheriff Valdez shouts.

The shadow raises his arm.

A shot rings out. Me an' Sheriff Valdez duck at the same time. Bits of stone rain down on us from where the bullets strike the cave wall. We raise our guns an' begin firin' back, but the shadow's gone. We take off runnin', chasin' him through the tunnels, 'til we come back out into the large flooded cave where we find Clint waitin', a gun pointed at each of us. We point ours back. I glance 'round the cave. There's no sign of Juanita or Megan.

"Give up," Sheriff Valdez says. "If you drop your guns now, I will arrest you and give you a fair trial."

Clint laughs. "Well, ain't you kind? But thanks, but no thanks, Sheriff. You can save that golden attitude fer when you're beggin' on your knees in hell." Ma whole body tenses as Clint looks Sheriff Valdez in the eye. "Say hello—"

Clint's body jerks ferward as two gunshots echo 'round the cave. As the guns fall from his hands, his mouth opens inna pained surprise. He falls ferward onto the sand, two patches of blood blossomin' on the back of his jacket, revealin' Megan an' Juanita standin' 'hind him, both their guns smokin'.

There's a moment when the four of us stare at Clint's body – a brief moment when all the tension drains from ma body – then we all remember what this final death means.

In the next second, all our guns're pointed at each other. Megan's gotta pistol each on Sheriff Valdez an' Juanita, I've ma gun on the sheriff, Sheriff Valdez's got his pointed at Megan, an' Juanita's sightin' at me down the barrel of her rifle.

"Wait!"

Ma eyes to shift away from Sheriff Valdez fer a moment. Cassidy's runnin' down the sand. She stands in the middle of our circle, arms spread wide, facin' Sheriff Valdez an' me.

"Don't do this," she begs.

"We've reached the end of our agreement," Sheriff Valdez says, lookin' past Cassidy to Megan. His eyes're hard an' resolute. "The Reckoners are no longer a threat. Now it's time to bring the Blood Twins to justice."

"That's the problem, Sheriff," Megan says. "'Cause the Blood Twins've no intention of bein' bought to justice."

"Please," Cassidy begs, lookin' 'tween me an' Sheriff Valdez with a pleadin' look that makes ma heart break. "There's no need for it to end this way."

I don't want it to end this way either. I don't want more bloodshed. The sheriff an' Juanita ain't bad people. They don't deserve to git hurt. An' I don't wanna hurt Cassidy.

But Megan's more important to me.

An' I'll kill anyone who threatens her.

"I can't let them go," Sheriff Valdez says, his voice low.

"An' we ain't givin' up the Blood Twins," I say. Cassidy meets ma eyes. The same sadness that's in ma eyes is reflected in hers. "You know we can't."

Summit changes in Cassidy's face. Her expression hardens, an' resolution enters her eyes. Fear fer what she's gonna do prickles 'cross ma skin.

An' I'm right to be afraid.

From the folds of her dress, Cassidy draws two guns.

An' points one at Sheriff Valdez an' one at Juanita.

I'm so shocked I almost drop ma gun, an' from the look on Sheriff Valdez's face he feels the same.

"Run! Megan! Cole!" Cassidy shouts.

"You fucking idiot," Juanita hisses.

"Cassidy," Sheriff Valdez whispers.

But their words only harden Cassidy's expression.

"Run!" she shouts again.

"You've gotta be shittin' me," I hear Megan mutter. She fires her guns.

As Sheriff Valdez an' Juanita duck, Megan rushes ferward an' presses a gun to Cassidy's head. She wraps her other arm 'round her body, pinnin' her arms to her sides.

"Drop your weapons!" Megan bellows. "All of you. That includes you, Miss Priss."

Sheriff Valdez an' Juanita exchange a quick glance an' lay their guns on the ground. Cassidy's tumble from her hands as tears leak from her eyes.

"Pick 'em up, Cole," Megan orders.

I collect Cassidy's first. From the weight of it, I can tell the cylinder's empty. Then I pick up the sheriff's pistol an' Juanita's rifle.

"Throw 'em in the lake," Megan orders.

The splash they make as they hit the water sounds loud an' clear 'round the cave.

"Now," Megan says, "where's that gold?"

"It's not here," Sheriff Valdez says. "Someone's likely stolen it. That's probably what all the shooting was about when we first got here."

Megan's eyes flick to Juanita, who shrugs. "I haven't sin it either."

Megan's face twists like she's tasted summit bitter. She spits on the ground.

"Fine," she says. "Then we're outta here. You stay here. If we so much as hear a footstep followin' us out, Miss Priss gits her brains blown out."

Megan starts backin' outta the cave 'wards the tunnel we came in by.

I back away with her, keepin' ma pistol pointin' at Sheriff Valdez an' Juanita so I don't hafta look at Cassidy's tear-streaked face.

The last thing I see is the resolution in Sheriff Valdez's eyes, an' I know he'll hunt us to the ends of the Earth.

Chapter 43

Promise

Antonio held off as long as he could, then grabbed a gun from Clint's body and sprinted after Cole, Cassidy and Megan. He raced through the tunnels, Juanita close on his heels. He knew he shouldn't get too close. He knew doing so would put Cassidy's life at risk, but he couldn't let them haul her off as a hostage again.

But he was too late.

By the time he made it out of the caves and back to the ledge, two of the horses were gone and Antonio's horse was dead. The handle of Clint's pistol bit into Antonio's palm. Juanita put a hand on his shoulder.

"We'll get them," she said.

Antonio nodded, although he felt numb.

"Did you get a chance to check on Ale?" he asked.

"Yes. He's alive but out cold."

Antonio blew out his cheeks. The numbness gave way

to a wave of relief. His hand went to the cross around his neck.

"Thank God," he muttered. "Let's grab him and get out of here."

They left the bodies in the caves, laid out on the sand side by side.

They had nothing to bury them with and nothing to build a pyre out of, so they thought it best to leave them there and come back for them later. Antonio would send a message to Little Point. Sheriff Conner could deal with them.

With no horses, the two of them walked back to Helena, Antonio carrying the unconscious Alejandro on his back and Juanita clutching her injured shoulder. Thankfully, the caves were not far from the town and along the road they met a wagon that allowed them to hitch a ride back. Antonio and Juanita dropped Alejandro off at the doctors, got the bullet removed from Juanita's shoulder, and then grabbed some spare guns from the sheriff's office and headed over to the Hayes house.

It was empty, of course.

There were no fresh hoof prints in the dirt or anything else to show that anyone had been near the house recently. They checked inside anyway, and also in the stables, to lay any suspicions to rest, but found them devoid of life.

Antonio wanted to scream. He kicked a bucket instead, sending it crashing into the side of the house. His foot throbbed along with his broken nose.

"We'll find them," Juanita said. "There can't be too many places they could've gone. I think that map of yours might come in handy again."

Antonio meant to start work on the map the moment he got back to the office, but he found Jason smoking outside. The grin he gave made Antonio's stomach drop like a stone.

"There's a man waitin' inside fer you," Jason said, blowing out a lungful of smoke. "A very well-to-do man. He looks inna mighty flap."

Antonio said nothing in reply as he strode into the office, but Jason's laugh followed him through the door.

Inside, as he suspected, he found Mr Scarborough pacing around. The hollows in his gaunt face were deeper than Antonio had ever seen them, and the dark circles under his eyes were more prominent than ever. But the wild look in them made Antonio take a step back.

"Where is she?" Mr Scarborough cried, striding across the room. His hands landed on Antonio's shoulders, squeezing them so hard Antonio's knees buckled. "Where is she? You said she'd arrived! You said she was at the house! Where's my daughter?"

Swallowing down his fear, Antonio said, "She was here, but she was kidnapped today by a pair of outlaws. I assure you, Mr Scarborough, my team and I are doing all we can to get her home. And we will get her home safe. I promise."

Mr Scarborough's wild eyes held Antonio's for a few moments more and then he sagged. Antonio caught him. With Juanita's help, he carried Mr Scarborough to a chair.

"Could you get some water?" Antonio asked Juanita. Juanita nodded and disappeared out the back. Antonio fanned Mr Scarborough's face with some paper. The older man's eyelids fluttered.

"Bring her home, Antonio," he murmured. "Bring her home safe."

"I promise I will, Mr Scarborough," Antonio said. "Don't you worry."

Chapter 44

Unmasked

We daren't go home.

Now that Sheriff Valdez knows where we live, the house's no longer safe. So we go to 'nother set of caves, not far from Helena, that Pa an' us'd discovered long ago, an' make our camp there. It means we're close to home to keep an' eye on what Sheriff Valdez an' Juanita are doin', but sumwhere they won't know 'bout.

Megan's inna right foul mood on the journey to the caves. She spits over Rosie's side an' then wheels her 'round an' checks the way we came, lookin' fer any sign of Sheriff Valdez or Juanita. But there's none. How can there be when we'd taken one of their horses an' shot the other. Or rather, Megan'd shot the other. I begged her not to, but she did it anyway.

"Grow sum," she told me.

I took Cassidy on the other horse, holdin' her in front

of me so she couldn't escape. She'd trembled all the way to the new cave. I wanna tell her I'm sorry – that I don't want things to go this way again – but those words are false. 'Cause she knows. She knows Megan means more to me 'n anythin' or anyone else. An' if I hafta do this to protect her, then I will.

The sun's high an' hot on the ride, an' all of us are glad to reach the cooler shadows of the cave. We drink our fill from our canteens an' I don't miss how Megan's arm shakes as she raises hers to her lips. Her face is sickly pale an' sweatin'. The blood that were on the inside of her shirt is now on the outside. Ma own clothes ain't any better off from where the fast horse ridin's re-opened ma wounds, an' every inch of ma skin *hurts* inna way I never thought could. Jest look at the infamous Blood Twins now.

Megan orders Cassidy to the back of the cave with Florence trained on her.

"What now?" Cassidy asks.

Megan gives her one of her looks. "You're gonna stay right there," she says, "while ma brother an' I work out what we're gonna do. An' if I hear one more peep outta you, your brains'll paint the back of that wall."

Cassidy returns Megan's look but keeps quiet.

"I still wanna find that gold," Megan says to me. "But if it warn't in the cave, then where the hell is it? Are you sure Pa meant *that* lake?"

I nod. "It could only be that one. There ain't 'nother like it."

Megan pulls a sour face. "Sumone from the gang musta taken it. I think we should go back to that fortress an' ransack the place."

"I don't think that's a good idea," I say.

"Why not? That gold's ours, ain't it? They stole it from us. It's ours by right. There ain't no court of law that could argue with our claim."

I have a feelin' that ain't the case, but I keep ma

mouth shut.

"But 'fore we go there," Megan says, "we're gonna need more supplies. We ain't got enough here to last us a day. I'll go into town an' pick sum stuff up." Her mouth pulls up into a smirk. "The rate it'll take the sheriff to git 'cross the desert on foot, I'll be in an' back here 'gain 'fore he even arrives in Helena." Stickin' her chin out, she gestures at Cassidy with her pistol. "Keep an' eye on her while I'm gone. An' don't you dare let her go."

Then she leaves Cassidy an' me alone in the cave. Cassidy's sittin' 'gainst the opposite wall to me. There's a feelin' 'tween us that ain't bin there since we first took her hostage.

I swallow, open ma mouth, but then shut it 'gain.

We sit in silence.

Cassidy whispers, "You know that day you took me from the train? Imagine if I'd just left the train when I should have done. None of this would have happened."

"It probably woulda done," I say. "Jest outta order. Megan woulda put her plan into action the moment your pa came back."

"What's going to happen now?"

I lick ma lips. "We're gonna wait fer Megan to come back an'..."

An' what? What would we do with Cassidy while we went back to the fortress to see if the gold were there? She'd hafta come with us, but how long would we keep her with us? When would Megan ever allow Cassidy to go free?

When would I ever be allowed to be free?

The thought hits me like a bullet to the gut an' digs its way deep.

'Cause that's it.

There's no version of ma life where I'll ever be free of the Blood Twins. I'll always be tellin' maself that one day we'd stop. That one day Megan'd tire of this life an' she'd settle down, then maybe I could as well. Start a horse ranch. Git married. Have a family.

But now, after everythin' we've done, that'll never happen.

Instead, one day, me an' Megan'll be caught. Cassidy'll go back to her family an' the Blood Twins'll swing from the gallows. An' I'll break ma promise to Pa, 'cause I've bin failin' to protect Megan from herself all this time. In protectin' her, I've bin drivin' her 'wards the gallows.

'Less I talk to Megan an' make her stop.

So I take inna breath an' say, "I'm gonna tell Megan. I'm gonna tell her that I wanna stop this. That I've had enough."

Cassidy looks up at me.

I take a deep breath. "I'm gonna finally tell her how much I hate this life. How much I don't want it anymore. How I wanna work onna horse ranch."

It feels good to finally say those words.

"Go for it, Cole," Cassidy says. Her voice's still quiet, but she's lookin' at me now.

I nod an' smile as ma chest lightens. Summit that could be hope.

"If you started your own horse ranch," Cassidy asks, "would Megan come with you?"

"I don't know. I don't know what she'll do. She ain't suited fer any sorta women's work. She's—" I swallow. "She's determined to keep the memory of our pa alive. An' she thinks that needs to be done through robbin'."

"That's stupid," Cassidy says. "There's no excuse that can justify causing misery to others."

We sit fer a little while in silence. The wind blowin' past the cave mouth makes a whistlin' sound.

"Do you ever think what our lives woulda bin like if I hadn't bin born into a poor family?" I ask.

"No," Cassidy says, "because it hurts too much to think our lives might have been that easy."

An' how I mighta hadda chance with Cassidy if I'd bin born into a wealthy family. The two of us woulda met at a ball, I woulda taken her fer escorted walks, sent her flowers an' chocolates. Never worryin' 'bout fallin' in love with her 'cause ma family were poor.

"We could have been together," Cassidy whispers, her voice thick.

"I know," I whisper back. There's a pause. "Why didja stand up fer us in the cave? You could've let the sheriff an' Juanita take us in. You'd be free from us if you had."

"I... I..." Cassidy sighs an' smooths down her skirt. "I'm not sure. I... know it makes no sense, but when I saw you caught up in that stand-off, I felt... conflicted. I know my feelings for you aren't real, but I do have feelings for you... even if they aren't real." She sighs an' presses her face into her knees. "I don't know. I'm all over the place."

Cassidy sniffs an' wipes her eyes on the back of her hand. I've a strange pain in ma chest. I don't wanna talk 'bout this no more. An' I'm tired. So tired.

"I'm gonna sleep," I say, takin' ma hat off an' restin' it over ma face. "Wake me if you need anythin'."

Even though I'm lent 'gainst a hard wall, I'm so bone weary that as soon as I shut ma eyes I drift off. Then summit warm an' solid presses up 'gainst ma side. Cassidy's hair tickles ma face as she lays her head on ma shoulder.

I've jest enough consciousness left to hear Cassidy whisper, "Let's pretend. Just for a little while," an' then I drift ofta sleep.

An' am woken by a rock strikin' ma temple. I start awake, disturbin' Cassidy. We look up an' find Megan standin' in the mouth of the cave. Her eyes're narrow. A cold feelin' rushes through me.

"Sis!" I say, feelin' ma cheeks flush. Cassidy scrambles off me an' both of us stand. "Didja git the supplies?"

"There's bin a change of plan." She draws a gun.

An' fires a bullet into ma leg.

White hot pain flares through me, whitin' out ma vision. I groan an' collapse. Cassidy screams.

"Didja really think you could hide her from me ferever?" I open ma eyes. Megan's standin' over me. Both her guns're out, one's pointin' at me an' the other at Cassidy, who's gone white.

"Are you that stupid that you thought I wouldn't find out that Miss Priss here is Cassidy Scarborough?"

"How?" I croak.

"There's missin' posters all over town, all includin' a lovely picture of Miss Cassidy here. Turns out that her Pa's also back in town an' is worried sick 'bout her." Megan's expression drops an' fer a moment she looks sad. Her eyes glisten inna way I haven't sin since the night Pa died. "How couldja do this to me, Cole? How couldja protect her knowin' who she were?"

"'Cause I love her," I say. I don't dare look at Cassidy as I say those words, but Megan needs to hear 'em. I wanna make her unnerstand. "I've loved her since we were children."

"Don't you love me, brother? Does that harlot mean more to you 'n I do?"

"No, Megan," I say. "You always come first. Always."

"Then why didn't you tell me? Why the hell didn't you tell me who she were?" Megan spits at Cassidy. "We coulda used her to git to Mr Scarborough. So we could avenge Pa. Didn't you love Pa, Cole?"

"'Course I did!" Tears form in ma eyes. Frustration, pain an' anger're all slippin' down ma cheeks. "He were our pa! He meant everythin' to me, so do you! An' so does Cassidy. It's bin hard lyin' to you knowin' one day you'd find out, but I hadda! Cassidy ain't done nuthin' to harm us. She'd nuthin' to do with Pa's death."

"Her pa has!" Megan's screamin' now. Her hands're shakin' an' I'm very aware of her fingers restin' on the triggers. "He murdered Pa, an' our grandpappy. We coulda used her! We coulda used her to git to him!"

"I don't wanna harm her, Megan! Why can't you unnerstand that?"

Megan stares at me like I've spoken to her in 'nother language.

"You know what, brother. I can't unnerstand it."

Megan's face hardens. I close ma eyes.

A scream echoes 'round the cave.

I hear the gunshot but feel nuthin'.

I open ma eyes an' find Cassidy tryina wrestle Florence outta Megan's hand.

"Cassidy, don't!" I shout, jest as Cassidy pulls the gun from Megan's hand. With a grim expression, she steps back an' levels the gun at ma sis. Megan fires Smithy. Cassidy screams an' Florence flies from her hand inna spray of blood.

"Megan!" I scream. "Leave her alone!"

Cassidy clutches her arm, blood seepin' through her fingers. She screams an' rushes once again at ma sis. Cassidy grabs Megan's remainin' gun an' points it away from me.

"Cassidy, don't!" I try to stand, but ma leg screams along with the rest of ma body. I ignore it an' pull maself up. I dive ferward, but Megan sees me comin' an' kicks out. I fall to the ground. I look up. Megan's got an arm 'round Cassidy's neck, an' a gun to her head. Cassidy's eyes are wide. Her an' Megan are breathin' hard.

"Two years we've bin waitin' fer this, Cole. Two years. An' when the time comes, you turned your back on me. Well, fine. I'll do this on ma own."

She smashes the handle of her gun 'gainst the side of ma head an' everythin' goes dark.

Chapter 45

Traitor

"Take a break," Juanita told him.

"I can't," he said.

"Toni, you won't make any progress in this state. You've been staring at that map for hours."

Antonio ran a hand down his face. "They can't be far from here. They'd stay close to town. I know they would, but *where*? I've marked and searched every shelter they could possibly hide in. There has to be something I'm missing."

"Then they must know somewhere only a local would know," Juanita said. "Perhaps you should ask Dean for help? He was helpful before."

Sighing, Antonio rested his forehead against the wall. "I think you're right."

"Let's go there now, then, but we should go see Ale on the way."

Antonio nodded.

Jason didn't spare them a glance as they walked through the office.

"Headin' out?" he said. "Anywhere you wanna tell your deputy 'bout? Or are you gonna keep sneakin' 'bout?"

"It's none of your damn business where I'm going," Antonio shot back at him. "Stay here, and do some work."

The door shut behind them. Juanita held up her hand and Antonio slapped his palm to hers. She interlaced their fingers and pressed the back of his hand to her lips.

"I love it when you use your authority," she whispered.

At Dr Fallon's, Antonio was so jittery waiting outside Alejandro's room that he barely caught what the doctor was telling him about his condition.

"I were 'bout to send fer you," Dr Fallon said. "Your friend's awake, but he won't be doin' anythin' too strenuous fer a while yet. Plenty of rest an' clean water to wash the wound twice a day. Change the bandages at the same time. I'll give you sum opium fer the pain."

"Thank you, Dr Fallon," Antonio said. Then to Juanita he said, "I want to talk to him alone. Would you mind waiting here?"

Juanita unshouldered her rifle. "Shout if he gets violent."

Antonio nodded. He took a deep breath and walked into the next room.

Ale sat up in bed. One side of his face was bloodied, the other side was ashen and drawn. There were dark circles under his eyes. Antonio paused in the doorway, afraid to approach the other man. He waited for Ale to reach for his gun, but he didn't, so Antonio sat down in the seat next to the bed.

"Feel like shit," Alejandro said in Spanish.

"You look like shit," Antonio replied. "How are you otherwise?"

There was a long pause. "Tired," Alejandro said. "Tired

of feeling angry, of carrying all that hate around with me."

"I'm sorry," Antonio said. "For making you feel that, and for my part in Elìas's death."

"I think I made myself feel it." Alejandro stretched his arms above his head. "I should have let it all go a long time ago. I think I blamed myself for Elìas's death, but it was so much easier blaming you than myself. It's always easier to blame someone else rather than yourself."

"So philosophical."

"Getting shot will do that to you." They exchanged weary smiles. Alejandro touched his own face. "What happened to your nose? Looks like someone docked you real good."

Antonio laughed and then winced. "No. Mother hit me in the face with a frying pan."

Alejandro blinked. "I mean, I would do the same if my son came home for the first time in thirteen years."

"Yeah. I deserved it."

"So you went back to the fort?"

"I did. With Juanita. We cleaned the last of The Reckoners out."

"Thank God." Alejandro crossed himself. "I'm glad they're all safe. I made such a mess out of everything."

Antonio thought about reaching over to give Alejandro a comforting pat on the shoulder, but decided he wasn't ready for that level of forgiveness.

"Juanita," Antonio said, "you can come in now."

Juanita entered the room with her rifle on her shoulder, pointing at Alejandro. She and Alejandro observed each other.

"You can put that away," Alejandro said. "I'm no longer rabid."

"I think I'll keep it out," she said. "Just in case."

Wanting to change the subject quickly, Antonio said, "Tell me, what happened in the cave. When we got there half The Reckoners were already dead. We couldn't find a hint of any gold."

Alejandro broke eye contact with Juanita. "That's because the white man turned on us and stole it all."

"What white man?" Antonio asked.

"This guy showed up at the fort about a week ago. Tall, skinny, old. Said he could help us find the gold – or at least he knew someone who could help us find it."

"And who was that?"

"That guy Clint had us kidnap."

"The one you tortured into telling you where the gold was?"

"Yeah. Turns out he was part of the duo that robbed that bank the same time as us. What a coincidence, eh? Once that guy gave us the information, the old white guy came with us to get the gold – said he could help us find the cave. But once we found it and the gold, the bastard shot us in the back and made off with it."

Antonio and Juanita exchanged a look, and Antonio knew she was thinking the same thing he was. "This old guy who came to the fortress," Antonio asked, "do you know what his name was?"

"Hmm..." Alejandro scratched his chin. "Dennis... ? Or Dom... ? No, Dean! It was Dean!"

"Of course." Antonio groaned.

"That bastard," Juanita hissed.

Dean must have known all along that Cole and Megan knew something about the gold. No wonder he'd been so pissed when Antonio had told him they were going to work with the Blood Twins rather than going after them. He must have had some plan to get the information out of them if Antonio arrested him.

"Wait," Alejandro said. "Do you know this Dean guy?"

"Oh, yes," Antonio said. "We know him, and we're about to pay him a little visit. Here." Antonio left some money on the bedside table. "Use that to pay the doctor. If he needs the bed, get someone to take you to the sheriff's office. You can use my room."

"Our room," Juanita corrected him as they left. Antonio raised his eyebrow at her in return. "What?" she asked. "How are we meant to get anything done if Alejandro's sleeping in our bed?"

"Hmm," Antonio said. "Good point. Perhaps I'll find him a room at the saloon."

He bumped Juanita's hip with his and she bumped his back in return.

"You got enough bullets on you?" Antonio asked, as they walked away from the doctor's house.

"Do you think it's going to get ugly?"

"I don't know, but Dean's an army veteran and an old mercenary. There's no way he's not going to fight back."

Juanita checked her belt. She had a whole case tucked into it. Antonio had half a case but decided it was enough. If they could catch Dean unawares, they should have no problem making him comply. Although the sinister sensation in his stomach told him otherwise.

As they approached Dean's house, the feeling in his gut intensified to the point Antonio was wincing in pain.

"Something's wrong," he whispered.

"Like what?" Juanita asked.

Then they heard the gunshot and both broke into a run.

Chapter 46

Dean

I wake to an empty cave.

Megan's taken all our supplies, Cassidy an' Rosie. She's shot the other horse an' left its body outside the cave entrance. Already flies're swarmin' all over it. I roll over. Summit digs into ma hip. With a mixture of relief an' fear, I find it's the gun Juanita gave me. I pull it from ma belt an' check the cylinder. It's full.

Fer ages, I sit lookin' down at the circle of bullets, ma mind blank an' ma body heavy.

What do I do now?

Megan's got Cassidy. She's gonna use her to git to Mr Scarborough.

I hafta stop her.

I hafta make sure Cassidy's safe.

But I hafta make sure Megan stays safe.

But how?

Where is Megan?

How am I gonna reason with her when she now hates ma guts?

The longer I stare at the circle of bullets, the more they seemed to be spinnin'. I snap the cylinder shut an' shove the gun into ma belt.

I need help.

That's what I need.

A second person to help me through this mess.

An' there's one person left who I can turn to.

I leave the cave an' limp to Dean an' Mary's house, draggin' ma right leg 'hind me. Ma head throbs an' I gotta mighty lump formin' where Megan smashed her gun barrel 'gainst ma head. A coupla times on the walk, ma vision whites out an' I hafta wait fer it to clear 'fore continuin' on. I find a stick an' use that to support maself.

It's gittin' dark an' the further I walk through the desert the harder it gits to see. I jest hope I don't tread on summit that'll bite me back.

But at the sight of Dean an' Mary's house, I don't feel the relief I normally do seein' it. Summit twists in ma gut makin' me slow, but I force maself ferward.

At the front door I raise a hand to knock but stop maself. Instead I move 'round the back. The door's unlocked. There's a pile of blankets an' a newspaper on the rockin' chair on the porch. Looks like sumone went to bed late an' fergot to lock the door.

Inside the house, there are packed bags on the floor. Walkin' past 'em, summit catches ma eye.

Summit round an' metallic.

A gold coin.

I pick it up. It's unlike anythin' I've sin. Thin, with a shield stamped on one side an' a cross on the other. It looks old. Very old.

Suspectin' summit, I ease the flap of one of the bags

open.

An' find it burstin' with gold.

More gold coins. Gold statues. Gold jewellery. Gold cups an' masks. All the items look like they'd once bin shiny but are now dull with age.

Is this the lost gold Pa'd hidden at the bottom of the lake?

If so, what's it doin' in Dean's house?

Then I remember summit.

That moment in the fort when I'd sin Clint talkin' to sumone else. Sumone I'd recognised but couldn't place.

Now, I know who that person were.

Who'd told Sheriff Valdez an' Juanita that me an' Megan are the Blood Twins.

Who'd gone to The Reckoners to git 'em to kidnap me.

Who'd then stolen the gold from 'em.

I draw ma pistol.

Slow an' steady I creep through the house. I know where everythin' is an' where Dean an' Mary sleep. Through the kitchen an' 'round to the front of the stairs. It's so dark I hafta trust ma memory more 'n ma senses.

I reach the bottom of the stairs. A light appears at the top. It's so sudden an' outta place in the darkness it takes me a few seconds to see there's a figure 'hind it. A male figure. Dean.

I bring ma gun up. He sees me an' freezes.

"Where's Mary?" I ask.

"Gone to her cousin's in Phoenix," he says.

"Good. Come outside."

I keep ma gun pointed at Dean as he walks downstairs. I let him walk in front of me but press the barrel of the gun to his lower back.

Outside the clouds have moved away from the moon. Me an' Dean stand out the back of the house on the porch. Half his face's in shadow, the other's illuminated by the lantern's yellow light.

Growin' up I always thought of Dean as an uncle. He'd always bin 'round, an' with the way he an' Pa'd acted togither it were easy to think they were brothers. But when I look at him now I feel empty. There's no family connection there anymore.

"What do you want, Cole?" Dean asks.

"You sold us out," I say. "To the sheriff an' to The Reckoners. Care to explain?"

Dean shrugs. "Not really."

I point the pistol at Dean's face an' bring down the hammer. "Wouldja care to explain *now*?"

"C'mon, Cole. Both of us know you ain't gonna use that thing. You ain't your sis." His eyes take in ma bruised, cut face an' then travel down to the bullet wound in ma leg. "Gawd you're a mess. Git in an argument with your sis, didja?"

I wanna shoot him, to coat the dirt with his blood, but instead I hiss, "Fer Gawd's sake! Will you jest fuckin' tell me why?"

I expect his expression to falter, fer him to cower a little, like people do when Megan says stuff like that to 'em, but his smile widens. He even laughs.

"Cussin' now, are you? You really are becomin' your sis."

"Jest tell me... please."

"You won't like it."

"I don't like it now. Megan's kidnapped Cassidy an' is gonna use her to git to—" Ma pain is causin' Dean pleasure, so I shut ma mouth.

"You reap what you sow, Cole. How the hell didja think you were gonna git away with hidin' Cassidy unner Megan's nose?"

He's right, but it makes ma stomach pang hearin' him say it. It were stupid of me to try to keep Cassidy safe from Megan.

Dean sits in the rockin' chair. He groans an' fer the

first time he looks old. His face's covered in lines, there're dark patches on the backs of his hands an' wisps of white hair escape from unner his hat.

"I sold you out to git the gold," Dean says. "I were tired of waitin' fer you to remember where your pa'd told you he'd stashed it. Thought a stint in jail an' a look at the noose would be enough to make you remember, but then that damn sheriff went cold turkey on me so I hadda go to the next interested party. Gawd, how dumb must you be to fergit summit like that? You were sittin' onna whole fortune an' you plain fergot all 'bout it."

"But how didja—"

"I saw your pa whisper summit to you the night he died, an' I assumed he were tellin' you where he'd hidden it."

"But how didja know he had it in the first place?"

"'Cause he wouldn't shut up 'bout it!" Dean snaps. I take a step back. Dean's eyes flick to ma pistol an' I steady maself. One show of weakness an' he'll be on me. "Ever since I met him, when we were both workin' at the Scarborough mine, all he'd go on an' on an' on 'bout were that fuckin' gold. His ma were the same apparently – her husband's death drove her mad. She made your pa promise to find the gold, told him all 'bout Scarborough, where to find him, an' how he should take revenge on him fer her husband's death. But your pa didn't believe her – he knew she were mad, so he thought she were talkin' horse shit. But then he moved to Helena an' met Scarborough. An' started thinkin' his ma's rantin's might be true."

"So he stole the gold from Mr Scarborough's house, an' Mr Scarborough shot him."

"No, Cole. Do you know what the dumb fuck did?" Dean leans ferward, his eyes sparklin'. "He *asked* Scarborough – his then *employer* – if the story were real."

Dean leans back an' laughs.

I keep a tight grip on ma gun as the hairs on the back of ma arms rise at the sound.

"Then guess what Benjamin did?" Dean asks, wipin' a finger unner his eye. "He fired him, an' then spread that damnin' rumour 'round town that your pa were a thief so no one'd hire him 'gain. *Then*, your pa decided to try sneakin' into Mr Scarborough's house to see if the gold were really there." Dean's eyes shine as he looks back 'wards the house an' the piles of gold that're there. "Turns out he were right, so he stole it an' hid it at the bottom of that damn lake."

"I don't unnerstand." I wanna appear strong, but ma voice comes out inna whisper an' shakes. "Why'd you'd sell us out? We were family. Pa trusted you like a brother."

Fer a moment Dean's expression falls, like ma words've finally struck him, but then his face hardens again.

"I've gotta greedy devil in me, Cole," he says. "Where there's money involved, I lose all sense. I guess it's jest part of ma nature."

I take inna deep, shakin' breath. "How didja work out we were the Blood Twins? How long've you known?"

"The moment the Blood Twins became known. It were right after yer pa died, an' the two of you never seemed to be workin'. It were jest too much of a coincidence, along with the descriptions of the Blood Twins. Any idiot shoulda sin it."

"You were spyin' on us."

"I like to keep an eye on ma enemies."

"We ain't your enemies."

"I didn't trust you. 'Specially that nutty sis of yours."

Ma fingers tighten on the trigger.

"What didja jest call Megan?"

"Oh, c'mon, Cole! Surely you must know? There ain't no place better fer you sis 'n the mad house. To be honest, you should be in there with her. Only a mad man follows his sis 'round when she's wavin' a gun an' pretendin' she hassa dick."

Ma eyes've gone all strange. Nuthin's in focus anymore. Ma heart thumps in ma ears.

"I shoulda sin it comin'. Your sis's nature's so much like your ma's. I shoulda done summit 'bout her 'fore it were too late, like slipped a scorpion in her boot."

"Stop it," I mutter.

"An' what were you doin' with Cassidy Scarborough fer all those weeks? Havin' a bit of fun, were you? I'd better tell Mr Scarborough to throw her out his house. Think 'bout what shame'll come to the family when his only daughter gits with child from a murderin', stealin' sunvabitch."

"Shut up!"

"When you were bein' so slow to remember where the gold's location were, I thought I'd hafta git The Reckoners to torture Megan or Cassidy to help you along. I were surprised you lasted so long without beggin' fer death since you're such a coward—"

A bang rips the air an' the pistol kicks in ma hand. Dean cries out as he slams back into the chair. He presses his hands to his stomach. Blood runs 'tween his fingers.

"Gawddammit, Cole! I didn't expect you to actually do it!"

Ma hands're shakin'. Pain radiates from ma wrist from the gun's kick. The night's spinnin' 'round me, but I clutch the gun tighter an' look down ma nose at Dean. I'm waitin' fer ma body to fail me, fer ma knees to knock togither, fer ma stomach to heave. Jest like they did when I realised we'd burnt all those folk alive in that church. But nuthin' happens. I'm strangely calm.

"You shouldn't've doubted me," I say. "I'm ma sis's brother, after all."

"You're not jest her brother – you're her Gawddamn twin! Fuck!" Dean spits. He slumps back in the chair. While one hand stays pressed to his stomach, the other slides inside his jacket an' fumbles fer summit. Ma hands clutch the gun tight, but I relax when Dean pulls out summit round. He keeps his fist closed, concealin' it. "You're jest like her. The same madness. Do you feel anythin', Cole? Are you feelin' anythin' 'wards the man you've killed?"

"You're not dead yet. An' I'm nuthin' like ma sis, 'cause Megan'd leave you to die."

I re-aim.

"But I'm merciful."

An' I shoot Dean in the head.

Chapter 47

Defeated

By the time Antonio and Juanita arrived at Dean's house, they found Cole standing over Dean's lifeless body slumped in a rocking chair on the porch, a gun in his hand.

Too late.

Juanita held her gun to Cole's head while Antonio disarmed him. The gun almost fell from his hand into Antonio's palm.

"Cole," Antonio asked. "Where are Megan and Cassidy?"

But Cole remained mute and motionless. Antonio could tell from his dull eyes that he wasn't all there.

"Stay here with him," he said to Juanita and went inside the house. He searched the two rooms upstairs and the two downstairs, checked around the front, but he found no one else. No trace of Dean's wife. Or of Cassidy or Megan.

The uneasy feeling in his stomach was back with a vengeance.

Something was wrong for Cole to be here without Megan.

Antonio spotted the pile of bags on the floor. The flap of one of them had been turned over, revealing the jumble of gold inside. Antonio's vision tunnelled as he looked down at the fortune sitting on Dean's parlour floor. His palms itched.

But he dragged his eyes away from it and went back outside, where he found Juanita and Cole in the same position as he'd left them.

"There's no one else inside the house," Antonio said. "The gold's there, though. Could you take Cole to the jailhouse? I've got some things to finish up here."

"Sure thing," Juanita said.

They found some rope inside Dean's house, which they used to tie Cole's arms to his sides. Although Antonio thought they needn't have bothered. Cole didn't even blink in protest. He left Juanita to lead Cole back to town while he dealt with Dean's body.

He had half hoped that the old man would be alive, but after getting a clear view of the hole in his head, Antonio knew there was no chance. Best get him inside the house before the animals smelt him.

As Antonio bent down to pick the old man up, something fell out of Dean's hand. It was a small woven turtle. From the look of it, Antonio guessed it was from a Native American tribe. Why did Dean have it?

Juanita returned and he showed it to her.

"It's a navel amulet," she said. "I've seen them before."

She pulled out a small notebook from inside her jacket. It was filled with sketches of people, items and scenery. Each one was marked with a date, location and the names of the people who appeared in the drawing.

"Is this from your travels?" Antonio asked.

Juanita nodded. "Wanted to record them somehow. Ah. Here." She stopped on a page which showed a rough sketch of a child standing beside his mother. An amulet like Dean's hung from the child's belt. Underneath Juanita had written, "Cheyenne".

"I saw them all over," Juanita said. "Not just in Cheyenne communities. They're protective charms..." Juanita looked down at Dean's body.

Staring down at the woven turtle, Antonio remembered the conversation he'd had with Dean in The Sleeping Racoon and thought that perhaps there was an untold story there. Not that he would ever learn it now.

"He told me his grandfather was a mountain man," Antonio said.

"It wasn't uncommon for mountain men to marry native women," Juanita said.

Antonio nodded. There was a pause. "We should move him into the house," he said.

They did so and moved the gold out of the house. Juanita had brought a horse with her from town.

"Thought we might need some help carrying some stuff back with us," she said, her eyes sliding over the pile of bags. "Have you taken a look?"

"Not yet," Antonio admitted.

Their eyes met and Antonio felt a shiver run through him. "Shall we?" Juanita asked.

Dry mouthed, Antonio nodded.

They flipped open the top of a bag each.

A rush ran through Antonio that made his hands shake as he reached out a hand to dip into the fortune, but then the feeling faded. And all Antonio saw was a bag full of rusted dull metal.

"I don't get it," Juanita said. "Why someone would murder for this."

"It's not that beautiful, is it?" Antonio said.

Juanita reached out and grabbed Antonio's hand. The

rush returned, only ten times stronger and didn't fade.

"What shall we do with it?" Juanita asked.

"I don't know. Let's get it back to the office for now. We can decide what to do with it later. Aside from us, Alejandro and Cole, no one else knows Dean stole it. Everyone else thinks it's lost."

They loaded the bags onto the horse and walked back to town.

"I told your deputy to watch Cole while I was gone," Juanita said, "as we don't know where the sister is. I don't think he was too happy taking orders from me."

"I'm surprised Jason was still in the office at this hour," Antonio said.

"He'd fallen asleep at his desk," Juanita said.

"Ah," Antonio said. "That sounds more like it."

"What's the plan now?"

Antonio sighed. "I don't know. The priority is getting Cassidy back safe, and I'm worried now that she's alone with Megan."

"Knowing that woman, she's got a plan," Juanita said. "And it's not going to be pretty."

"At least we have Cole," Antonio said. "Hopefully we can make him talk."

"Clint was able to," Juanita said.

Antonio winced. "I'm hoping not to have to resort to that level of violence."

Back at the office they unloaded the saddle bags. Antonio had Juanita take them around the back of the building so that Jason wouldn't see them, and then he went in the front.

Jason sat in front of the cell bars, pistol in his lap pointing at Cole, but he was asleep again. Antonio gently pulled the pistol from Jason's fingers and kicked his chair. Jason's fingers squeezed as though they were reaching for the trigger, but they just grabbed empty air. Confused, he looked around and found Antonio dangling his gun from his fingers.

"Go home," Antonio said, pushing the pistol into Jason's hand.

"You... er... You back, then?" Jason asked, his eyes still bleary as he returned his gun to its holster.

"Yes. We're back. Go home."

"Oh, er, good." Jason thumbed his nose and sniffed. "You know, er, I've had ma eye on this fella all night. Vicious bastard, ain't he? Never woulda thought the Hayes siblings were the Blood Twins, but it, er, makes sense now, don't it? I mean, the sis's a right crazy bitch—"

"Go home, Jason."

Jason held up his hands "All right, all right. I'm jest sayin' is all."

Once the door shut behind him, Antonio took his seat in front of the cell door. Cole sat on the bed, his back slumped, staring at the opposite wall. His right trouser leg soaked with blood. His eyes unfocused and dull. Defeated.

"Cole," Antonio said, "I know you're in shock right now, but I need your help. Megan has Cassidy, doesn't she? Do you know where they are?"

On the other side of the cell bars, Cole made no motion to show he had heard Antonio. He didn't even twitch.

"Cole," Antonio said, "please. I need to get Cassidy home safe. You love her, don't you? If you do, tell me where Megan's keeping her."

Still Cole did not move.

A hot flare of anger rose up in Antonio.

He was so done.

He was exhausted.

He was tired of all the lies, of the gold, of the kidnapping and the torture, the deceit and seeing the gravestones of his loved ones.

His muscles bunched. He stood up, seized the back of his chair and smashed it against the cell bars. The metal rang as pieces of wood spun across the room. Antonio continued to hit it against the bars until there was nothing but two pieces of thin wood left in his hands.

Seeing the destruction around him sobered Antonio. He took a deep, shuddering breath before looking up. He expected Cole to be staring at him in shock.

But still Cole had not moved.

"Fine," Antonio said, throwing the remaining pieces of chair away. "Have it your way."

Juanita waited for him in the kitchen, the bags of gold at her feet.

"What did that poor chair ever do to you?" she asked.

"It had the misfortune of being the closest thing to me. Sorry you had to see that."

Juanita's silence was like a knife in Antonio's gut. A new rush of heat went through him, but this time it was an emotion far from anger. He remembered his father destroying a side table like that once in one of his fits.

"I promise I won't do it again," he said. "I... I lost myself there for a moment."

"You'd better not," Juanita said. Her look and icy tone doubled Antonio's feeling of shame. "I'm guessing you didn't get an answer out of him."

"No," Antonio said, picking up two bags. "He didn't say anything."

"Then we're still at square one." Juanita picked up two bags. "What are we doing with this?"

"For now, hiding it."

"Keeping it for yourself?"

"No," Antonio said firmly. "I don't know what we should do with it yet, but I know Mr Scarborough doesn't deserve it. So we'll keep it quiet from him."

They hid the bags in the ceiling of Antonio's room, removing a nail from the boards and pushing the bags into the gap.

As they slid the final bag in, Juanita said, "Someone's knocking."

"I'll go."

Downstairs, he found a man dressed in smart servant clothes.

"Mr Scarborough asks that you come to his house," he said.

Antonio's mouth felt very dry, but he nodded. "I'll be right there."

If it was possible, Mr Scarborough's cheeks had sunk further, and the circles under his eyes had grown bigger and darker. With the translucent pallor of his skin, he looked almost skeletal.

"Have you found her?" Mr Scarborough demanded the moment Antonio walked into the parlour.

"Not yet, sir," Antonio said. "But we've captured one half of the Blood Twins. We believe Cassidy is with the other."

"What do they want?" Mr Scarborough cried. "What do they want with my little girl?"

"I don't know, sir," Antonio said. "But rest assured, I am doing everything I can to find her."

"The man you've captured," Mr Scarborough said, his hands twisting together, "does he know anything?"

"He's playing mute at the moment, sir."

"But you know how to get him to talk?"

Antonio stiffened. "I'm rather hoping it will not come to that, sir."

Mr Scarborough's eyes were wide and wild as they met Antonio's. "But you would, wouldn't you, if needs must."

Antonio swallowed. "Yes," he admitted. "If needs must."

Chapter 48

Exchange

In his dream, Antonio was caught in a crocodile's jaws. It had hold of his leg and was shaking his body for all it was worth.

Then the crocodile started calling his name in Juanita's voice, and Antonio knew he needed to wake up.

"Are you secretly a crocodile?" he murmured once he had opened his eyes.

"What?" Juanita asked.

"Never mind. What's going on?"

"Someone's banging on the front door."

Now that he was awake, Antonio could hear it. Eyes bleary from sleep, he climbed over Juanita and got out of his bed. Their bed, now. If the person banging on the front door didn't have an urgent reason, he was going to murder them.

He pulled the window open with far more force than

necessary and stuck his head outside into the night.

"What?" he hissed. "What? What is it?"

The banging downstairs stopped and a figure moved in the dark.

"Beggin' your pardon, Sheriff," they said, and Antonio recognised the voice as Mr Scarborough's servant. "But you need to come to Mr Scarborough's house right away."

"I was there only a few hours ago," Antonio said. "Can't it wait?"

"No, Sheriff. The matter is very urgent."

Sighing, Antonio ran a hand down his face. "Fine," he snapped and slammed the window shut. "I'm going to the Scarboroughs'," he said, looking around for his pants. He had been in such a hurry to get them off last night, he couldn't remember where he'd thrown them.

"Can't wait to see what this urgent matter is," Juanita said, sliding her hand down the side of the bed and pulling out his pants. Antonio bent down and kissed her as he took them from her. "It'd better be worth getting up for."

"Hmm," Juanita said and kissed him back in a way that almost made Antonio push her back down onto the bed. Instead, he sighed and put his pants on.

"It was pinned to my front door," Mr Scarborough said, pacing up and down the salon. "We were woken up by a gunshot, and when William went downstairs to see what the matter was he found this."

Antonio looked down at the piece of paper in his hand.

The writing on it was neat and cursive – the type of writing that came from years of being taught how to fit into the higher levels of society. Cassidy's writing.

It has been demanded that I, Cassidy Scarborough, write these terms.
In exchange for my safe return, my captor demands that they receive Benjamin Scarborough.

The handover will happen on the west side of town, near the old hanging tree at the cross roads at noon tomorrow.
If these terms are not met in any way, I will pay for it with my life.
I pray to God that an agreement can be met between the two sides that stops this from happening and that sense can be seen by all.
Miss Cassidy Scarborough

"It's them, isn't it?" Mr Scarborough said. The edges of the paper crumbled in Antonio's hands. "It's the Blood Twins."

"Or one half of them," Antonio said.

"What would they do to me," Mr Scarborough asked, his voice a harsh whisper, "do you think, if you handed me over to them?"

"You would most certainly be killed," Antonio said.

Mr Scarborough's face turned white. His servant and Antonio rushed over to him as he swayed and helped him sit on one of the sofas.

"We can't give in to their demands!" Mr Scarborough cried. He was twisting his hands again. There were scratches on the back of them and around his wrists, overlaying the scars that were already there. "I'm too important to the economy! Thousands of people rely on me for their jobs! I-I can't die! But my poor, poor Cassidy," he murmured, his voice growing distant. "My dear sweet girl. Held captive by that villain! What should we do, Antonio? What should we do?"

Antonio took a deep breath. As he did, his head cleared.

"I have an idea," he said. "But we'll need to play along with the game – just at first. I will get Cassidy back for you, Mr Scarborough, and I will not lose you in the process."

Just before noon the next day, Antonio found himself sat at the cross roads astride a horse beside an old twisted tree on which swayed frayed pieces of rope. Behind him, two other horses sweated in the hot sun, their riders fidgeting. Mr Scarborough drooped in the sun like an overripe sunflower. The other figure pulled at the collar of their dress.

"How the hell do women cope in these things?" Alejandro demanded. "It's so hot. The skirts are heavy. I'm sweating in places I didn't know I could sweat."

He moved to unbutton his sleeves, but Antonio caught his arm.

"Don't," he hissed. "You can't expose any skin. Otherwise Megan will know you're not Juanita. Just sit there quietly and keep your head down. The hat will do the rest."

Alejandro muttered something Antonio didn't catch, but he returned his hands to the saddle horn.

As Antonio watched the horizon in front of them, he tried not to glance at the spot where he knew Juanita was hiding. Or at least, where he thought he remembered helping her hide. The blanket covered in sand was such fantastic camouflage that he had lost her in the landscape. He just hoped nothing stung or bit her while she was lying there and she didn't get too hot under her pile of sand.

A movement caught his eye on the horizon.

It was a horse, with a figure sat astride it, and another figure walking alongside with a rope tied around their hands. Antonio knew them to be Megan and Cassidy, even before they were close enough that he could make out their features.

"Afternoon, Sheriff," Megan called from the horse, coming to a stop. She was in her usual shirt and pants, rather than her red Blood Twins clothes, but she'd tied a strip of cloth over her face, obscuring her features. Cassidy looked tired, but Antonio was pleased the fight hadn't gone from her eyes. Then he noticed the bloodied bandage wrapped around her hand and his stomach burned hot.

As Megan's eyes slid from Antonio to Mr Scarborough, Antonio saw the hatred ignite in them.

"Afternoon, Benjamin Scarborough," she hissed, shifting in her seat. Antonio knew it was taking all her effort not to draw her gun from her belt and shoot Mr Scarborough where he stood. Mr Scarborough let out a quiet whimper.

"Shall we get this over with?" Antonio said.

"I'd be happy to. I've waited two long years fer this moment. No sense in prolongin' it any further."

"On your count," Antonio said, "we will start the exchange."

"An' if I see a flicker of movement from you or your woman," Megan said, "I'll shoot Cassidy through the head 'fore you can draw your gun. Is that clear?"

"Crystal." To Mr Scarborough, he said, "You need to get off your horse now, sir."

Mr Scarborough let out another whimper. He sat still for such a long time that Antonio thought he wasn't going to do it, but then, slowly with shaking hands, he got down from his horse.

"On the count of three, start walkin'," Megan shouted. "No runnin' or else I shoot, all right? One... Two... Three."

She dropped Cassidy's rope. Cassidy and Mr Scarborough began their walk towards each other. Antonio sat very still, watching them. The hammering of his heart intensified the closer they became. As they passed each other, he noticed father and daughter exchange a look. Mr Scarborough's body twisted slightly, and for one sickening moment Antonio thought he was going to ruin everything, but he walked on.

As Cassidy pulled up beside Antonio's horse, the sheriff let out a long-held breath. He dismounted and used his knife to cut Cassidy's hands free.

"What happened?" he asked, holding her injured hand.

"I'm fine," Cassidy insisted, pulling away.

As much as Antonio didn't want to drop it, he knew now was not the time. "Get ready," Antonio whispered. Cassidy's eyes widened, full of questions, but she just nodded. Across the way, Mr Scarborough had stopped beside Megan's horse. Megan had one gun pointed at him.

"Much obliged to you, Sheriff," Megan called out. "Thanks to you, I can fin—"

A gunshot boomed across the desert. The gun went flying from Megan's hand in a spray of blood.

"Run, Mr Scarborough!" Antonio yelled.

Mr Scarborough didn't need telling twice. For someone who looked like he might get blown away by a strong gust of wind, he sure as hell pegged it back towards them. Megan's face twisted into a snarl. Using her undamaged hand, she reached for her other gun.

From her hiding spot, Juanita fired a second shot.

Antonio spurred his horse forward as Megan toppled to the ground. There was a bloody hole in her shoulder. Antonio dismounted and pulled his gun from its holster. Holding the pistol to Megan's head, Antonio removed the second gun from her belt and threw it as far as he could.

"Megan Hayes," he said. "I arrest you for murder, kidnapping, blackmail and theft. You will face trial tomorrow and if you are found guilty, you will hang."

Antonio brought Megan back to the group, gagged and bound. Juanita walked beside them, her face and clothes covered in dirt.

"What are you doing?" Mr Scarborough demanded. "Shoot her now! Didn't you see what she tried to do to me?!"

"With all due respect, I'm the sheriff in this town, sir," Antonio said. "We will do things my way, and that is by judge and jury. Not by cold-blooded murder."

Antonio knew he had spoken out of turn, that Mr

Scarborough could strip him of his sheriff's star then and there, but something in Antonio's words must have hit home, because Mr Scarborough kept quiet.

Chapter 49

Jail Break

I'm aware of Sheriff Valdez leavin' in the middle of the night, called sumwhere by a knockin' on the door an' shoutin' outside, but I go back to sleep soon afterwards.

I've spent most of ma time asleep since bein' thrown in the jail cell, when the pains in ma body let me. Sleepin' means I don't hafta feel the pain coursin' through ma body or listen to the thoughts rotatin' in ma head.

But no matter how much I sleep, they're always there when I wake up.

Megan has Cassidy now an' Gawd only knows what kinda revenge she's got in mind fer Benjamin Scarborough.

An' then there's Dean. I still can't believe it. He'd bin Pa's best friend. They'd loved each other like brothers. He an' Mary'd taken us in when Pa'd bin in jail, an' then they'd kept an eye on us after he died. It didn't make any sense.

An' now Mary'll come home from Pheonix an' find her husband dead.

Dead by ma hand.

A sharp pain grips ma stomach. I curl onto ma side with ma hands over ma head.

Dean's right.

I'm a murderin', stealin' sunvabitch.

In the moments I'm awake, I pray sumtimes, beggin' fer His fergiveness, beggin' Him to keep Cassidy safe, beggin' Him to save Megan.

But Gawd ain't gonna listen to me now. I'd broken a promise to Him. I'd made a deal with Him – Megan's life fer a life free of robbin' an' killin' – an' I'd broken it by killin' that person in the caves, an' then killin' Dean. All our bad luck – Megan findin' out 'bout Cassidy an' Dean betrayin' us – were all 'cause Gawd were punishin' me fer breakin' ma promise.

I curl up on ma bed an' pull the thin sheet over ma head.

It's all ma fault.

Sheriff Valdez didn't come back 'til the next afternoon. Juanita left 'fore he came back, waitin' fer the deputy to arrive 'fore she did. The deputy's bin in the office all day, but he's spent most of it with his feet up on the desk an' his hat over his face while he snores.

While Sheriff Valdez an' Juanita are still out, he comes over to ma cell an' leans on the bars.

"We caught your sis today," he says.

I keep ma mouth shut.

"She tried to trade that girl back to her pa. Made a right mess of it. They tricked her – got the girl back unharmed an' your sis's locked up." I smell the smoke from his cigar on his breath. I risk a glance at him. Our eyes meet an' the deputy smiles at me. He holds his cigar, breathes deep an' lets out a cloud of smoke into ma cell.

The smell reminds me of the burnin' church.

"You ready to die, boy? 'Cause you will, along with your sis. A double hangin'. Now, won't that be summit to see?" He gives me one last smile an' walks away.

I retreat unner ma thin itchy blanket an' try to go to sleep. I'm glad Cassidy's safe, but I feel sick with fear fer Megan's life.

Returnin' to the office, Sheriff Valdez dismisses the deputy an' sits in the chair outside ma cell.

"Cole," he says, "we've arrested Megan. She tried to trade Cassidy for Mr Scarborough in a hostage exchange, but she's in our custody now. Cassidy's safe with her father. Megan goes on trial tomorrow. If she's found guilty, she'll be hanged. You'll go on trial the day after."

There's a long pause. Sheriff Valdez sighs, gits up an' walks away.

Several times durin' the day, folks come to the sheriff's office. I hear 'em talkin' to him, congratulatin' him on capturin' the Blood Twins. Sum of 'em are surprised that it were me an' Megan 'hind the masks, but sum of 'em say they ain't surprised, not with how our pa turned out. Sheriff Valdez keeps 'em away from ma cell, 'though I've a feelin' his deputy would let 'em have a nose at me fer a dollar. At least I don't hafta worry 'bout a vigilante group draggin' me early to the gallows with the sheriff 'round.

I don't sleep well that night. It's so cold in ma cell an' the growin' pain in ma leg from where Megan shot me doesn't help. I need to remove the bullet, an' wash an' treat the wound, but I can't bring maself to look at it. It don't matter anyway. Not if I'm on ma way to the gallows.

The next day, Sheriff Valdez an' Juanita leave the sheriff's office dressed in smart clothes. They come back several hours later. I hear the sheriff stop outside ma cell.

"Megan was found guilty. She'll be hanged tomorrow at dawn. Your trial will start at noon."

I wait 'til he's walked away fer burstin' into tears.

That night, I dream I own a horse ranch. It's sumwhere green with lots of mountains. Cassidy's with me, smilin' an' happy. We both have gold bands on our fingers. She kisses me an' tells me that she loves me. Then she puts a hand on ma chest an' pushes me off the edge of a cliff.

I wake to the sound of clinkin' keys an' soft footsteps approachin' me. Sumone stops outside ma cell. I sit up.

"Hello?" I whisper. There's a rustle of clothin', the hiss of a match bein' struck an' the clank of a lantern bein' lit.

"Cassidy!"

"Shh!" She puts a finger to her lips an' points upstairs, where Sheriff Valdez an' Juanita sleep.

I nod, but ma heart's anythin' but calm.

What's she doin' here?

Cassidy fumbles with the keys, tryin' to find the one that fits the lock on ma door. There's a bandage 'round her hand where Megan shot her. The sight of it makes ma stomach clench. At last, she finds one that makes the lock click. Slowly, to lessen the sound of the door squeakin', she opens the cell door. As I slip through it, she gestures at the door to the outside with her head an' I follow her out into the night.

She leads me 'round the side of the buildin' next door where Rosie's waitin' loaded with supply bags an' a rifle hangin' from the saddle. I cry an' hug her neck an' press ma face into her mane.

"I asked Antonio if I could have her," Cassidy says. I hear the smile in her voice an' right then know that I will never deserve her. "I knew you'd want her back."

I wipe away a fallin' tear. "You shouldn't've let me out. You'll git into trouble."

Cassidy grins at me. "My father isn't letting anything happen to me after he's just got me back."

"Are you..." I swallow. "Are you all right? I mean, after

what Megan did—"

"I don't want to talk about it!" Cassidy snaps an' then winces. "I'm sorry, Cole," she says, wipin' her hand unner her eyes. "But it was awful."

"I'm sorry," I say. "I'm so sorry."

Cassidy nods an' looks at Rosie. "I bought some supplies. I'm not sure how much you need – or what you need, really. I took a bit of a guess, but there's food and water. I thought you could go somewhere far away. Somewhere with a ranch and you can have the life you've always wanted."

I run a hand over Rosie's side an' through her mane. Feelin' her warmth unner ma fingers an' her soft breathin' calms ma thoughts.

'Cause I wanna go.

I wanna take this chance an' run.

I want a life away from this mess. Away from sheriffs an' lost gold an' guns an' heartache an' death.

I want a quiet life surrounded by horses an' fields.

But then I think 'bout Dean, slumped in that chair, with the hole in his head that I put there. 'Bout the burnin' church, an' the other six folks I've killed.

An' know the life I'm longin' fer is far from ma reach.

It's too late to turn back now.

"But I can't abandon Megan," I say. "I can't leave her to die while I run away."

Cassidy sighs. "I should have known you'd say that."

I ignore the stab of pain in ma chest her words cause. "Do you know where they're keepin' her?"

There's resignation in Cassidy's expression as she replies, "I don't know. They've got her locked up somewhere in town. What are you going to do?"

"I don't know, but I hafta help her."

The night's very still. Nuthin' seems to be movin'. There ain't a sound. Even Rosie's quiet.

"What are you gonna do now?" I ask. "Are you stayin'

with your pa?"

"No," Cassidy says. "I... I talked to him today. Or, rather, I told him everything I felt about him." She laughs. "I poured it all out. All my frustration and anger towards him. How much I hate him for keeping me locked inside my whole life. I got so angry, Cole. He shouted at me, told me how ungrateful I was, how he was only trying to protect me from the evils of the world. So I told him. I told him I knew what he did to those men in California."

Cassidy falls silent.

"What did he say?" I prompt.

"Nothing." She laughs again. I so desperately wanna take her hand, to give her summit to hold onto, but I keep ma hands pressed to ma sides. "I struck him dumb. So I told him what I wanted – a house in Los Angeles that's mine, the freedom to do what I wanted, money of my own and a future where I have the chance to change the world for the better. And if he didn't give those things to me, I would tell every newspaper from here to New York what he'd done. Of course, he agreed to my demands after that."

I look away while Cassidy takes a handkerchief from inside her sleeve an' blows her nose.

"I guess I have to thank you," she says. "For making me realise how trapped I really was."

"You've got nuthin' to thank us fer," I say. "Don't ever think that you do."

Cassidy nods an' blows her nose again.

"So," she says. "I guess this is goodbye."

"Yes," I say. "This is goodbye."

Our gazes hold. I should break away, but I have a feelin' that once I do I'll never see those dark green eyes – dark as a pine forest – again. Each second I look at 'em I feel a strange mixture of love an' pain – fer the love I've invested in her an' the pain from knowin' that after tonight I ain't gonna see her again.

"Don't come back to Helena, Cole," Cassidy says.

Then she's walkin' away. I shiver in the cold air an' wrap ma arms 'round ma body, huggin' maself, watchin' 'til Cassidy's lost in the darkness. Hot wet tears form in ma eyes as I climb into Rosie's saddle. I wipe 'em away, but they keep comin'. I grip Rosie's saddle horn tight an' let 'em run dry, sobbin' every last drop of water outta me, cussin' the world an' prayin' that when I open ma eyes we'll be children again, with Pa an' Dean still alive, Megan an' me playin' at Cassidy's house, never havin' known the feelin' of a gun in our hands.

But, course, I'm still swayin' in Rosie's saddle as she walks the moonlit streets of Helena, bloodied an' bruised, with an impossible task ahead of me.

I'm gonna hafta hide sumwhere overnight. Sumwhere I ain't gonna be sin 'fore I put the world to right tomorrow mornin'.

Chapter 50

The Last Stand

The next mornin's one of those hot, bright ones with plenty of wind. It ain't the sorta day I want it to be. I want cloud an' rain – I want the world to cry fer Megan an' me, but it's sunny, fer which I should be grateful. I have a clear view of the hangin' tree in front of the town hall.

Last night I put Rosie in an empty stable stall in the saloon, thinkin' that if there were gonna be a manhunt fer me, a horse among a load of other horses were gonna draw less attention 'n one standin' on its own. Then I dragged maself onto the roof of the saloon, which hadda clear view of the gallows. I didn't sleep. Ma body aches an' feels full of lead, an' ma head's whirrin'.

It's the longest night of ma life.

At the break of dawn I expect to be tired, but ma hopes rise with the dawn. I hafta be ready an' alert. If I miss this shot, Megan'll hang an' I'll have a whole town after me.

But if I make it, we might've a chance.

If I can make it. Which I don't think I can.

As the sky's starts to lighten with the first rays of dawn, folk arrive in the square. I know so many of 'em – Mr Bergman who runs the store, Joe from The Racoon, Miss Martin who taught me an' Megan at school. Are they sad or happy that Megan's gonna die? I spot a number of folks who'd swung by the sheriff's office yesterday to try to git a glimpse of me in ma cell.

I watch 'em from ma hidin' place on the roof, peepin' over the lip of the false front.

Then as the first curve of the sun appears 'bove the horizon, they bring Megan into the square. She's ridin' a black stallion, led by a man on 'nother horse. There're two men ridin' 'hind her, an' there's at least 'nother dozen armed folk in the square scannin' the surroundin's, includin' Juanita, the sheriff, an' his deputy. I've never sin so many guards at a hangin'. I guess it's protection 'gainst me since they musta discovered ma empty cell this mornin'.

Megan's hands're tied in front of her. Her face's bloodied an' swollen, like sumone's beaten her. The front of her shirt's dyed red with blood from her side wound. There's a bloody hole in her shoulder, an' her right hand's wrapped in stained bandages. Ma stomach boils in anger, but I grip the rifle's barrel an' take a deep breath. I hafta keep calm. Everythin's ridin' on me bein' able to make this shot. I look at Megan again. She's pale, paler 'n I've ever sin her. There're dark circles unner her eyes, like she hasn't slept in days, but if she's tired, she don't show it. She sits on her horse with a straight back, her eyes starin' at the gallows with the look that's made dozens of grown men cower.

They pull Megan up to the hangin' tree. Two men who'd bin waitin' lead Megan's horse unner the noose, slip the loop over her head an' tighten the knot unner her chin. Megan keeps her back straight.

Up to the end she's gonna keep her pride.

The town mayor, dressed in his fine clothes, steps ferward.

"Ladies an' gentlemen, today we bear witness to the hangin' of Megan Hayes, half of the notorious Blood Twins. She has bin tried for murder, theft, arson, blackmail, kidnappin', destruction of a house of Gawd an' destruction of property. She has bin found guilty of all these charges an' has bin sentenced to hang by the neck 'til dead."

I glance back at Megan. Even though she's strainin' 'gainst the noose, she's smilin'. It's a wolfish smile, like she's sin summit that she wants to hunt. She ain't afraid. She's proud of everythin' the mayor's reain' out.

One of the men puts a bag over Megan's head.

I line up the rifle. Ma hands're shakin', but I force 'em to be calm. I can't mess this up. If I do, I could end up hittin' sumone in the crowd, the mayor or Megan. Megan would be able to make this shot easy, but I ain't her. I'm sure I can't do it, but I hafta try.

Then the mayor says, "May Gawd've mercy on your soul."

An' he raises his ridin' crop to hit the black stallion on the rear.

To make the horse bolt.

To snap Megan's neck 'gainst the rope.

I take the shot.

Fer a heartbeat I think I've failed.

That I've missed.

But the horse bolts an' takes Megan with it, leavin' a frayed rope hangin' from the tree.

I whoop out loud, not carin' if sumone hears.

Fer a moment everyone stands still, no one unnerstandin' what's jest happened. Then everyone with a gun starts shootin'. I fire ma last shot at one of 'em an' then slot more bullets into the barrel. Megan's now far enough away, but I continue pickin' off the men after her.

I hit a man in the shoulder an' 'nother in the leg.

"Look! Up there! It's the other one!" Sumone's pointin' at me. They've finally spotted me. I duck 'hind the false front jest as a bullet whizzes past where ma head were a moment 'fore. Several more hit the false front, splinterin' the wood. It's time I were gone.

I crawl 'cross the roof, the rifle gripped in ma hand. I climb down quickly an' jump the last few feet. I fall on ma ankle. I holler as pain shoots through it an' ma leg. But I don't have time to check it. I hafta catch up to Megan. I limp into the saloon stables. Seein' me, Rosie snorts. I swing maself up into the saddle, ignorin' the screamin' in ma whole body. As I do so a load of bullets fall from ma pocket. I begin to git down again, but two men enter the stables.

"There he is!"

I kick Rosie into a gallop. The men fire at me. I press maself flat 'gainst Rosie's back an' urge her on. The two men dive out the way as Rosie an' I tear outta the stables.

I push Rosie harder 'n I've ever pushed her 'fore. I ride through the crowd of folk hangin' 'round the gallows, partin' 'em like a wind through a field of crops. I lie flat in the saddle, the rifle 'cross ma legs, listenin' to more bullets bein' fired in ma direction.

I follow Megan's hoof prints. Soon I see her in the distance, the bag gone from her head. I pull Rosie 'round, so I'll approach her from the side. Both ma ankle an' ma leg scream at the horse's motion an' the weight I'm puttin' on 'em. I jest hope Rosie ain't shot from unner me, 'cause I'll have no chance on foot.

I catch up with Megan an' find a different person from who I'd sin by the hangin' tree. She ain't smilin' no more. Her cheeks're streaked with tears an' she looks real pale. But she gives me a weak smile. I smile back.

"Nice shootin' back there," Megan says.

"Thanks," I say an' a rush of pride courses through me.

Megan glances 'hind us an' frowns.

"We've got company."

I look 'hind us. There are a dozen horses approachin' us in the distance. We push our mounts even harder, streakin' through the desert, trailin' a dust cloud of red 'hind us.

It ain't long 'fore Rosie begins to slow. She's gittin' tired, as is Megan's stallion. They can't keep this pace up ferever. I glance 'hind. The others're catchin' up fast.

Then I see it ahead of us.

"Megan, is that...?"

"It sure is."

I pull on the reins, forcin' Rosie to stop a few feet away from the edge of the cliff. Megan pulls her horse up beside me. We stare down at the ragin' river several hundred feet below us in the canyon.

"Fuck." Megan glances up an' downstream, but this is it. There ain't nuthin' we can do now. The horses can't jump the canyon, there's no point headin' up or down it – the men would catch up to us easy. We're trapped.

I grip ma rifle. I rummage in ma pocket an' pull out three bullets. I look inside the magazine. There ain't any in there. We've three bullets to defend ourselves with. I look up at the dozen men approachin' us fast.

"Here." I reach inside ma boot an' pull out a knife. I cut Megan's hands free, an' then hold the gun out to her. "You'd better take this."

"You were a pretty good shot back when ma head were inna noose."

"But you're still better. You'll do the most damage."

Megan nods an' takes the gun from me.

"Three bullets ain't gonna be much use 'gainst twelve men."

"There's always hope."

Megan spits. "I guess there is."

We watch the men git closer. Sum of 'em've their guns

drawn an' 're wavin' 'em in the air, whoopin'.

I'd secretly hoped to die inna bed, old an' wrinkled. But there were no way I were gonna git a death like that, not with the life me an' Megan lead.

I'm thankful Megan's with me. We entered the world togither, an' we should leave it togither.

I hear a screech an' look up. A golden eagle's flyin' over us.

To ma right, Megan's lookin' down the sights of the rifle. She's bitin' her bottom lip, her face's a stone wall of concentration. Her eyes flick to the side. She's watchin' me.

"Cole?"

"Yeah, sis?"

"You were right. When they were leadin' me to the noose, I thought 'bout what you said. An' you were right. I started robbin' 'cause I were angry at Pa's death. It warn't nuthin' to do with wantin' to make him proud."

I suck inna deep breath as ma eyes water. I wanna reach out an' grab Megan's hand, but she wouldn't wanna be touched, so I keep ma hand on ma saddle an' grip it hard as the surge of emotion runs through me.

"I shouldn't've dragged you into it," she says.

"It's all right," I say.

The eagle 'bove us screeches again. Megan cocks the rifle.

"I'm lookin' ferward to seein' Pa an' Ma again," she says.

I smile an' look up at the clear blue sky. An' even though there ain't no way Gawd'll allow us into Heaven to see 'em, I say, "Me too."

Chapter 51

Silver and Gold

They patrolled the side of the canyon several times, walking the horses up and down the same stretch of land, scouring the fast-flowing river below. Someone from Helena even climbed down the cliff face and searched along the bottom.

But they found no traces of the Blood Twins.

They'd disappeared into the pages of history.

Antonio called off the search as the sun started to set.

"Either they'll show up again," he said to Juanita as they rode back to town, "or they won't. And if they do, I won't let them slip through my fingers again."

"I don't think they're coming back," Juanita said.

They ate dinner and then sat outside, watching the stars together and listening to the sounds of the animals and insects calling in the night.

"What should we do about the gold?" Juanita asked.

Antonio tightened his arms around her and pressed his face into her shoulder.

"I don't know," he said, his voice soft against her back. "But I do know I don't want it, and I have a feeling that anyone else who gets hold of it will only feel misery."

"Then we should get rid of it."

"I don't want to sell it."

Juanita twisted in his arms so she could meet his eyes. "Then don't," she said.

Her thoughts connected with Antonio's like a static shock. Understanding, Antonio nodded.

"All right," he said.

They went up to their room and brought the bags of gold down from the ceiling. Hearing the clink of metal on metal and feeling the weight of all that wealth in his hands, Antonio felt his resolve waver, but then he remembered Dean slumped in the chair with a hole through his skull, and he threw two of the bags onto the floor. Outside, they attached the bags to the horses and rode into the desert, two lanterns and the moonlight lighting their way.

They'd walked up and down the same stretch of land so many times that day they knew where to direct the horses even in the dark. They dismounted and led the horses to the edge of the canyon where they could hear the rushing of the river below.

Antonio leaned over the edge, staring down into the gaping maw. Juanita pressed a bag into each of his hands.

"Come on," she said and threw her bags over the edge.

Antonio held on for a moment longer, grappling with the whispering voice in his head, with the greed that made him want to hug the gold to his chest, and then he was throwing the bags over the edge. Juanita brought the last two bags over and they threw them over together. There was no sound as the bags hit the river, at least not one that Antonio heard. He took a deep breath and realised his shoulders felt lighter. He took Juanita's hand and she squeezed it in reply.

"What now?" she asked.

"What now?" he repeated. Then a stone hit the bottom of his stomach. He swallowed. "You're thinking about leaving."

A sharp pain bit into Antonio's hand. He gasped and pulled it out of Juanita's, thinking something had stung him, but from the look on Juanita's face he knew she had pinched him.

"No," she said. "I wasn't, actually, but I was wondering if you were?"

Antonio opened his mouth to deny her claim, but something stopped him. A thought that had been taking root in the back of his mind over the past few days.

"I don't know," he admitted. "I wasn't, but..." He sighed and ran a hand down his face. "These past few weeks have been hard. I believed in Mr Scarborough – I knew something was off with the way he treated Cassidy, but he never treated me poorly. And then I learnt that he was the one who murdered my great-uncle, Hu's grandfather, and Cole and Megan's grandfather... And now that the Blood Twins have gone I feel... empty. Like I have no purpose anymore. And, to be honest, I... I don't think I want to be a sheriff anymore. I like helping people, but I feel this isn't the place I should be – or want to be."

Juanita slid her arms around his shoulders and pressed him to her. Antonio breathed in her scent and felt something inside him loosen.

"We don't have to stay here," she said. "There's a whole world out there for us to find somewhere to call home."

Antonio nodded into her shoulder.

"You're right," he said and kissed her. It was nothing deep or passionate – just something to show how much she meant to him.

"You know I always am," she whispered. He laughed, gave her one last squeeze and let her go.

"What do you want to do now?" Antonio asked.

Juanita sighed. "To be honest, I'm not sure either."

"Perhaps," Antonio said, "we can work out what we want together?"

"I'd like that."

They walked back to Helena, hand in hand, leading the horses by their reins, the silver moon shining above them and the river of gold flowing behind them.

About the author

Adelaide Newton is an author based in Bristol, UK. They are a Bath Spa Creative Writing BA graduate. At the crack of dawn and at the weekend, you can find them typing away at their WIP. By day, they work in marketing. You can find them online at www.adelaidenewton.co.uk. You can connect with Adelaide on Twitter, Instagram, and TikTok at @bookworm_scribe. Or you can drop them an email at adelaide.newton@hotmail.co.uk. And although they use Adelaide on their covers, they much prefer being called Addy.

Enjoyed this book?

As a self-published author, I don't have the powerful machine of a publishing company behind me to generate a buzz around my books - a buzz that will put my book into the hands of more readers. Therefore, if you enjoyed this book, I would be very grateful if you could spend a couple of minutes leaving a review on the Amazon page. This will help bring the book to the attention of future readers. Thank you.